# The Beer Cook Book

Susan Nowak is the Chairman of the British Guild of Beer Writers and editor of the Campaign for Real Ale's bestselling guidebook *Good Pub Food*. She is past winner of the Beer Writer of the Year Silver and Pewter Tankards. She has written numerous features on cooking with beer and pub food for the *Telegraph*, *Daily Mirror*, BBC *Good Food* and *Vegetarian* magazine, CAMRA's *What's Brewing* and *Sainsbury's Magazine*.

In addition to her many television and radio appearances on cooking with beer and pub food, she has judged international beer and pub food competitions, originated beer recipes for major breweries and devised beer banquets for the British Guild of Beer Writers.

by the same author

Campaign for Real Ale's *Good Pub Food* (editor)

# THE BEER COOK BOOK

## Susan Nowak

*faber and faber*

*With thanks to my husband Fran and son Taddy
for tasting so many beer dishes!*

First published in 1999
by Faber and Faber Limited
3 Queen Square London WC1N 3AU
Typeset by Faber and Faber
Printed in England by Clays Ltd, St Ives plc

Beers and glasses courtesy of The Beer Shop,
14 Pitfield Street, London N16 EY

A CIP record for this book
is available from the British Library

ISBN 0–571–19291–X

2 4 6 8 10 9 7 5 3 1

# Contents

# Acknowledgements

I would like to thank the following for their help:

Martin Barry of the Salopian Brewing Company; from Belgo's, joint founder Denis Blais, head chef of Belgo Centraal Charles Noorland and beer sommelier Mark Stroebandt (see also the *Belgo Cookbook*); beer expert Mark Dorber of the White Horse, Parsons Green, London, sw6; Martin Kemp of The Beer Shop and Pitfield Brewery; vegetarian chef and writer Leon Lewis, author of *More Vegetarian Dinner Parties*; 'Beer Hunter' Michael Jackson, who has caried out pioneering work on beer cuisine, with books including the *Pocket Beer Book*, *Great Beers of Belgium* and, most recently, *Beer*; Benjamin Myers, author of beer books, including *Ben Myers' Best American Beers*; beer author and broadcaster Barrie Pepper; beer author and broadcaster Roger Protz, whose numerous works include the *Real Ale Drinker's Almanac* and, most recently, *The Tase of Beer*; Lucy Saunders, author of *Cooking with Beer,* in the USA.

And a special Thank You to the celebrity chefs, restaurant and pub chefs who donated recipes for this book.

# Introduction

Beer. A flat, brown, murky, lukewarm liquid slopping about in heavy pint tankards in a public bar where real men exhale smoke and throw darts? Where have you been? Today's ales and beers are a miracle of taste, texture, complexity and character. Delicate, dry pilsners; lip-smacking full-bodied bitters as round as a ripe Burgundy; sparkling pink cherry beers as luscious as a kir royale; black, viscous stouts and dark chocolate porters; smoked beers the colour of kippers hanging in a chimney; tart, lemony wheat beers frothing up the glass like champagne . . . an explosion of yeast, malt and hops turned to sheer nectar by craft brewers.

It demands more effort, skill and knowledge to create a superb beer than a fine wine. And the tradition is as old, if not older. I once asked a Bavarian brewer just what it was that produced the wonderful blend of flavours, the sheer mouth-filling depth in his famous dark wheat beer of awesome strength. 'I suppose it is because we have been making it for nearly 400 years – we should have got it right by now!' he said. And you can taste those centuries in a beer that takes the nose and tastebuds through layer upon layer of flavour.

Beer comes in all shades from pale straw through topaz, amber, rich chestnut, ruby red, mahogany brown and pitch-black. You can savour ales the colour of moonlight falling on a hayrick, or hold up to the light a glass that glows with claret crimson. I'm told somebody produced an emerald beer for St Patrick's Day, but happily I never saw it. There are limits.

In the past year I've probably passed them. I've drunk heather beer, gooseberry beer, a mint beer as syrupy as a julep, elderberry beer, honey beer, grapefruit beer, damson beer; even, Lord help me, tea beer! I've talked to brewers who have found inspiration in the beer recipes of the Elizabethans to start flavouring their ales with herbs and spices such as nutmeg, root ginger and coriander.

When the Romans arrived they found us brewing beer. Perhaps that's why they stayed so long. Through the ages beer has played a pivotal role in the life of the nation. In medieval times every manor house and farm brewed its own ale, which was drunk with every meal including breakfast. Even the children (and servants) were given 'small beer' – the weaker ale resulting from the second or third fermentation. Its relationship to the kitchen was close. At one time baker's and brewer's yeasts were more or less interchangeable until it became clear that one made a satisfying loaf, and the other a satisfying pint – I think both come close to being the staff of life.

Today we can rejoice that the wheel has turned full circle and microbreweries in pubs, off-licences, cow sheds and small industrial units are once more brewing for their local community – and showing such idiosyncrasy. The fruits of their labours can be some weird and wonderful brews with even more weird and wonderful names – Doris's 90th Birthday Ale, Rudolph the Red Nose Reinbeer, Sneck Lifter, Tempus Fugit, Midsummer Passion, Monkey Wrench, Bodger's Barley Wine, Myrtle's Temper, Honey Bunny, Hopnosis, Bishop's Tipple, Tipsy Toad, Whistle Belly Vengeance, Headcracker, Ale Mary . . . et al. If they were just names, though, there'd be nothing to celebrate. All these ales have different characteristics and their own distinctive taste.

A few centuries ago beer was quite closely allied to food. It was heated to make possets, using a red-hot poker, and put into syllabubs; beer batter goes back to Tudor times, when it was used for apple or spinach fritters; the Elizabethans used to casserole lamb in ale with prunes and raisins. Sadly, the advent of drinking houses seemed to divorce beer from the kitchen in this country, apart from that drop of bitter in the 'landlord's' beef stew or steak and kidney pie.

In other countries, however, the tradition continued uninterrupted. In Germany and Austria, for instance, brewery taps are often found in restaurants and the beers make superb accompaniments to robust local dishes and those splendid hams and sausages – the Zum Uerige brewery in Düsseldorf has its own sausage kitchen making blutwurst and brawn, producing rich dripping which is served with their knock-your-socks-off Mainzer cheese marinated in beer. In Holland, too, you will find some outstanding beer cafés, where a wide selection of beers complements simple, filling snacks and more ambitious dishes.

America started late, but now its burgeoning craft-brew pubs/restaurants enthusiastically create outstanding beer on the premises. You can watch it being brewed behind floor to ceiling windows as you drink it alongside every style of cuisine imaginable. Never ones for moderation, the American approach to beer cuisine has been unrestrained. Even the Waldorf-Astoria decided it was gastronomically acceptable to serve up tiramisu made with porter, while a bistro in Philadelphia is credited with purée of roast garlic soup and red pepper coulis with Young's Winter Ale. In Hawaii I found a modern brew pub not far from Waikiki Beach, where German-style lagers and heavier dark dunkels are being brewed to partner some of the most exotic flavours under the sun, from local Kaola pig to Pacific Rim cuisine, embracing Japanese sushi and American all-beef burgers. Here, too, local products are used to flavour their beers, such as their famous Kona coffee beans and hula berries. Definitely beers to cook with.

But it is really to Belgium we must turn for the whole culture of beer and food known as *cuisine à la bière*. It is mind-boggling to wander round ornate bars in the old part of Brussels and find beer lists over a hundred long, from the strong, vinous Trappist beers brewed by monks to cloudy wheat beers impregnated by wild yeasts, from the powerful fruit beers to the sour Flemish brown beers used to create a classic beef carbonnade. Beer *sommeliers* in long, formal aprons talk to you knowledgeably about the different styles, suggesting a beer to your taste or to accompany your meal.

As snow falls outside, it is one of life's great pleasures to sit by a roaring fire in an ancient Belgian bar, often below a stained-glass window, like those of the great abbeys where the genuine Trappist beers are brewed. One such monastery is Orval, which has its own beer cookbook, where monks produce a heavenly brew and also make their own bread, cheese and honey. Alongside the beer lists are menus with entire sections devoted to beer cookery – the inimitable Belgian mussels cooked with bacon and beer, rabbit braised with prunes in beer, fish with a wheat-beer sauce, *foie gras* on a raspberry beer *gelée*, duck breasts with cherry beer glaze, peasant stews with dumplings soaking up the beer stock.

I have visited the Hoegaarden brewery in Brussels, which has a vast beer hall serving its beers and beer dishes. You'll find some of their recipes in this book. One of the best-known beer restaurants, Spinnekopke in Brussels, has its own recipe book: *Cuisine facile à la biere*. The Belgians even put fruit beer in their gorgeous chocolate liqueurs.

But it is catching on in this country. Fuelled by the vast array of different styles of beer now being brewed here, or imported, offering such rewarding flavour and texture possibilities in cooking, we are seeing beer take its rightful place on the dinner table – both as a drink and an ingredient. Beer cuisine *est arrivée* in the UK!

It has also become far more accessible; Britain now has a brilliant range of bottled beers, which can be bought easily as an ingredient. Tesco has enabled small brewers to get their products into its national chain and has introduced a twice-yearly contest for brewers to produce a new summer and winter beer. Pubs and many breweries are now offering more ale in special 'carry out' packs, so you can use live beer in your cooking.

Top chefs from Rick Stein to Albert Roux are taking an interest; they have both donated recipes for this book. And we are now seeing restaurants which give beer the recognition it deserves, such as Belgo's London beer hall/restaurants with their Belgian beers and beer cuisine – their recipe for mussels, beer and bacon is on page 23. Two more London brew restaurants opened in 1998, Mash and Air near Oxford Circus and Soho Brewing Company, both brewing ale on the premises which is served alongside their food.

In this book you'll find sections on cooking with beer, beer to drink with food, a dictionary of beer styles, how to serve beer and the different glasses to use, beer feasts and menus, how beer is brewed and where to find some of the rarer ales you might want to cook with. I hope it brings you a flavour of what Dickens called 'stonking ale' and of some of the crusading characters who brew it, cook with it and drink it. Cheers!

# Hops and How Beer is Brewed

Hops are extraordinary plants. Those fragrant, cone-like flowers are related to the cannabis family – but that has absolutely nothing to do with getting drunk. The climbing vines have been called the grapes of brewing and I take the point, but I prefer to think of them as herbs. Their main role in ale is to give the brew its bitterness, hence a pint of bitter, but this is by no means their only role.

I can claim some justification for comparing hops with herbs because in the early days of brewing – and the Romans found us at it when they came to see and conquer – a sort of ale was made with grain, using herbs as flavouring; by all accounts it was an inferior brew. The Elizabethans began using spices such as coriander and ginger as well. As it happens, we've now come full circle and brewers are experimenting with herbs and spices again to create a cornucopia of flavours – one of the reasons for this book. But whatever else they add today it is as well as, not instead of, hops.

A very early reference puts hops in England in the first century, but they did not come into regular use in brewing until the end of the fifteenth century. There are all kinds of hops; some are used for bitterness, others for aroma. As described on page xiv, hops are boiled up with the sweet liquor produced from barley malt and water; a bit like brewing tea. The great art of the brewer is to combine different varieties of hop, and add them at different stages of the brew, to create an almost infinite palette of flavours, from the subtle to the robust. In this respect, hops can be compared to grapes, as wine-makers blend grape varieties in the same way as brewers blend hop varieties.

Even as I write, brewers have been carrying out trail-blazing work on creating beers using just one kind of hop to give a strong, pure flavour; like wines produced with a single variety of grape. I spent an enthralling night at an event called Cordon Hop, where one of the country's most respected brewers, Sean Franklin of Rooster's Brewery in Harrogate, was persuaded to make five beers specially for the occasion, each with only one variety of hop in the brew.

So we tasted a beer made exclusively with Fuggles hops, which Sean said smelt of 'dried grass until rubbed in the hand, then it had a smell of peaches and raspberries'. The beer in our glasses was vinous, deeply bitter and with more than a hint of apple. Described by the Hop Association as 'the most famous and revered of English hops', it gives a roundness, depth and bitterness to ale. At the same tasting we also revisited two beers which are both made entirely with Fuggles – Vaux's Harvest Moon, dark, smooth and well rounded and Whitbread's Fuggles Imperial, an updated India Pale Ale with lots of hop bitterness and depth. And if you get such extremes of flavour with just one type of hop, imagine what happens when you start to blend.

In fact, Fuggles is often blended with another famous hop, Goldings. But when Sean brewed solely with this fragrant hop his early results identified a citrus character which came through as delicate and refreshing in the final brew.

And then he brewed with First Gold, a new hop developed in 1995 by the Hop Research Department at Wye College, which Sean reckoned had an intense peach/apricot flavour as it went into the fermenter. Fruity, spicy beers may well contain First Gold – a prime example being Fuller's bottle-conditioned 1845; so thick, dark and spicy you could almost spread it on bread like Marmite! We also tasted King and Barnes's Harvest Ale, also made entirely with Goldings, though this time with the new green hops, and enjoyed a golden beer, soft and mellow as autumn itself.

Target hops, used for bitterness, unexpectedly flower in Caledonian's Golden Promise, one of the very few wholly organic ales using organic hop flowers as well as organic malt. Bramling Cross is a gorgeous hop which often puts the intense berry fruitiness into spicy winter ales; Challenger hops are perfumed and valued as a versatile blending hop producing well-balanced bitter depth. And so it goes on.

Different varieties of hop are added at different stages of the brew, again to enable the brewer to create even more flavours, perhaps putting in one type of hop at the start of boiling, then another later. And at the end of the brewing process, when the beer is conditioning in tanks, many brewers will add an extra measure of hops to strengthen the flavour, a practice called 'dry hopping'.

Hops can actually be used in cooking in their own right. In Belgium it has long been the custom to steam tender young hop shoots, which taste a little like asparagus, and this is being tried over here in hop-growing areas such as Hereford and Kent. You can use hops as flavouring in a recipe, but do so sparingly as they taste so bitter. Buy them from home-brew shops and crumble them in your fingers – a pinch can go into a salad dressing or home-made chutney or, best of all, horseradish; one of the recipes in this book includes a tiny amount in a lemon sorbet, helping to cleanse the palate. Ushers Brewery of Trowbridge wanted to sell beer sausages in their pubs, but found a judicious use of hops was preferable to adding liquid beer. The resulting organic pork-beer bangers are a triumph. Hop essence or oil is sometimes used in brewing instead of fresh hops, a method frowned upon by craft brewers, but it can certainly be used in cooking, perhaps to flavour a stir-fry, or even intensify a salad dressing; taste it first and you'll know you need to adopt the minimalist approach.

A Hereford cheesemaker hit on the cracking idea of embedding hops in the cheese rind, and I see no reason why you should not sprinkle a few on top of beer-bread dough before putting it in the oven. But be warned. I thought of flavouring a meat loaf with neat hops as a recipe for this book and clearly used too many. The result was disgusting!

I am always struck by how many terms brewing and cooking have in common – words like mashing, brewing, porridge, kettle – indeed, award-winning beer writer Roger Protz states in the introduction to an edition of his useful *The Real Ale Drinker's Almanac*, 'Brewing beer is like making tea. Both are the result of a simple infusion of basic ingredient and hot water.'

The basic ingredients of ale are barley, hops, yeast and water; in weiss or wheat beers a proportion of the grain is wheat. The starting point is barley, which specialist maltsters turn into malt by saturating the grain in water, then spreading it out in warm rooms to germinate so that the starch can be converted to sugar, which is crucial to the fermentation process. The maltster then roasts the malt: for pale, straw-hued beers less heat is used to produce a paler malt; dark beers such as porter contain a proportion of more intensely roasted malt, though ordinary grains of unmalted barley are also roasted and added to give greater depth of colour and flavour.

Now the malt is milled to produce a coarse sort of flour called grist – hence the expression grist to the mill. Part of the brewer's art then lies in mixing together various types of malt to get the desired taste and colour; often a little crystal malt is added, in which the sugar has been crystallized by kilning damp barley at a very high temperature immediately after germination, skipping the slow, drying process.

The grist goes into a vessel called a mash tun, where hot water is added – some breweries draw their own water from an underground well; again, the water used affects the character of the beer. Grist and water are mixed together into a kind of porridge. At this stage the malt releases sugars which are absorbed into the water, then the liquid (called wort) flows into the brew kettle (or copper), leaving the thick mush behind.

Now comes the process like making tea. The sweet wort is boiled in the copper with hops to provide the traditional beer bitterness and flavour. The hopped liquid is cooled and piped to fermenting vessels, where the yeast, a live fungus, creates a fierce reaction, its live cells gobbling up the sugar in the brew to turn it into alcohol and carbon dioxide. In British ales a top-fermenting yeast is used, creating a great, heaving crust on the top, a mind-blowing sight, accompanied by the warm aromas of malt, hops, bread and alcohol. This process takes about a week; after that most of the yeast is removed and the young beer transferred to tanks and left to mature or 'condition'.

To make lagers or pilsners a bottom-fermenting yeast is used – literally, a yeast that sinks to the bottom; the process takes longer, sometimes many months, because it is carried out at a cooler temperature.

During the conditioning, finings, from the air bladder of sturgeon, are added to make the yeast settle and give the brew its clarity. The liquid then goes into casks (barrels), or bottles.

And then comes, for me, one of the wonders of beer. This is a living product and the small amount of yeast left in the ale allows it to undergo a second fermentation in the cask in the pub cellar, or in the bottle. Sometimes extra sugar is added to encourage this process. That is the difference between real ale and keg beer, which is filtered and pasteurized. In the pub carbon dioxide is injected under pressure into keg beer to give the product fizz and head. With real ale the natural carbon dioxide produced by the yeast provides the sparkle and head; it has a rounded maturity and complexity you will not find in keg beers.

Here I have to nail my colours to the mast. I am a member of the Campaign for Real Ale, which saved live beer in this country and celebrated its Silver Jubilee in 1996, and which also encourages the smaller and regional brewers who originate many of the craft styles used in this book. Where I give recipes using draught beers I am always talking about real cask ale, never keg. In the case of bottled beers, many of the styles used in these pages are available bottle-conditioned; but to get the full palate of all the different flavoured beers now available I also cook with beer which is not bottle-conditioned. In my view there are some good bottled beers albeit not bottle-conditioned, and they are certainly preferable to keg beer. I use no canned beer in cooking. I find it an unpleasant product which tastes tinny, a flavour that seems to be accentuated during the cooking process.

# Beer Styles

Happily, beer styles are growing in number even as I write. It would take far too much space to give a full list, but here are the main ones to be found in this book. Beer strengths given as percentages refer to amount of alcohol by volume (ABV).

**Barley wine:** the brandy of the beer world, spirited and complex, extremely high in strength – usually at least 7 per cent and sometimes over 15 per cent (stronger than wine). Available bottled year round, and sometimes in small casks around Christmas.

**Bière de Garde:** strong, wine-like beers from northern France, best bottle-conditioned and often in corked bottles; can be above 7 per cent.

**Bitter:** an absurd term used to describe the whole gamut of English ales. This broad description is not just applied to beers with hop bitterness but to everything from delicate, light beers through those with floral, spicy, fruity and herbal flavours. Strength generally from just under 4 per cent to around 5 per cent. Best bitter and special bitter are the stronger versions.

**Brown ale:** a sweetish, dark brown beer with surprising body for its low strength of up to 3.5 per cent; flavour comes through well in cooking.

**Christmas or Winter ale:** strong, dark, spicy brews often found in small casks in pubs around Christmas or throughout winter to add jollity to our festivities or cheer us in the winter months

– usually 6–7 per cent, but can be stronger.

**Dunkel**: a German term for dark beer, which can be strong and spicy; *bock* is the German term for a strong beer, usually bottom-fermented.

**Festive Ales**: strong, often dark beers, at their best featuring all the Christmas pudding spices like nutmeg, cinnamon and ginger, and very often served around that time of year (see Christmas or Winter ale).

**Fruit beers**: for a long time the province of Belgium, which sends us a brilliant range, including cherry (kriek), raspberry (framboise), strawberry, plum, apricot, and many more, even banana, some very sweet, others with the sourer notes of Flanders brown beers. In the UK we are now brewing excellent but very different fruit ales, in which the fruit flavour is far more elusive and secondary to the hops – ours include damson and gooseberry.

**Ginger beer**: real ginger beer is a proper beer, often brewed with wheat, but noticeably flavoured with either grated root ginger or dried ginger. Great in cuisine.

**Gueuze**: one of those acquired tastes definitely worth acquiring. From Belgium, it is a sour, lambic style of beer, wonderfully vinous – to my mind the beer that comes nearest to wine.

**India Pale Ale (IPA)**: a strong ale originally produced for shipping out to the British Empire, and highly hopped to withstand the long passage, usually around 5.5 per cent.

**Lager**: a bottom-fermented beer with a clean taste which is, at its best, splendid. At its worst it is an all-embracing homogenous product which constitutes the basic bar drink. It can be golden or dark; pilsner is a more rounded, characterful version.

**Mild**: often dark but can be light, the UK's most lightly hopped weakest beers (perhaps 3 per cent) which can nonetheless be extremely quaffable and cook well, but are under-appreciated and, sadly, an endangered species.

**Old ale**: the term old is often misused by marketing men trying to give added cred. It is a medium-strength dark ale, the cousin to pale ale, which is not pale but mid-hued and also around 6 per cent.

**Porter:** said to be named after the London porters who drank it, this most marvellous of brews has made a strong comeback; it is a dark brew with a creamy head and a roast grain flavour often erupting into chocolate and coffee notes.

**Scotch ale:** the beers of Scotland, often referred to as 'wee heavies', have their own evolving tradition, but their main characteristic makes them one of my favourites – a malty flavour superb in cooking.

**Smoked beer:** often referred to as rauchbiers because they normally come from Germany – specifically northern Bavaria – smoked beers are made with smoked instead of roasted malt and have a pronounced, smoky flavour. English brewers are now taking up the style with a lighter hand to create a sweeter beer with a whiff of smoke.

**Stout:** similar to porter but stronger and darker – sometimes a real Bible black, with more body, made with higher roasted malts. There are sweet stouts and the Irish-style dry stouts, the classic accompaniment to oysters. Can be as strong as 14 per cent.

**Trappist beers:** heavenly by definition because they are brewed by Trappist monks in their abbey breweries at only six places: five in Belgium and one in France. These are beers of really huge character, strength (up to 14 per cent) and complexity; Chimay is probably the best known. When bottle-conditioned, they can be laid down. Abbaye beers imitate the style, but are generally brewed to a similar recipe not by monks but in commercial breweries; nonetheless, at their best they are excellent beers.

**Wheat beer or weissbier (sometimes called white):** made with a high proportion of wheat; this is one of the few beers meant to be served cloudy, the bottled sediment tipped vigorously into the glasss. From Belgium come pale, spicy wheat beers, of which Hoegaarden is probably the best known, and lambic wheat beers. These are open to the air so they spontaneously ferment with wild yeasts (fruit beers are often lambic). From Germany come top-fermenting wheat beers both pale and very dark, often with a pronounced banana or apple and boiled-sweet or bubblegum characteristic – quite delicious. The style is growing apace in England, where brewers are mixing wheat and barley with hops to create a rather different taste.

## Beers to Drink with Food

It's time to call time on the notion that wine is the only serious partner to a serious meal. Or even a frivolous one! Sparkle, depth, fruitiness, character; big, bold, smooth, sharp; sweet, dry, rounded, spirited; complex, acidic, spicy, spritzy; mellow, rich, aromatic, and, yes, even presumptuous . . . the descriptions that go with grapes are equally at home with hops.

Certainly the language of beer is as evocative as that of wine. Mown grass, butterscotch, sulphur, camphor, espresso, chocolate, tobacco, hazelnut, lemon, coriander, bubblegum, raisin, toast and treacle are all bandied about at beer tastings. And beer can boast its own vocabulary – malty, yeasty, hoppy, oaty and chewy.

There is a beer for every stage of the meal and for every dish, starting with a palate-titillating apéritif with the effervescence of champagne or the nuttiness of a dry sherry, through the big beers with a complex bouquet and those with the breadth of a brandy. A 'decent malt' isn't just a twenty-year-old whisky, now that beer has such bottle. For instance, Marston's Brewery have produced a beer called Single Malt, so named because it uses only Golden Promise malt, an older barley once used in the distilling industry.

The first rule when choosing a beer to go with your meal is: there are no rules. Have we escaped from the tyranny of the wine snob only to fall prey to the beer buff? I hope not. Choosing beer is intensely personal. Just as it is now perfectly acceptable to drink red wine with fish if that's what you like, the most important aspect of beer selection is identifying the styles and tastes that you enjoy. But your meal will be enhanced if you choose a beer which either complements the menu or is a clever contrast. You can deliberately partner strong flavours with an unassertive beer so that the food takes centre-stage, or choose a big beer that stands up to the dish.

When I'm matching beer to food, be it for drinking or cooking, I like to get family or friends to taste the beer first, describe the flavours they find, and suggest which foods might go with it.

At a beer tasting, pour two to three inches into a glass, leaving plenty of room above it for a swirl to release the aroma. Tippler's tip – put the glass on a flat table (or bar) to swirl, then it will stay in the glass; if you hold it up and swirl you'll get an eyeful! After the swirl, get your nose into the glass and have a good sniff; this will tell you if the beer is malty, bitter with hops, yeasty, fruity, and so on. Real beer experts can recognize the style and region of the beer simply from the aroma – and often know which brewery has produced it. Taste first through the tastebuds on the tip of your tongue, then swirl the beer all around your mouth to let the flavours develop. With beer, the aftertaste is important too. Sometimes a seemingly full-bodied beer tails away disappointingly, or you are left with a nasty tang; that's why at a beer tasting you won't see as many tasters spitting out the beer as you do at a wine tasting. That's my excuse, anyway!

As an apéritif, you might like a palate-cleanser such as a pale lager, pilsner or a slightly tart wheat beer full of champagne bubbles. Alternatively, a dark creamy mild is low in alcohol – sensible at the start of a meal – and often has a fino finish to take the place of sherry. Those who enjoy a kir royale will love a flute of Lindemans Framboise raspberry beer, pink and sparkling, served chilled – ridiculously cheap, at around £1 a bottle, for such a beautifully crafted beer still conditioning in the bottle.

Here are some broad outlines for drinking beer with food, roughly in order of weight, strength and where they might fit into a meal – follow or ignore them as you wish.

**Pale Dry Lager or Pilsner; Belgian Sparkling Wheat Beer:** more delicate fish such as sole, plaice and poached salmon. Do what the Belgians do and put a slice of lemon on the rim of the glass. Some white meats such as chicken breast, or pork and veal escalopes. Vegetarian dishes like tomato flans and asparagus with hollandaise. Clean, stronger lagers and pilsners are also good with curries.

**Lighter Cask Ales and Bitters:** fuller-flavoured chunky fish such as cod or haddock in batter; milder cheeses either raw or in a light cheese quiche or soufflé; fresh fruits such as apples and plums; chicken and ham pie; more delicate vegetable, fish or meat terrines.

**Dark and Light Milds:** low in alcohol, so good early in the meal, a dark mild can be surprisingly robust and might go with chicken liver or mushroom pâté and onion soup. A light mild can be lovely with a bowl of bacon and spinach salad or savoury pancakes.

**Floral Ales – the beers with a hint of clover, heather or blossom:** summery beers to go with summer foods, such as salads, roast peppers, goat's cheese tart topped with olives, juicy fruits like melon and peach, tomatoes sliced with mozzarella.

**Ales Flavoured with Herbs and Spices:** beers are now brewed with everything from coriander to mint. Wonderful with food and to cook with. Match the strongest flavour in the beer to the food.

**Full-bodied Hoppy Bitter:** not surprisingly, pub dishes – home-cooked ham and chutney, pork pies, ploughman's, steak and kidney pie, toad-in-the-hole, braised beef. The strongest, most characterful cask beers can partner roasts – maybe Yorkshire beers with beef and Yorkshire pudding.

**Malty Ales (often a Scottish characteristic):** a wonderful food accompaniment, smooth and full-bodied. Delicious with red meats, venison and stronger game birds, also with good malty bread, a mellow Cheddar and desserts such as treacle pudding.

**Porter:** a dark, roasted brew, like stout, porter can be drunk with shellfish, but is delightful with meat dishes such as gammon, or roast leg of pork with crackling. Conversely, its frequent bitter coffee and chocolate notes make it wonderful with chocolate pudding, coffee ice cream and raspberry and strawberry desserts.

**Stout:** traditional accompaniment to seafood. A black stout with a thick, creamy head and hint of either saltiness or sweetness brings oysters, lobsters, crab and mussels out of their shells (though weissbier is good with moules marinière). Some of the strong imperial stouts can be drunk with red meats like grilled steak, braised collops of beef or a mixed game pie, or at the end of a meal.

**Fruit Beers:** covers a multitude of – no, not sins – virtues. From Belgium comes a huge range of fruit beers. Some are cherry sweet, such as Timmermans and Lindemans, or on the sour side, such as Liefmans. Cherry, or kriek, is the most common and can be drunk in place of red wine with duck, but is also superb with chocolate puddings, as is raspberry beer. Other fruit beers include peach, plum, damson and blackberry beers. British fruit beers tend to put the hops first with just a hint of the fruit, making them appropriate with main dishes, both meat and vegetarian.

**Ginger Beer**: not the sweet, non-alcoholic, soapy pop but a proper, strong beer flavoured with root or dried ginger, often in a wheat beer, generally dark and aromatic. Excellent accompaniment to spicy foods.

**Wheat – or Weiss – Beers**: pale, tangy wheat beers from Belgium with delicate acidity are perfect with white fish and a marriage in heaven with poached salmon; lighter starters (asparagus with hollandaise); lightly spiced foods such as some of the more delicate Thai flavours; chicken or almost any white meat in a cream sauce; lentil and tomato pâté. Bavarian wheat beers are deeper-hued and more rounded with a boiled sweet and apple/banana palate, quite strong and refreshing with stronger fish such as tuna, and salty meats like gammon, or pork cooked with apples, sausages and appley desserts. Hefty, dark wheat beers are on a par with our dark festive ales and can stand up to much stronger flavours such as game.

**India Pale Ale**: a recently revived style of a beer that was deliberately highly hopped and strong to withstand passage to India during Empire days, bitter and full of body – *the* drink to accompany hot curries.

**Smoked – or Rauch – Beers**: until quite recently only brewed in Germany, where they have a throat-catching, tongue-curling intensity which makes them an acquired taste, but they are good with some of the powerful German hams and sausages, strong-tasting smoked fish, robust cheese and, conversely, an intensely sweet dessert like treacle tart. New in the past year or so are more mellow versions from the UK and USA, with just a whiff of smoke, which can be drunk in larger quantities, perhaps at a barbecue.

**Trappist or Abbey-style Beers**: wonderfully complex vinous beers of great diversity and strength – from around 6 to 12 per cent. They are some of the world's very greatest beers (see page xvii), and are absolutely superb with strong-tasting meats such as haunch of venison, rich game pie, well-hung game birds, roast beef and turkey on festive occasions, and big, ripe cheeses such as Stilton and really oozy Camembert or Gorgonzola.

**Winter or Christmas Ales:** produced by breweries for those dark times of the year when we need cheering up – or festive occasions when their strength makes us merry and adds to the festivity! Often both bottled and on draught (you'll sometimes see a small cask on the bar), these are dark, feisty beers redolent of all the Christmas cake ingredients such as cinnamon, nutmeg, raisins and candied peel. They make perfect companions to rich fruit cake, plum pudding, mince pies and, with port-like notes, a game casserole, jugged hare, or even roast pork with caramelized crackling.

**Barley Wine:** the brandy of the beer world, so strong it can reach 15 per cent and top the strength of wine, rounded and with more than a hint of the distillery. An end-of-the-meal drink when your toes are on the fender and you are at your most philosophic.

A one-to-one with beer *sommelier* Mark Stroebandt, at Belgo's, is an eye – or palate – opener. He'll suddenly say: 'Have you tried X with X?' and call for yet another Belgian beer and a small plate of edibles, which set each other alight. Mark has been on beer courses in the same way Masters of Wine go on wine courses; he's also trained at various breweries. 'There are no golden rules. If someone likes moules marinière with a pineapple beer, then that's fine.' Surely not.

'The most important aspect in pairing beer with food is always to find a balance. When you are dealing with delicate flavours such as asparagus, for instance, then you need a subtle, delicate beer and that is one type of balance. The other is to look for a contrast – a sweetish meat such as rabbit can be served with Rodenbach (a sour, red, winey beer from Flanders), while Rodenbach Alexandre, cherry-flavoured, is good with venison – though a beer I find people need to be convinced about.'

One of the great taste twinnings I learned from Mark was to sip a small Gueuze – again a sour, brown beer from Flanders, used by Belgians to make their classic carbonnade – alongside a salad with a simple vinaigrette dressing. The sourness in the beer exactly echoes the acerbity of the vinegar. Magic.

Some of Mark's suggestions for classic couplings involving Belgian beers include creamy, sweet, dark Gouden Carolus (named after Holy Roman Emperor Charles V) alongside dark, Belgian chocolate; for white chocolate he suggests raspberry beer. Strong, Trappist Chimay Bleu he recommends with big cheeses and as an after-dinner beer; Lindemans tea beer, flavoured with tea leaves, is served as a refreshing drink with a slice of lemon – perhaps the definitive accompaniment to cucumber sandwiches (Mark also suggests it in a sorbet). He twins Leffe Blonde, one of the few sweet blonde beers, with some fruit dishes, while a Trappist Chimay Blonde goes with Indian dishes – and with spicy food in general the Belgian Saison-style beer, with its peppery aftertaste, is perfect.

## Tips on Cooking with Beer

Beer is brilliant in the kitchen – far more versatile than wine. You can use it for marinating, basting, baking; long, slow casseroles – and quick stir-fries; sauces and soups; breads and batters; crisp fritters and melting moments; to add tartness to a salad dressing, spice to a curry and pungency to a pickle. It glazes, caramelizes, tenderizes, lifts, enriches. It can flavour – or accompany – fish, game, meat, molluscs, poultry, vegetables, fruit, cheese, chocolate, cakes, puddings and pies. Keep your mind open, a bottle opener to hand, and be creative. Here are some of the ways of using beer you'll find in this book.

**Aspic:** certain beers work well as a setting agent. Pale, zesty wheat beers with their acidity and citrus notes make a fine aspic that can be used to pot fish or meat, as a jellied glaze such as the whole salmon in beer aspic you'll find in the fish chapter – or a dessert like my porter jelly (see page 240).

**Baste:** on top of the stove or in the oven, basting with beer adds flavour, colour and sheen to roast meat and game, or vegetables turned and turned in ale.

**Batter:** putting beer in the batter when you deep-fry fish produces the best cod and chips in the world – the yeast in live ales helps make the batter light, fluffy and crisp, while the hops provide just a touch of brewery in the aroma. Then again, it's brilliant in sweet and savoury pancakes and crêpes. And whisk real ale into your

Yorkshire pudding batter and see it hit the top of the oven.

**Bread**: again, flavour and texture. Beer breads are the staff of life, malty and yeasty. Use the dregs of a bottle-conditioned beer, containing the yeast sediment, to prove your own yeast as an interesting kitchen experiment – then use the liquid beer in the dough itself.

**Cakes**: an eye-opener. A light beer makes a light sponge; a dark porter or stout a chocolate cake to die for (see my drowning by porter cake, page 253); and a strong, spicy barley wine or Christmas ale the definitive solid-with-fruit cake.

**Caramelize**: you get a wonderful mahogany varnish on vegetables and fruit when you sauté with butter and beer; beer brings out their sweetness, too.

**Casserole or braise**: beer is brilliant for long, slow cooking in the oven, adding richness and a great depth of flavour to meat and game, tenderizing even the toughest old birds or beasts in the process.

**Grill**: fish and meat can be brushed with beer under the grill – such as smoked beer on pork ribs; fruity bitter mixed with mustard on gammon; honey, ale and rosemary blended to flavour lamb chops.

**Marinate**: a robust beer marinade is every bit as good as red wine for flavouring and tenderizing meat and game, choosing your beer as appropriate, then either using the marinade in long, slow cooking or preparing separately to make a gravy.

**Neat**: alcohol evaporates during cooking – but if you use beer raw in a salad dressing or a fruit beer in a cold desert such as a syllabub of trifle, it stays alcoholic. Equally good in ice creams and sorbets.

**Pastry**: the right beer lends lightness and flavour to pastry – a hoppy one for a savoury dish, fruit for a pudding; good choux pastry and suet pastry, too.

**Poach**: an excellent way to flavour fish and fruit (maybe fruit beer but not always) which can be left to chill in the poaching liquor; or poach chicken fillets and vegetables such as chicory and asparagus, then use the hot liquor to make a sauce.

**Pot roast:** a whole joint of meat, game or poultry emerges brown and succulent from a casserole, with root vegetables and beer in the bottom forming the base of an accompanying sauce or gravy.

**Preserving:** ale can be used in chutney and in mustard; hops can flavour the vinegar. Sliced red onions can be soaked in chilli beer to accompany spiced dishes.

**Roast:** brush a joint with beer while roasting for a crisp, dark finish – and use it to flavour the pan juices for the gravy.

**Sauce:** yes, beer can be delicate as well as robust. Use golden lagers and wheat beers in a white sauce with fish and vegetables, fruit beers in sauces with game, duck and puddings.

**Steam:** steaming in beer – not to be confused with American Steam Beer – is the way to cook mussels; use a pale wheat beer for its lemon edge.

**Steep:** soak dried fruit from currants and raisins to figs and apricots in beer to either serve neat or use in cooking – works well with dried mushrooms and chestnuts, too.

**Stir-fry:** fling a gingerbeer or oyster stout in your wok with the same abandon as you would soy or oyster sauce.

**Stock:** simmer meat bones and mollusc shells in a mixture of beer and water to make stock which you can freeze in small quantities and use to enrich soups, sauces and stews.

The pzazz comes in deciding which beer to use and which method to use. There are no hard and fast rules, any more than you stick to 'white wine with fish, red wine with meat'. If that was the criterion, whoever would have thought of pairing stout with oysters? It is the texture and flavour of each ingredient, not its type, which determines the beer you should use.

Albert Roux put it most succinctly: 'When I am cooking with beer I always taste it first, as you would do with wine, to see what will go with it,' he told me. He's quite right. Every time I come across a new beer I taste it with my husband and son and we all call out the flavours we find – could be anything from candyfloss to compost – say what we'd like to cook with it and what we'd like to drink it with, which may not be the same thing at all.

But there are some guidelines. First, it's a myth that wine is more successful in cooking because it is higher in alcohol and acidity. Alcohol disappears in cooking and in any case today's trend is towards stronger beers. And beer actually has quite a respectable level of acidity from both the hops and malt.

What is important is to use a beer with plenty of flavour, especially if it is for long, slow cooking, so that you can still identify beer in the finished dish. In slow-cooked dishes, I add a drop of the neat beer at the end of cooking time just before serving to 'bring back' the flavour. In some dishes prepared with beer you cannot actually identify the beer; but it has somehow contributed – to texture, to aroma, to colour, to some elusive flavour at the back of the palate you cannot quite place.

Here are a few helpful hints when cooking with beer, some of them passed on to me by chefs and brewers. In fact, I have found that some of the most brilliant ale creators are both chefs and brewers. One such is Martin Barry who bravely founded the Salopian Brewery in a hotchpotch building on the edge of Shrewsbury, where I found not just hops and barley but piles of fresh root ginger, Chinese spices, soft fruit and herbs – all used to create beers in which the culinary process meets brewing. Martin has produced bottles of live ale which continue to ferment on the shelves of beer stores and supermarkets. He cast off his brewer's apron and donned his chef's hat to help me with some hints on using live ales in cooking: 'Draught bitter, as its name suggests, tends to have a dryness and bitterness due to acidity from the hops and malt, and because most of the sugar in it is consumed by the yeast. Most bitters should not constitute more than a third to a half of the total liquid needed in a dish due to tannin in the hops, which is the most likely reason for a beer dish to develop a slightly bitter tang.' So avoid some of the hoppier, more uncompromising bitters in casseroles and stews; but they are fine in a batter which is cooked rapidly, or in pastry and glazes, where a relatively small amount is used. Similarly, highly hopped beers should be avoided in dishes where the liquid is reduced over a high heat, as this can concentrate the bitterness.

However, there are plenty of other beer styles which do lend themselves to casseroles, in particular stout and porter, smoked beers, barley wines and fruit beers which are lovely with game. Fruit beers are also sexy in sauces, as are the golden spritzy wheat beers.

Martin says that cereals, such as flour and oats, work especially well as thickening agents in beer dishes because they disperse the concentration of hop flavours and create a smoother taste. 'Salts in beer have a part to play. They make the flour cells harden round the edge and produce a crisper batter. Add a little extra baking powder in baking because it reacts with the acid in the beer and fluffs it up. Avoid lighter beers in casseroles and stocks because the flavour disappears and all you're left with is the hops.'

While Martin has deserted food recipes for beer recipes, one man cooking with beer every working day is Charles Noorland, Head Chef at Belgo Centraal in London's Covent Garden. Charles is from Holland, another country with a noble beer tradition, so he joined Belgo in 1995 with a great respect for *cuisine à la bière*, and is an expert at using beer in cooking and designing dishes to accompany beer. At Belgo, only Belgian beers are served – hardly a restriction since they stock around a hundred different makes, from the tangy lambic brews impregnated with wild yeast to the intense fruit beers such as banana and strawberry, from skull crackingly potent Trappist beers, to sour Flemish brown ales and delicate wheat beers – not forgetting mint beer and even tea beer! Charles's menu encompasses beer dishes both robust and subtle, ranging from a filling Flemish beef stew, traditionally prepared with the sour brown ales of the region – he uses Liefmans extraordinary Goudenband brown ale – to monkfish in a wheat beer and cream sauce. Above all, he is a man who believes in the pleasure of beer. 'Cooking with beer should be fun. You should be adventurous and open to different flavours. Don't take it too seriously,' is his advice.

At Belgo he uses beer in modern dishes such as chicken liver parfait with a raspberry beer *gelée* alongside, fruit salad with a white beer sorbet, grilled lobster with a beurre blanc sauce made with an abbey-style 'tripel' (literally, triple strength). Belgo's diners are equally at home with everyday Belgian dishes, such as rabbit or venison stew made with kriek – dark sweet and sour cherry beer – or chicken cooked with beer and mustard.

'There should be a balance of flavours – a beer sauce should complement the dish, never overpower it,' he said. 'Balance a strong taste. You don't want to be eating beer, it just has to be there somewhere in the background.' While I like to add the yeast sediment in the bottle to recipes involving flour such as bread and batter, it should never be used in sauces because it can make a cream sauce curdle or separate. When Charles is using a very hoppy beer he likes to balance the bitterness by sweetening the sauce with a little sugar or honey, and he favours dark, malty beers for long, slow cooking. With very strong, full-flavoured beers, such as the Trappist brews, he reckons a little goes a long way.

'Right at the end, just before serving, elevate the flavour by adding a drop of beer neat from the bottle. A fruit beer, for instance, will change to something more savoury during cooking so bring it back at the end.'

The Belgians use beer in many more ways than we do over here. Chocolates, for instance, can contain Belgian fruit beer; most breweries make a beer with a cheese connection, such as Orval. Belgo hold beer tastings, pairing 10–18 different cheeses with beer, and Belgian bars serve the beer of the month with the cheese of the month. English landlords, take note!

# Keeping Beer

### Cask-conditioned Ale
This can be bought direct from the pub or from a brewery which sells to the public. Pubs and breweries now have special re-usable containers for supplying their draught ales to domestic customers, or you can take your own containers, after rinsing then out thoroughly. Whether for cooking or drinking with food, buy on the day you need it and keep it somewhere cool until use, preferably out of the light; do not unscrew the top until you want to drink or cook. Serve 'cellar' cool, around 12°C, rather than chilled – if a beer is ice cold you lose the different strands of flavour that go with your meal.

### Bottled Ale
A huge range of beer styles and brands is now supplied bottled, everywhere from off-licences, specialist beer stores and wine chains to leading supermarkets. Many bottled ales have been filtered to remove the yeast sediment, and you should follow the 'use by' date on the bottle, or use within six months. Store upright in a cool, dark place.

## Bottle-conditioned Beers

For my money, the best bottle to serve on the dinner table. These are live beers undergoing a secondary fermentation in the bottle, which gives them a superb complexity and rounded character that can compete with wine. Strong bottle-conditioned beers will keep indefinitely; I have had the privilege of drinking a 14 per cent Thomas Hardy's Ale bottled in the 1950s and found it superb, and some bottled beers nearly a century old have been found to be still drinkable. Like a fine wine, their character changes as they age. Always buy more bottle-conditioned Festive or Winter Ale than you need and keep it for next year or the year after. Again, store in a cool, dark place, ideally a cellar, and keep upright, even in the case of corked beer bottles, because if laid down on the side the yeast sediment can harden along the inside of the bottle.

# Serving Beer

## Draft Beer

If in a container with a small tap on the bottom, tip the glass at an angle by the base of the tap and turn it on slowly and gently or it will suddenly flood out all over your feet. For the table, you can fill a big jug for people to serve themselves. If pouring from the top of the container, again tip the glass at an angle and pour, slowly straightening the glass to get a head on the top.

## Bottled Beer

Some bottled beers, such as golden lagers, pilsners and pale wheat beers, should be slightly chilled in the fridge; serve others cellar-cool; strong and dark beers to accompany red meat, game and some hot puddings should be at room temperature. Do not remove cap or cork in advance to 'breathe', as you would with wine – the beer will actually lose its life. When pouring, hold the glass at an angle to the beer, again slowly straightening to form a head. Always stand bottle-conditioned beer upright for at least a day so that the yeast can settle; pour slowly and smoothly, leaving the final half-inch of yeast sediment in the bottle, or it will cloud the beer. This yeast sediment can be used in cooking, especially in batters and bread, but not in sauces, which may curdle.

## Glasses

The key to enjoying beer with your meal. Unless it is a one-course meal of hearty, pub-style food such as ploughman's or steak and kidney pie, you will very rarely use pint – or even half-pint – glasses or tankards. Not only do they look clumsy on the dinner table, and somehow relegate the occasion to the public bar, but a whole pint of ale is almost a food in itself. It will fill you up and satisfy your appetite so that you can't enjoy the food on your plate.

Instead, suit your glass to the beer and the stage of the meal. Serve a dark mild before a meal in a large schooner, an effervescent pale wheat beer or raspberry beer as an aperitif in a champagne flute.

Many Belgian and Bavarian beers have their own glasses, which are exquisite and a joy to collect. Even so, they are generally large enough to take the whole bottle and you may not want a whole bottle with one dish, so go for a wine glass. Stemmed white-wine glasses are fine for pale wheat beers; larger, slender glasses widening towards the rim are excellent for lagers and pilsners. Big beers to accompany big meat and game dishes require those really big-bowled red-wine glasses – and don't fill them, leave space above for the beer to release all its aroma.

I often use some of the slightly larger, heavier whisky-shot-style tumblers for dark beers such as stout and porter served with a meal; the cut crystal ones, especially, look beautiful on the dining table. Triangular dessert wine glasses are ideal for fruit beers at the end of a meal, but stay with the tumbler for a drop of porter or Festive Ale with the pudding.

Brandy glasses are absolutely fine to swirl and warm a barley wine or a really strong Scotch malt ale in your hands at the end of a meal. Although you would pour out more than a brandy shot, you certainly don't want a half pint – often sold in tipple-sized third or half-pint bottles, two of these are quite sufficient between six people at the end of a meal. Just enough to put the world to rights.

# STARTERS

To talk about using beer in starters is a subject as big as a whole cookbook, because first courses embrace as many flavours as main courses. They are actually my favourite part of the meal and I quite often have a second starter instead of a main course when eating out. Since a starter is small I feel it should have a concentrated flavour and beer has a role to play here. Quality not quantity, pared down and to the point. A zingy, pale wheat beer is wonderful in aspic on a salmon tartlet or a hollandaise with asparagus; a strong fruit beer is perfect in a sweet and savoury jelly to accompany a robust game terrine; and a dark spicy beer is delicious in an onion marmalade alongside thin slices of smoked venison. Try a sweet stout glaze on oysters, or use beer as an ingredient in vinaigrette to accompany all sorts of starters – a summer roast-cod salad, for example.

Beer is equally valuable in helping to fluff up thick little pancakes which can be bases for a savoury topping – smoked trout and horseradish, perhaps – or in thin pancakes wrapped around a delicious filling. And in another kind of batter, the deep-fried variety, a golden bitter or pale pilsner adds crispness to a coating for mushrooms or vegetables with dips, or even for quails' eggs in beer batter.

Beer is also brilliant in a huge range of pâtés and terrines; tart wheat beers are used with dill in fish terrines, deep spicy ales in layered game terrines and a dark porter makes a surprise appearance in a chicken liver pâté.

Alternatively, if you are having an informal lunch or supper with just a light main course, beer is ideal for making a starter more substantial. The recipe for mussels with beer and bacon, for instance, is almost a meal in itself.

Ideally, beers to accompany should not only suit the starter but also the stage of the meal – they should stimulate the appetite. A hearty starter which demands a heavy beer should be served with just a drop in a sherry schooner or a spirits shot glass.

# Ale Choux Filled with Horseradish Cheese (serves 6)

One area where beer comes into its own is in pastry making. All kinds of pastry can be improved by adding ale including choux, both savoury and sweet (see page 243). Here I used Golden Promise brewed by Caledonian in Edinburgh, a fruity, ripe ale with some malt in the flavour, made entirely from organic ingredients and available both cask and bottle-conditioned. It produces a light, caramel-coloured choux with just a hint of hops, making a perfect bun for a savoury filling. I have mixed cream cheese with a dash of horseradish, but you could equally fill the buns with a Stilton and broccoli sauce, spiced fish mousse, crème fraîche mixed with chopped prawns, creamed wild mushrooms – whatever you like.

150 ml (¼ pint) fruity, malty bitter
50 g (2 oz) unsalted butter
65 g (2½ oz) plain flour
2 medium eggs, beaten

175 g (6 oz) cream cheese
A little pouring yoghurt
1 tsp horseradish sauce or ½ tsp grated fresh horseradish

Sift flour into a bowl; put beer and butter into a pan and bring to the boil. Remove from heat and quickly tip the flour into the pan all at once, then beat with a wooden spoon until the mixture forms a ball. Set aside to cool slightly for about 10 minutes, then heat the oven to 400°F, 200°C, gas mark 6.

While it is heating, trickle a little egg at a time into the mixture and beat it in, continuing until the mixture reaches piping consistency. Line a baking dish with buttered foil and either pipe blobs or éclair shapes – or just drop heaped tsps – on to the lined baking tray.

Bake towards the top of the oven for 25 minutes, resisting any impulse to open the oven door. The buns should be puffed and golden brown. Turn off the oven, remove buns and make a slit in each, partly opening them, then return to the oven for 10 minutes, leaving the door open so they can dry out.

While the choux are cooking, stir a little yoghurt into the cream cheese to thin it slightly, then add the horseradish sauce or grated horseradish. Let the choux cool, then fill them with the mixture. Makes around 12 – serve 2 each as a starter, accompanied by a salad with a walnut-oil dressing, or you can pipe tiny walnut-sized choux to make about 24 and use them as part of a buffet.

*To drink: Golden Promise is excellent, but at 4.9 per cent fairly strong for the start of a meal, so chill it slightly and serve in a wine glass. Or try a light draught bitter with a clean citrus hint to offset the horseradish, such as prize-winning Ridley's IPA, which tastes stronger than its 3.5 per cent.*

# Black Pudding Baked with Mustard and Mild
## (serves 6)

Black pudding is much loved in the Black Country – and so is mild, in particular Banks's mild, which is brewed in Wolverhampton, though they just call it Banks's now because mild doesn't seem sexy enough to the marketing men. I've eaten black pudding with ale in it and splendid it was. In this recipe the black pudding is cooked in the oven in a mustard sauce made with mild simmered with onion. I find that the combination of beautifully balanced Banks's with its elusive sulphuric tang, and rich black pudding, encapsulates the flavour of the Midlands. There are various milds you can use, but choose one with a good balance between malt and hops, and a dry finish, such as Hanby's Black Magic Mild or Harvey's XX Mild; the darker the mild, the darker the sauce.

1 large onion, peeled and chopped roughly
300 ml (½ pint) dry mild
1 large cooking apple, peeled, cored and sliced
50 g (2 oz) butter for frying

1 tbsp cider vinegar
3 level tbsps plain flour
1 dstsp English mustard powder
350 g (12 oz) black pudding links

Place onion and mild in a pan, cover, and slowly bring to simmering point. Leave to cook very gently for 30 minutes without boiling. Strain beer off and discard onion.
Melt 15 g (½ oz) butter in a frying pan and, when foaming, add apple slices and fry briefly on one side until brown. Turn over to brown the underside, sprinkling over the cider vinegar.

Divide slices between 6 individual ovenproof dishes – 3–4 in each. Carefully skin the black pudding links, halve them along their length, and place 2 pieces in each dish on top of the apple, flat side down.

Melt remaining butter in a pan and stir in flour, cooking for 2 minutes. Add the mild liquor and give a good stir, then transfer to a liquidizer with the mustard and liquidize. Spoon this sauce into the dishes to cover the black pudding, then bake above the centre of a warm oven (375°F, 190°C, gas mark 5) until a dark crust has formed on the top and the sauce underneath is bubbling.

Serve with chunks of malted grain bread to soak up the sauce.

*To drink: a dish where the cooking mild is an excellent accompaniment or Ballard's zestful Trotton Bitter with a bit of fruit to match the apple (also available bottled), served in a sipping tumbler.*

# Boozy Fennel Baskets (serves 6)

I first met Alistair and Joy Shaw when they were reluctantly leaving the pub where they – and Alistair's father before them – had been tenants for years, to take the risky step of owning a freehouse. Needless to say, they were feeling a little apprehensive. Apparently I stiffened their morale by telling them that a year hence they'd wonder why they ever hesitated. It took a little longer than that, but eighteen months later they invited me to lunch at the Froize (or Friar's Inn) at Chillesford near Woodbridge in Suffolk, where Alistair's clever cooking and fresh local ingredients are now packing them in. Here is a starter he created for me.

| | |
|---|---|
| 6 fennel bulbs | Approx 1 litre (1¾ pints) light |
| Sunflower oil to fry | summer ale* |
| 3 medium potatoes, peeled | Vegetable oil |
| 12 tomatoes, skinned and | Salt and pepper |
| chopped finely | Dill fronds to garnish |

Halve fennel bulbs, top and tail them. Heat sunflower oil and pan-fry fennel until browned on both sides. Season to taste. Place browned fennel in a deep oven tray and cover with summer ale. Cover with foil and place in a pre-heated oven at 335°F, 170°C, gas mark 3½ for about 1½ hours.

Slice potatoes, using a mandolin to gaufrette cut. Place 1 potato slice at the bottom of a lightly greased gaufrette mould and put 3 slices of potato around the sides. Close over the gaufrette mould and deep-fry for about 3 minutes. Repeat 6 times, placing each on kitchen paper to cool.

To serve: divide tomatoes between 6 serving dishes to create a bed of tomato crush. Place gaufrette baskets stuffed with braised

*Alistair used Adnams' Regatta brewed in Southwold, a pale, clean summer beer made with 100 per cent English malted barley and Golding hops, which was launched as a seasonal beer in summer 1996. You could also try Blackawton's summery Devon Gold. More and more breweries are now bringing out a summer beer – look for ripening barley hues and light bitter or floral flavours.

fennel on top, and pour a little of the cooking jus over the top. Garnish with dill fronds.

*To drink: either a cellar-cool summer ale or a slightly chilled bottled wheat beer with a tart citrus flavour, such as Hoegaarden.*

## Chestnuts Roasted in 1824 Particular

I generally devise the menu for the British Guild of Beer Writers' annual banquet, held in Ironmongers' Hall – six courses all cooked with ale and served with ale. The menu is different every year, naturally. However, ever since I first suggested them, beer-glazed roast chestnuts as nibbles have become a must. They make a welcoming start to a festive evening on a chill winter's night; the chestnuts are cooked with a rich, spicy Christmas Ale. I've used several – Ushers' 1824 Particular, their Christmas Ale, with its own nutty flavour works well, as do Ballard's Wassail and Young's Winter Warmer. These are quickly made and keep warm for ages.

1 tin cooked, peeled chestnuts    Christmas or Winter Ale
 (contains about 18)    1 tbsp clear honey

Arrange chestnuts in a single layer in a shallow oven-proof dish or meat tin. Pour over enough ale to just cover the bottom of the dish and add the honey. Place towards the top of a warm oven (375°F, 190°C, gas mark 5) and cook for around 40 minutes, turning the chestnuts over from time to time so that they are well coated in the beer, which will slowly cook to a dark glaze.

You could, of course, roast chestnuts in their shells if you have an open fire, then remove the shells and beer-glaze the chestnuts in a metal dish by the glowing coals. But you've probably got a life!

*To drink: Christmas or Winter Ale of course, preferably sitting round the fire after a cold walk on Boxing Day.*

# Chicken Liver Pâté with Dark Horse Porter (serves 6)

The Skirrid Mountain Inn near Abergavenny in Gwent is an ancient hostelry with a massive staircase from which Judge Jeffreys hung miscreants after trying them in the bar below. His ghost is said to linger here, but has little effect on the cooking skills of land-lady Heather Gant, a winner of Ushers' Brewery pub food awards. As a judge, I've enjoyed her creativity more than once, but never more so than in this dish, which won the prize for best beer dish. It's a recipe that breaks all the rules because Ushers' Dark Horse Porter is full-bodied and a trifle heavy for the first course, but it works brilliantly here. I will not soon forget sitting by an inglenook fire while snow fell outside, scooping up this rich, almost gamey pâté with an endless supply of hot melba toast.

Unsalted butter for frying and mixing
1 medium onion, peeled and chopped
2 cloves garlic, crushed with a little salt

450 g (1lb) chicken livers, cleaned and chopped
1 tsp dried thyme
Dash brandy or sherry
Salt and freshly ground black pepper
300 ml (½ pint) porter

Melt a knob of butter in a large frying pan. Add onion, garlic, chicken livers and thyme and sauté gently for about 5 minutes. Add porter and continue to simmer for a further 15 minutes until cooked through. Remove from heat and leave to cool slightly.

Process in a food processor or blender until mixed but not too smooth. Work in a knob of softened butter and the brandy or sherry. Press firmly into a serving dish or individual ramekins, melt more unsalted butter, and pour it over the top in a thin layer.

Chill until the pâté is firm and the clarified butter has set, then serve with a young leaf salad with walnut oil dressing, and lashings of hot, thin toast.

*To drink: Dark Horse Porter, available bottled, goes surprisingly well with this, considering it has a bitter chocolate edge. Other options for drinking or preparing the pâté include King and Barnes's bottle-conditioned Old Porter and the historic Old Growler, an intensely plain chocolate-edged porter, brewed by Nethergate Brewery at Clare in Suffolk to recreate the oldest known porter from London of the 1750s. They're all quite chunky, so a wine glassful is ample.*

## Chilled Melon with Cherry Beer (serves 6)

More of a tip than a recipe, and I only discovered it when using up some cherry beer – but it is such a delicious summery starter that it seemed a shame not to share it. The only advice I can give is on the ingredients: the melon must be a really ripe, sugary, bright orange Charentais and the cherry beer should be lusciously deep red and sweet but with just that sharp, almondy edge you get from a Belgian kriek (cherry lambic beer) to offset the sweetness – Lindemans, brewed in traditional farmhouse style, or Timmermans, are both good examples on sale here.

For 6 people chill 3 small to medium Charentais melons, cut in half round their diameter and scoop out the seeds, then fill with cherry beer. And that's it – except that I'd be very surprised if the diners recognize it as beer. It could almost be a liqueur.

Alternatively, scoop out melon balls and place in a container with thinly sliced mango or peach, pour over cherry beer and leave to macerate in the fridge for a few hours, then pile the fruit into tall glasses, drizzle over the steeping liquor, sprinkle on a little very finely chopped mint, loop a couple of fresh cherries over the rim and serve.

You can also dress thinly sliced melon in cherry beer and serve it with Parma ham and a red leaf salad. Or, for another delicious starter soak dried figs in a dark, spicy beer and serve them with Parma or similar ham and salad.

*To drink: I wouldn't drink anything with this as the drink is in the melon; if you must, have a small wine glass of well-chilled dry lager that won't try to compete with the cherries.*

# Duck Liver and Pancetta Salad with Gueuze Dressing
## (serves 6)

Gueuze is perhaps the Belgian beer for the connoisseur – where beer truly meets wine. It is produced in a small area outside Brussels and is a blend of young and mature lambic beers fermented with wild yeast and then stored in oak casks, where more microorganisms in the wood again attack the beer. The result is tart and acidic with some cider sourness leading to a fino finish; if this is an acquired taste, it is one definitely worth acquiring. The famous beer, wine and food pub, the White Horse at Parson's Green in London is a great supporter of Belgian beers and chose a classic of the style brewed by the Cantillon working Gueuze Museum in Brussels to create a dressing to perfectly balance the richness of the duck in its coating of spice and smoked paprika.

450 g (1 lb) fresh duck livers
1 tbsp smoked paprika
1 tbsp ground ginger
½ tbsp cinnamon
Salt to taste
100 g (4 oz) wild rocket
100 g (4 oz) washed pousse
150 ml (¼ pint) Cantillon Gueuze
1 tbsp wholegrain mustard
Ground black pepper
150 ml (6 fl oz) extra virgin olive oil
225 g (8 oz) pancetta or smoked streaky bacon
½ bunch basil, shredded finely

Quickly rinse duck livers and pat dry in kitchen paper. Trim off white fat and roll in a mixture of smoked paprika, cinnamon, ginger and salt, then set aside.

Wash pousse and rocket in a sinkful of cold water, discarding any discoloured leaves, and leave in a colander to drain.

Whisk together Cantillon Gueuze, wholegrain mustard and a grating of black pepper in a mixing bowl, then gradually whisk in 100 ml (4 fl oz) of the oil to give a creamy dressing.

Place a thick-based frying pan on a low heat with 50 ml (2 fl oz) olive oil and pancetta or bacon cut into small pieces and increase heat to high. When slightly browned, remove pancetta/bacon, drain on kitchen paper, and add directly to the dressing. Return pan to the stove and when oil is lightly smoking add the duck livers and cook for 1–1½ minutes on each side (slightly longer if you prefer them better done), then also drain on kitchen paper.

Add rocket and pousse to the dressing and mix well. Divide between 6 plates, top with the warm duck livers and serve immediately, garnished with shredded basil.

*To drink: definitely Gueuze, which perfectly complements classic oil/wine vinegar salad dressings. Alternatively sip a lightly smoked beer to pick up the smoked paprika. A non-sweet Belgian cherry beer in small glasses is also good.*

# Duet of Smoked Salmon and Smoked Halibut Laced with Stout Vinaigrette (serves 6)

Stout is the traditional accompaniment to seafood though, given its substance and dark hue, perhaps an unlikely one. Historically, it was swigged down with oysters – at a time when they were cheap and cheerful – and perhaps it is the hint of sweetness with underlying dryness, and the smoothness of drinking it through the creamy head, that  makes it the perfect partner for salty molluscs. I like it most of all with smoked fish, as in this recipe from cook and food writer Phillip Buswell, head chef of the Tollemache Arms in Harrington, Northants, a sixteenth-century country inn.

| | |
|---|---|
| 175 g (6 oz) smoked salmon | 1 tsp English mustard |
| 175 g (6 oz) smoked halibut | 50 g (2 oz) fresh coriander |
| Oakleaf lettuce for garnish | 100 ml (4 fl oz) stout |
| *Vinaigrette* | 50 ml (2 fl oz) vinegar |
| 2 egg yolks | 50 ml (2 fl oz) olive oil |

Make the vinaigrette by blending all the ingredients, except the olive oil, in a food processor, then add the olive oil very slowly, a little at a time, and correct seasoning.

Arrange smoked salmon and halibut on 6 plates and decorate with oakleaf lettuce; drizzle vinaigrette over the fish and serve.

*To drink: there is nothing wrong in serving stout, slightly chilled, but only a wine-glass full as it is rather filling. I think I might go for something lower in alcohol to start the meal, such as a dark mild, which will refresh without competing with the fish.*

## Fennel in Weissbier Mayonnaise (serves 6)

German weissbiers are top-fermenting wheat beers with a tart spiciness which comes from the yeast. One of the best known over here is Schneider Weisse, brewed at the George Schneider family brewery in Bavaria. It has earned itself a permanent place on the shelves of some of our best-known drinks chains – despite competition from all the other German weissbiers now on sale in the UK, including supermarket own brands. It's a powerfully perfumed and flavoured, amber-hued, sparkling drink with hints of banana and bubblegum, some of which disappear in heating. But used neat in this dressing the characteristic acid-drop fruitiness of south German wheat beers complements fennel's aniseed flavour to create an interesting mayonnaise.

6 medium heads fennel
1 bottle German weissbier

*Mayonnaise*
2 egg yolks
1 tsp dry mustard
1 tsp salt

1 tsp sugar
½ tsp freshly ground black pepper
Up to 220 ml (8 fl oz) hazelnut oil
2 small pickled gherkins, diced finely

Remove tough outer leaves from fennel, and put fronds aside for later use. Place bulbs in a pan and half-cover with weissbier, then simmer, covered, for around 15 minutes until tender. Drain fennel, reserving stock, cool, then chill.

Make mayonnaise by mixing egg yolks with mustard, salt, pepper and sugar, then whisk in the oil very slowly, a few drops at a time (if it becomes too thick add a little of the beer stock from cooking the fennel). When most of the oil is incorporated and the mayonnaise is thick and smooth, stir in enough neat Schneider Weisse to reach the right consistency. Finally, stir in the chopped gherkins.

Cut each fennel bulb into several slices but without cutting right through the base, then fan on to a plate. Spoon mayonnaise in a semi-circle below and garnish with fennel fronds.

Serve as a starter with rye breadsticks.

*To drink: has to be the Schneider you have used in the dressing, which is the link between the vinaigrette and the fennel. Serve it just chilled in a tall glass (it has a magnificent one of its own).*

## Giant Yorkies with Beer and Onion Gravy (serves 6)

Yorkshire pudding is an institution, normally served with roast beef on Sunday – and many boast about how high their puddings rise. But the lightest, puffiest, crispest Yorkshire puddings contain beer; a fairly light golden beer to give air and lightness with just a hint of the brewery – a draught beer from Yorkshire itself such as Timothy Taylor's golden-hued best bitter, which uses Golden Promise malt. You can use this recipe to produce puddings to accompany the roast, or to make an even better version of a popular pub starter – giant Yorkies filled with onion gravy. Sadly, many pubs buy in ready-made frozen puddings and the tinned gravy to accompany them. These are the real McCoy, and with beer in both puddings and gravy.

| Pudding batter | Onion gravy |
|---|---|
| 225 g (8 oz) plain flour | 1 large onion, peeled and |
| 1 tsp salt | sliced |
| 2 medium eggs | 1 tbsp plain flour |
| 175 ml (6 fl oz) milk | 300 ml (½ pint) sweet stout |
| 175 ml (6 fl oz) light bitter, chilled | 300 ml (½ pint) beef stock or water |
| Dripping or vegetable fat (for cooking) | 1 sprig fresh thyme |

Put first 5 batter ingredients in a liquidizer and liquidize until light and covered with air bubbles, or mix in a mixing bowl.

If cooking for a starter, put a little dripping or vegetable fat into each of 6 round tins, about 4 inches (10 cm) across the base. If accompanying roast beef, either put fat into a meat tin to make one large pudding or into 12 bun tin compartments. Put on the top shelf of a hot oven (425°F, 220°C, gas mark 6) for 3–4 minutes until the fat is smoking hot. Pour in the pudding batter and bake for about 30 minutes until well risen, crisp and browned.

To make onion gravy, sweat sliced onion in dripping, stir in plain flour for and cook for 2 minutes. Add stout and simmer fairly briskly until thickened and reduced. Add stock or water, a sprig of thyme and simmer for 5 minutes, seasoning to taste, then remove thyme.

To serve as a starter, place one of the round puddings on a plate and fill with onion gravy.

*To drink: drink Taylor Landlord whenever you can get it, that's my advice. Otherwise have a half pint of a well-balanced York-shire bitter, preferably draught from the pub. Another treat would be bottled Black Sheep brewed at Masham near Ripon by Paul Theakston, ex-Theakston's brewery following its takeover by one of the nationals.*

## Jellied Weissbier Rillettes (serves 6)

The process of poaching either meat or fish in zestful, acerbic wheat beer produces a rich jellied stock – in the fish chapter I use it to coat a whole salmon in aspic (page 65). I discovered this dish quite by chance when I simmered a duck carcass in a half and half mixture of wheat beer and water to make a soup stock. After straining, I left it overnight to clear and next morning found a well-set savoury jelly, so gave up the idea of soup and used it to create potted duck and ham as a refreshing starter. I used a pale German Weissbier – Franziskaner Hefe-Weissbier (Hefe means it still contains the yeast) is spicy, tart and excellent; most supermarkets now sell their own brand of German weissbier.

Roast duck carcass with some meat left on it
Any giblets that came with the duck
1 small onion
1 bottle (approx 450 ml or ¾ pint) German wheat beer
Cold water

100 g (4 oz) gammon, cooked and diced
1 orange
Salt and pepper
2 tbsps chopped parsley
Watercress and orange segments to garnish

Place duck carcass, giblets and onion in a large pan and pour over weissbier. Add enough water to cover, then cover and simmer gently for around 1 hour. Remove duck carcass and pour stock through a sieve. When the carcass is cool, remove all the meat you can and cut into small pieces with any edible bits of giblets.

Place meat in a pan with diced gammon and zest from half the orange, then cover with stock and heat through gently, seasoning to taste with salt and pepper. Remove from heat, sprinkle chopped parsley in 6 individual starter-sized bowls along with a thin round of orange (peel and pith removed), then divide the duck and gammon mixture between them.

Allow to cool, then chill in the fridge until jellied – overnight is fine. To turn out place the bottom of the bowl briefly in hot water, then reverse on to a plate. Garnish with watercress and orange segments.

*To drink: a tulip-shaped glass of the chilled weissbier will be refreshing, a thin slice of orange floating in it. Or a good, golden lager such as Freedom Lager produced in south London at the UK's first lager microbrewery, made with yeast from the Stein Brewery in Bavaria and Saaz pilsner hops, and available bottled in High Street chains.*

# Mushrooms Marinated in Merman XXX (serves 6)

Mushrooms steeped in Merman XXX slither down your throat like juicy oysters. I first enjoyed this concentrated starter at a beer dinner for enthusiasts devised by pub landlady Heather Humphreys, a convert to beer cookery who has given me two or three recipes from her banquets. Licensee of the Rising Sun at Woodland near Ashburton in Devon, she used draught Merman XXX, an interesting beer brewed by Caledonian in Edinburgh to a Victorian recipe for India Pale Ale (also bottled in one of the main supermarkets). It is full and ripe with a mix of malt, fruit and biscuity caramel in the mouth. A spicy porter would serve as well.

2 rashers smoked, streaky bacon, diced
2 tbsps oil
1 fat clove garlic, chopped finely
1 shallot, chopped finely
175 ml (6 fl oz) Merman XXX
275 g (10 oz) button chestnut mushrooms (or mixed mushrooms)
1 bay leaf
Salt and freshly ground black pepper
1 heaped tbsp parsley, chopped

Sauté bacon in oil until crisp; remove with a slotted spoon. In same pan, fry garlic and shallot gently until soft but not brown; add mushrooms (whole if very small, otherwise sliced or quartered). Continue cooking gently until the juices begin to run. Add the Merman, bay leaf and seasonings, bring to the boil then turn down and simmer gently for 3–4 minutes, giving the pan an occasional shake.

Leave to cool, then remove bay leaf, stir in bacon, and refrigerate. Serve in 6 small dishes sprinkled with parsley and accompanied by hot, herby ciabatta.

*To drink: for a contrast you could chill a bottle of Merman's sister beer Golden Promise, a pale beer brewed with organic hops and barley – the well-balanced fruit and hop dryness will set off the dark, spicy mushrooms. Or choose a sweeter porter than the one you cooked with to underline the flavour of the mushrooms.*

# Mussels with Beer and Bacon (serves 6)

Cooking with beer is the norm in most Belgian bars, and mussels with beer is the most widely served dish (flippantly accompanied by frites). On a winter's night, to sit in one of Brussels's ornate, Gothic-style taverns by a roaring log fire, with a steaming cauldron of mussels set before you throwing off beer fumes, is one of life's great pleasures. London restaurant Belgo's triumphantly brought the style over here at their cavernous underground emporium in Covent Garden and their original restaurant in Chalk Farm, where waiters are garbed in monks' habits in the style of Trappists. Here is Belgo's version.

2 kg (4 lb) fresh mussels
2 sticks celery, chopped
½ large onion, diced
600 ml (1 pint) Belgian wheat
  beer*

200 g (7 oz) smoked bacon,
  cooked and diced
2 tbsps parsley, chopped
50 g (2 oz) butter

Clean and beard mussels; lightly sauté celery and onion in butter. Add mussels and then beer, bring to the boil and simmer briskly for around 4 minutes until the mussels open. Sprinkle bacon on at the end of cooking, otherwise it will make the mussels too salty. Sprinkle with parsley and serve with hot baguette to soak up the juices.

'In Belgium they would serve this with a bowl of frites – and a beer, of course,' says Belgo's executive chef Philippe Blaise.

*To drink: in Belgo's you might well drink Hoegaarden wheat beer, which is sparkling and aromatic. Personally I prefer a dark, dry stout, brilliant with shellfish, and a good partner to a dish more robust than the normal moules marinières.*

*At Belgo's they use Hoegaarden to create this dish, available there (and many pubs) on draught, but extensively available as a bottle-conditioned real ale in High Street chains and supermarkets ridiculously cheap for this craft product.

## Quails' Eggs in Rice Beer Batter (makes 24)

What goes best with spicy foods? Beer, of course – though preferably something a little more subtle than six pints of keg lager with the bhoona gosht! Both the Indian and Chinese cultures produce lighter, more aromatic pilsners, often made with rice, which more perfectly complement their food. Some of these are now imported bottled, but British brewers have also risen to the challenge of this lucrative Asian restaurant market by producing their own. It is usually a light, golden, aerated brew which makes batter as good as the batter you find round king prawns and banana fritters in Chinese restaurants. I've used it here to make exotic nibbles, and another version with fish (see page 54). Indian/Chinese pilsners on the market incorporating rice include Lal Toofan brewed by Ushers, Sun Lik produced in the UK by Shepherd Neame, and Tiger from Singapore.

| | |
|---|---|
| 24 quails' eggs | Pinch five-spice powder |
| ½ cup self-raising flour | 2 dstsps sesame seeds |
| ½ cup Lal Toofan (chilled) | Oil for deep frying |
| Pinch salt | |

Hardboil quails' eggs for 5 minutes, drain and plunge into cold water. Leave for 30 minutes, then shell carefully to avoid damaging the egg white. Put the next 4 ingredients into a liquidizer goblet and liquidize to produce a batter the consistency of stiff cream – add a little more flour or beer if necessary. Pour into a bowl and stir in the sesame seeds. Add in the shelled hardboiled quails' eggs and mix well to make sure all are thickly coated with the batter.

Heat oil to very hot and drop in the batter-coated eggs – they'll be ready in about 2 minutes when risen to the surface and golden brown. Remove with a slotted spoon and drain on kitchen paper, then pile in a bowl and serve hot with poppadums, spicy dips and chutneys.

*To drink: an instance where the beer in the batter, chilled, is the ideal choice to serve with the food – the beer will taste stronger than the batter but will not get confused with the pickles and, at 5 per cent, has plenty of body.*

# Real Ale Pancakes Wrapped Round 'Hop Shoots'
## (serves 6)

Batter with a head on it! Beer really comes into its own in so many batters from Yorkshire pudding to fish and chips. The yeast and sparkle in ale enhance both the taste and texture and give off a wonderfully satisfying aroma during cooking. In Belgium they like to steam the young hop shoots as a dish – and if you live in a hop-producing area like Kent perhaps you can get hold of some. But they actually taste rather like asparagus, so that's what I'm using here. In fact a strong Belgian ale or French bière de garde in bottles with wired corks, from both specialist beer shops and supermarkets, are good – equally, go for a yeasty, hoppy beer like award-winning Woodforde's Wherry Best Bitter from Norfolk or Charles Wells's Eagle Bitter. At any rate use a live beer, whether bottle- or cask-conditioned, so the yeast is still working. However much you make just stick to equal quantities of beer and flour and you can't go far wrong.

*Pancakes*
1 cup yeasty live ale
1 cup plain flour
2 medium eggs
1 heaped dstsp cornflour
½ tsp salt

2 tbsps melted butter
1 tbsp cold water

*Filling*
12 asparagus spears
warm hollandaise sauce

Place all the pancake ingredients in a blender, and blend until smooth (or make in a mixing bowl in the usual way). Leave in the fridge for 3 hours, or even overnight, then stir, adding a little very cold water to thin down the mixture, which will have thickened. Make pancakes in the usual way, using 3 tbsps batter per pancake, and keep warm.

Meanwhile steam the asparagus until just cooked and prepare the hollandaise sauce.

To serve: Spread sauce on a pancake, then roll around 2 asparagus spears each pointing in opposite directions. Accompany with lemon wedges.

You can serve these savoury pancakes with all sorts of fillings – a hot pancake filled with cold cream cheese mixed with smoked salmon strips as an elegant starter; smoked bacon in a rich cheese sauce; spinach and ricotta or wild mushrooms with pine nuts as a vegetarian dish; smoked haddock with parsley sauce. Sweet beer pancakes are equally fine at the end of a meal – see page 211.

*To drink: a lighter beer than the one used in the batter. To reflect the delicate asparagus and hollandaise sauce, serve a flute of chilled Belgian wheat beer with a slice of lemon on the rim.*

# Shark, Salmon and Swordfish Potted in Witbier
## (serves 6)

Every December the British Guild of Beer Writers stages a thoroughly decadent banquet. It's an unashamedly gargantuan feast where every course is cooked with beer and accompanied by beer. Catering for some 120 diners at this event is a daunting task, but is carried out with skill and good will by professional chefs from Focus on Food, whose director Terry Smith has the job of making our ideas work. One of the best starters he ever helped us develop was this trio of fish layered in an aspic made with cloudy Belgian wheat beer Hoegaarden, one of the classic beers of the world and wonderful for cooking – especially with fish. It has a fresh spiciness and delicacy that zizzes on the tongue, imbued with fresh coriander and dried orange pith, snapped open to release its zest during brewing. This is one of my Desert Island Beers; drink it appreciatively with this starter.

75 g (6 oz) each of salmon fillet, shark fillet and loin of swordfish
300 ml (½ pint) aspic, made with Hoegaarden and fish stock
Cucumber
Radishes

6 black olives
25–30 capers, chopped
6 tomatoes concassées (blanch and skin 6 tomatoes, remove seeds, retaining any juice. Finely chop tomatoes and mix with juice)

Poach the fish gently in water until cooked, then remove carefully and set aside. Use equal quantities of fish stock and Hoegaarden to make around ½ pint aspic and let it cool slightly.

Rinse ramekin dishes or small moulds with cold water, decorate the insides by lining the bases with thin, fancy-cut slices of cucumber and radish, and 1 stoned black olive in the centre and set in a spoonful of the cooling aspic. Arrange the fish in alternate layers, starting with a piece of salmon, followed by swordfish then shark, and a little tomato concassé and chopped capers between the second and third layers. Fill up the moulds with the aspic/Hoegaarden mixture, then chill until set.

To turn out, dip ramekin bases in boiling water for 10–20 seconds, turn on to a serving plate and garnish with lemon and a crisp mixed-leaf green and red salad.

*To drink: Hoegaarden in a champagne flute, lightly chilled, with a lemon slice perched on the rim.*

# Toasted Hop and Lemon Sorbet
## (makes just over 1 pint)

Hops, which put the bitterness and aroma into beer, are also related to cannabis and nettles, so should have a culinary use. In theory at any rate. In practice, hops have such an intense bitterness that they have to be used very sparingly – but used judiciously they can add piquancy to some dishes. This sorbet is a perfect example, with the tiny pinch of dried hops giving the bite that helps clear the palate between starter and main course. It was devised by Stephen Coggins, Head Chef of the Vine Hotel in Skegness as part of a brewery beer banquet. Since it's a Bateman's Brewery house, no doubt he used either Goldings or Challenger hops, as they use in their ales. You can buy dried hops from home-brew stores.

| | |
|---|---|
| 15 g (½ oz) dried hops | 600 ml (1 pint) water |
| 3 lemons | Fresh lemon balm (optional) |
| 225 g (8 oz) caster sugar | 5 egg whites (optional) |

Scatter dried hops in a clean frying pan and dry-cook them over a moderate heat for 2–3 minutes until lightly browned, then leave to cool. Carefully remove zest from 2 lemons and extract their juice. Place juice, zest, sugar and water in a pan with toasted hops and heat gently until the sugar has dissolved, then remove from the heat. If using, chop 2–3 sprigs lemon balm and add to the hot liquor. Leave to infuse for 30 minutes, then pass through a fine sieve.

Place zest and juice from remaining lemon and egg whites, if used, in a liquidizer and 'blitz' until smooth. Add a little hop syrup to the liquidized mixture and pass through a fine sieve to remove any unwanted lumps, then mix with remaining syrup. Pour mixture into a clean container and freeze, beating with a whisk every hour until sorbet is set (or place in an ice-cream maker and churn until mixture has virtually set).

Shape frozen sorbet into little balls with a melon baller and place in chilled wine glasses, frosting the rims by dipping in a little beaten egg white then caster sugar, and serve decorated with a sprig of lemon balm and maybe a dried hop flower so that diners can see what it's all about.

*To drink: nothing. You're supposed to be cleansing your palate before the next course with its own beer.*

# SOUPS

I am sometimes asked to judge pub food competitions. This involves visiting hostelries and choosing arbitrarily from their menus. (In the course of judging I have been known to visit three pubs, one after the other, tasting at least fifteen dishes and becoming a legend in my own lunchtime, but I digress.) I might have something as simple as a sandwich, a public bar staple which can be much abused, or a sophisticated dish like lobster ravioli in a pub which has aspirations. But I have one golden rule. I always choose the soup. 'By their soup shall ye judge them,' I cry to fellow judges, for there is nothing like home-made soup and sadly some of the soups I slurp in pubs are nothing like home-made soup because they have come out of a packet. But good home-made soup at its best is one of the great soul foods, and is greatly enhanced by a drop of the hop stuff.

Use a light golden ale with a herby or flowery bouquet in a delicate vegetable soup; a Belgian wheat beer with a citrus edge in a light fish and mussel or cream of chicken soup; a heavier, more malty beer in a soup containing dark poultry; a dash of stout in a more robust fish bouillabaisse; or barley wine or spicy Christmas ale to enrich a game soup.

I don't really go much on meat soups (apart from oxtail, from which we are temporarily – I trust – estranged), regarding them as stews, but I do like using beef, lamb, duck and game bones to make a well-flavoured stock with a mix of beer and water, about one-third beer to water, then strained and used as a soup base for anything from beetroot to dark mushroom consommé. Do not choose too hoppy a beer for this because the bitterness will be accentuated in the cooking; likewise simmer the soup gently without letting it reach the boil.

The possibilities are endless. You might use a ripe cherry beer in a tomato soup, a real ginger beer with red peppers in a chilled soup, a mint beer in a cucumber soup, a French bière de garde in an onion soup, a smoked beer in a peasant potato and frankfurter soup. Tiny dumplings are luscious because they soak up the beer flavour; thickening with oatmeal also works very well with beer.

You can drink beer with soup, but drink it in a wine glass not a tankard or you'll be bloated with liquid and ruin your appetite for the rest of the meal.

In this chapter you'll find soups from beer and boletus broth to the spiced beer soup created by well-known one-time Gavroche head chef Mark Prescott, who now runs a good food pub.

# Beer and Boletus Broth with Mushroom Dumplings
## (serves 6)

In autumn, within a mile of my home in Hertfordshire I pick a rich harvest of edible fungi, from ceps and shaggy parasols to puffballs, honey fungus, oyster mushrooms, and even glorious chanterelles. One of my favourites is the dark brown, fleshy, bay boletus, which I slice and dry to last me through winter. A soup made of fresh, dark-gilled field mushrooms and dried wild mushrooms, now in most food stores, is superb; and especially savoury when flavoured with a dark, spicy bitter. I used draught Theakston's Old Peculier, prize-winning and gently hopped (also available bottled), but we have no shortage of strong, dark bitters!

1 large onion, peeled and chopped roughly
600 ml (1 pint) dark, spicy bitter
600 ml (1 pint) water
225 g (8 oz) dark field mushrooms, wiped and chopped
50 g (2 oz) dried ceps or boletus

2 tbsps fresh parsley, chopped
Salt, pepper and grating of nutmeg for seasoning

*Dumplings*
1 cup self-raising flour
½ cup shredded suet
pinch salt
cold water

Place all broth ingredients apart from salt, pepper and nutmeg in a large, heavy pan and simmer gently for about 1 hour to make a dark broth smelling like a brewery in the woodlands. Strain, retaining cooked onion and mushrooms. Season the broth to taste with salt, pepper and nutmeg. You should have a clear, dark, aromatic mushroom consommé.

Make dumplings by mixing the flour, shredded suet and salt, and a little of the mushroom mix, chopped finely; add just enough cold water to turn it into a soft dough. Bring the broth to a brisk simmer and drop in walnut-sized balls of the dumpling mix. Lower heat, cover and simmer for around 15 minutes until the dumplings are cooked and rise to the surface.

The dumplings tend to thicken the broth. If you want it to

remain a consommé, cook the dumplings separately in water and add at the end, or cook in deep hot oil until swollen and crisp, then drain on kitchen paper and serve separately.

*To drink: try a dark, nutty brew with enough body to echo the soup but not too strong as this is the start of the meal. So choose an almost black mild with a creamy head and serve it in a round-bowled wine glass.*

## Bortsch 'n' Beer (serves 6)

Being Polish, my husband tried to persuade me that this should be made with Polish beer. But there are few to be had over here – and anyway I think a full-bodied stout to echo the Imperial Stouts brewed for export to Russia during the tsarist Empire (Samuel Smith's Imperial Stout is available bottled, but there are many stouts now being brewed) is a better choice, the sweetness emphasizing the sweetness of the vegetable and darkening the colour from deep pink to ruby.

600 ml (1 pint) good meat
 stock
300 ml ( pint) Imperial Stout
450 g (1 lb) raw beetroot,
 peeled and chopped roughly
1 medium onion, peeled
1 carrot, peeled and cut in 2
1 stick celery, chopped roughly

5 allspice berries
1 tbsp dark soft brown sugar
Salt and freshly ground black
 pepper
*To serve*
Crème fraîche flavoured with
 grated horseradish, made
 earlier and chilled

Put all ingredients apart from sugar and seasoning in a large pan. Bring to bubbling point, then turn heat down very low, cover and simmer very gently for 1½–2 hours, until all the colour is cooked out of the beetroot into the stock.

Strain into a bowl, then return the deep red broth to a pan. Stir in sugar, bring to simmering point and season to taste.

Put a steaming tureen of this fragrant consommé on the table so that diners can serve themselves, along with a small bowl of the crème fraîche and horseradish, and some dark rye bread. (If you prefer a thicker, heartier soup then liquidize the vegetables and about ½ the beetroot in the stock after cooking.)

*To drink: the Imperial Stout is a noble accompaniment; alternatively a mini tankard of smoked beer would round it off – or a wine glass of cherry beer to match the colour and sweetness of the fruit. After all, they have cherry vodka in Poland and Russia!*

## Brewer's Soup (serves 6)

There's a north–south divide with brown ale. In southern Britain it's a fairly low alcohol beer, yet surprisingly thick, and with a sweet, malty edge. In the north it is drier, about 1 per cent stronger, and with a slightly sharper edge. Manns Brown Ale is a classic example of the first variety – a real working man's beer, which is why Ushers, who now brew it, wanted some recipes under the Andy Capp theme and asked me to originate them. I was surprised to find just how much power this 3.3 per-center packs in cooking. Here's one of the recipes I devised, in which the sweetness caramelizes to great effect – Mackeson Stout is a good alternative.

3 large onions, peeled and chopped
2 shallots, peeled and chopped
2 cloves garlic, peeled and crushed
Butter for frying
1 dstsp plain flour
1 bottle (500 ml) Manns
Cold water
1 tbsp fresh parsley, chopped
Salt and pepper
French stick
Garlic butter
75 g (3 oz) Gruyère cheese, grated

Sweat onions, shallots and garlic gently in butter in a heavy, covered saucepan for 20–30 minutes until soft. Then cook uncovered for a few minutes more until the onion starts to colour and is slightly caramelized.

Sprinkle over plain flour and cook gently for 2 minutes, stirring all the time. Pour over Manns and bring to simmering point; add parsley, cover and cook for 5 minutes. Fill the empty beer bottle with cold water and add slowly to the soup, stirring. Simmer gently, covered, for around 30 minutes, then season to taste.

Cut French stick into thick slices and lightly toast on one side; turn over, spread with garlic butter, sprinkled with grated Gruyère, and toast until golden. Top each bowl of soup with a slice.

*To drink: a dark mild, low enough in alcohol to start the meal, and not as sweet as the beer in the soup.*

# Cock a Leekie with Oatmeal Ale and Toasted Oats
## (serves 6)

I have taken great liberties with this Scottish soup, which traditionally has a fairly clear broth, by thickening it with a mixture of Scottish Oatmeal Stout, brewed by Broughton in the Borders, and Scotch oats, to make a hearty and extremely savoury soup. There are several oatmeal stouts and, when I was devising this recipe, just one oatmeal ale brewed by my local brewery, McMullen, in Hertford, using oats as well as barley in the brewing process. The stout adds a whisky smoothness to the broth, and oats work well in beer recipes, offsetting the hops' bitterness. In the original recipes a whole chicken is used to provide more of a meal than a soup, but it is thriftier to simmer the carcass after you've had roast chicken and freeze the stock until you make the soup.

900 ml (1½ pints) chicken stock (made by simmering chicken bones or carcass with an onion)

3–4 boned chicken thighs, cut into small chunks (or leftover roast chicken)

1 medium carrot, peeled and diced

1 medium turnip, peeled and diced

350 g (12 oz) leeks, washed and shredded

300 ml (½ pint) Scottish Oatmeal Stout or Oatmeal Ale

50 g (2 oz) oats

Salt and pepper to season

Add raw chicken, carrot and turnip to chicken stock in a large pan and bring to simmering point. Cover and cook gently for 15 minutes. Add leeks and cook for a further 10 minutes. (If using cooked chicken add with the leeks.)

Liquidize most of the oats in some of the beer. Add the rest of the beer to the pan and bring back to simmering point, then season to taste with salt and freshly ground black pepper. Stir in the beer/oats mix and cook gently until the soup thickens.

Meanwhile, toast the remaining oats by cooking them for a few minutes in a dry frying pan, turning frequently. Serve the soup with toasted oats scattered on top, accompanied by hunks of oaty bread.

*To drink: bottled Scottish Oatmeal Stout, Sam Smith's fine bottled Oatmeal Stout or Maclay's draught Oat Malt Stout with a delicate sweetness, made to a recipe dating back to the last century.*

# Lady Chatterley's Wheat Beer and Cheese Soup
## (serves 6)

Quite a number of UK-brewed wheat beers are available now, but several years ago, when most of the wheat beers I had tasted came from Belgium or Germany, the first English variety I tried was the uncompromising Chatterley Wheat Beer brewed at the little Steam Packet Brewery in Yorkshire, where the brewer, Mellors, was inspired by D. H. Lawrence. Susan Richardson, outstanding cook at the Star Inn in Weaverthorpe, North Yorkshire (the pub I visit when body and soul need a bit of succour), combined Chatterley wheat beer with Gruyère to make a delicate cheese and ale soup.

1 large, mild onion, peeled and chopped quite small

1 large potato, peeled and diced finely

1 stick celery, wiped and chopped

50 g (2 oz) butter

A little olive oil

25 g (1 oz) plain flour

300 ml (½ pint) strained chicken stock (or vegetable stock for vegetarians)

300 ml (½ pint) English wheat beer

75 g (3 oz) Gruyère, grated finely

85 ml (3 fl oz) double cream

Salt

White pepper

Nutmeg

*To garnish*

Garlic croûtons

Parsley, chopped

Melt butter with a little olive oil in a heavy pan. Add onion and sauté gently until soft but not coloured; add potato and celery and sauté for a few minutes. Sprinkle on flour and cook for a few more minutes, stirring in the flour. Add beer and stock and whisk until simmering point is reached. Season with salt, white pepper and freshly grated nutmeg. Simmer very gently for 15–20 minutes until the vegetables are soft, then liquidize.

Reheat gently, adjust seasoning, add cream and grated Gruyère and stir in over a low heat – do not allow to boil or the cheese will become stringy. Serve garnished with garlic croûtons, parsley and extra grated cheese if desired.

*To drink: don't miss the chance to drink draught Lady Chatterley if you can find it as a pub guest beer; otherwise choose a delicate straw-coloured English bitter or an English-style wheat beer.*

# Otter Chowder (serves 6)

No, not made with Toad's chum but with an unusual beer called Otter Bright. Pale lagers make good partners for fish and are mostly brewed on the continent, using 'bottom-fermenting' yeasts, which sink to the bottom during fermentation, while British ales use 'top-fermenting' yeasts that rise to the top. This lager-type beer (now available bottled) is produced by the top-fermentation method at the little Otter Brewery near Honiton in Devon, which has recently enjoyed great success at beer festivals. To me it tastes like a cross between lager and ale and is perfect sipped with white fish – and in this seafood chowder. You could also use a light, flowery bitter or a rounded golden lager.

175 g (6 oz) shell-on prawns
50 g (2 oz) smoked streaky
  bacon, diced
1 large onion, chopped finely
2 cloves garlic, crushed
2 sticks celery, sliced
1 medium carrot, sliced thinly
Butter for frying
300 ml (½ pint) stock (made
  from prawn shells)
225 g (8 oz) floury old
  potatoes, peeled and cut in
  large chunks
225 g (8 oz) naturally smoked
  hake (or haddock) fillet, cut
  in chunks

350 g (12 oz) white fish fillets,
  de-skinned and cut in chunks
225 ml (8 fl oz) Otter Bright or
  alternative
50 g (2 oz) small white button
  mushrooms, sliced
Pinch cayenne pepper
Salt and freshly ground black
  pepper
75 g (3 oz) queenie scallops
  (shelled)
2 tbsps fresh parsley, chopped
  finely
50 ml (2 fl oz) thick cream
Paprika for garnish

Shell 100 g (4 oz) of the prawns and set aside. Rinse shells and sauté for a few minutes. Add 450 ml (¾ pint) water plus any fish skin and simmer for 20 minutes to create stock; discard shells and skin and reserve stock.

Sauté bacon gently until crisp and remove from pan with a slotted spoon. Add a little butter to the bacon fat and sweat the onion, garlic and celery gently for around 10 minutes until softened and barely golden. Add sliced carrot and sauté for a few minutes more. Stir in stock, add potatoes and cook gently until tender. Liquidize around one-third of this to thicken and return to the pan.

Add all the prepared smoked and white fish and the beer, cover and simmer very gently for around 45 minutes. Stir in the mushrooms and immediately remove from the heat, cover, and set aside for a few hours for flavours to develop (thus far this can be prepared the day before).

Return to simmering point, add a hint of cayenne, then taste and season with salt and pepper. Add crisp bacon, scallops, halved shelled prawns and half the parsley and continue to cook for another 10–15 minutes; taste again for seasoning, then stir in the thick cream.

Serve in a tureen garnished with a circle of fresh parsley surrounding a sprinkling of paprika, with unshelled prawns perched on the rim.

*To drink: chilled Otter Bright in a wine glass with a thin slice of lemon is lovely, or you might enjoy a bitter with citrus notes such as Charles Wells's Eagle or Fuller's Chiswick, which is brewed in London.*

# A Real (Ale) Pea Souper (serves 10–12)

You'll have lashings of gorgeous ham and beer stock left over from the Mash Tun Gammon (see page 140), and with all that beer in it's too good to waste. So turn it into a soup which is not only a real winter warmer, but a magic hangover cure – keep some in the freezer for just such an occasion. If you used green gammon you can use all the stock and the level of salt will be just right – add water to make up the quantity. If you used smoked gammon because you wanted a stronger flavour, the stock will probably be very salty, so use less stock and more water – that way you can make two batches and freeze some. Before you start, leave the stock somewhere cold overnight so that you can remove fat from the surface before making the soup.

450 g (1 lb) dried marrowfat (not split) peas*
2.25 litres (4 pints) gammon/beer stock and water
1 large onion, peeled and chopped
1 stick celery, peeled and diced small
1 large carrot, peeled and diced small

*To garnish*
Fresh parsley, chopped
Thick single cream

Soak peas overnight in cold water (with 'tablet' if provided), then drain through a colander and rinse. Place in a pan with beer/ham stock and water and bring to the boil. Continue to boil for 10 minutes, skimming off any scum.

Add onion, celery and carrot, then cover and simmer for around 2 hours until the peas are tender; stir with a wooden spoon to break up some of the peas, thickening the stock, and leaving some whole. The soup will be a lovely bronzed green colour so, after ladling it into bowls, garnish with a little parsley, surrounded by a swirl of cream and serve with trenchers of mixed malt bread.

*I don't use split peas because they dissolve altogether. But you can use yellow split peas with some of this stock to make a beery pease pudding, which you might serve with boiled gammon and mashed potatoes for a real Cockney meal.

*To drink: a robust half pint (or even a pint) tankard of a good British quaffing bitter, medium strength, hoppy and savoury, to make this a complete meal.*

# Spiced Beer Soup (serves 6)

'I first tried this recipe as a bit of a lark for some friends who had been out shooting . . . they loved it. Now it is a very popular winter special,' says Mark Prescott, renowned chef-proprietor of the White Hart at Nayland near Colchester. Actually, he may unwittingly have created a modern version of a medieval mulled ale. At any rate, he's right about it being a cheering winter warmer. Being in Suffolk, Mark chose local brewer Greene King's IPA; you could equally use a rounded, dryish draught bitter.

1 litre (1¾ pints) IPA
1 stick cinnamon
4 star anise
2 cloves
1 heaped tbsp plain flour

50 ml (2 fl oz) water
4 medium egg yolks
60 g (2½ oz) sugar
400 ml (13 fl oz) milk

Bring beer to the boil with spices. Mix flour and water to a paste, stir into the soup and boil rapidly. Beat egg yolks and sugar together and whisk into the boiling milk.

Remove the soup from the heat and pass it through a chinois (conical strainer); vigorously whisk in the egg mix and serve immediately in hot bowls.

*To drink: nothing. This is a drink in itself.*

# FISH

Now here's a pretty kettle of fish – brewed up in the beer kettle. If you find the idea of pairing fish and beer surprising, then read on. Yes, some fish are delicate, but so are many beers, and this chapter should convince you that beer can be as versatile and sophisticated with fish and seafood as wine.

To start with a traditional treat, beer comes into its own in fish and chips, creating the best batter in the world – light, crisp and with just that savoury hop hint which goes beautifully with a thick fillet of fresh cod or haddock.

Sparkling, citrus-edged wheat beers are a great discovery with fish. Over the past couple of years these tangy, beautifully crafted beers from Belgium and Bavaria have really caught on over here – so much so that British brewers have begun to produce copies of the imports as well as a more English version. They are superb with the more delicate white fish, both as an accompanying drink and in a sauce. The slightly acidic edge also cuts across the oil to perfection in a richer fish like salmon – and in this chapter I have used the most famous wheat beer of all, Hoegaarden, now easily available in the UK, in an aspic with a showpiece whole salmon. Smoked beers are terrific for marinating barbecued fish, from swordfish steaks to sardines – and a marinade of porter and honey is luscious for brushing giant prawns.

But fish is not just delicate. There are all kinds of fuller-flavoured fish and seafood which go with the stronger, fuller-flavoured beers – crab cakes with stout, for instance, and the hearty, rustic combination of pale ale, cod, bacon and cabbage from the country's most famous seafood cook, Rick Stein.

In this chapter you will find dishes as unusual as gurnard with wild mushrooms, saffron and Old Ale, created by Alistair Shaw, chef/proprietor of the 1998 Seafood Pub of the Year; Ram Tam Salmon with a stunning Yorkshire ale by ex-Miller Howe chef Bob Lyons; skate with black beer and scallops in beer batter.

So whether it's in fish cakes, batter, a subtle accompanying sauce or a robust fish stew, beer has a great role to play in the fish course. And the best accompaniment to fish and chips is still a pint of bitter!

# Blackened Salmon with Ram Tam Beer (serves 6)

At Canal Foot, Ulverston, in the heel of Cumbria, is a pub called the Bay Horse. It is extraordinarily hard to find in an unpromising industrial estate, but you turn a final corner and suddenly the whole of Morecambe Bay opens in front of you with this brilliant pub on its shore. The Bay Horse is in my top ten British pubs for food. The chef/proprietor is Robert Lyons, who produces a blackboard of treats every day using local ingredients from air-dried Waberthwaite ham to sea trout. He learned his art at Miller Howe, working with TV chef and writer John Tovey, who supports him at the Bay Horse. Bob has been very enthusiastic about this book and created three recipes for me, using fine cask ales. This one is flavoured with Timothy Taylor's Ram Tam, based on their complex Taylor Landlord; Ram Tam is made by adding caramel to produce a sweeter, deeper brew. Bob says, if you can't get it, go for a good dark porter.

| | |
|---|---|
| 6 225 g (8 oz) fresh salmon escalopes | *Marinade* |
| | Juice and rind of 2 limes |
| 50 g (2 oz) unsalted butter | 4 pieces stem ginger in syrup |
| Salt; freshly ground black pepper | 300 ml (½ pt) Taylor's Ram Tam |

To make the marinade grate the stem ginger and the rind from the limes. Add lime juice to grated lime rind and ginger along with 2 tbsps syrup from the stem ginger and all the Ram Tam. Mix well. Pour marinade over salmon and marinate for several hours or overnight, turning from time to time, and making sure that all sides of the fish are well coated in the mixture.

To cook: place butter in a heavy-based frying pan over quite a high heat. Season the salmon escalopes with salt and black pepper. Cook quickly on both sides until the outside of the fish is black and charred, the inside pink.

*To drink: a cold dry porter poured slowly into a wine flute is an offbeat choice that works as a good foil to the delicacy of the fish, with its salty skin and richness of the lime/ginger. To be more conventional, chill a dark gold lager and serve with a slice of lime.*

# Cod and Potato Lager Bake with Crispy Crumb and Bacon Topping (serves 6)

The oldest secular building in Newcastle upon Tyne is the Cooper-age on the quayside, now a pub and restaurant with huge wooden beams and exposed stone walls. They have long used beer in their cooking, from pies to fish – here is head chef Colin Cunningham's recipe for a cod and vegetable hotpot cooked in lager with a crispy topping.

1 kg (2 lb) potatoes, peeled and sliced thinly
1 medium onion, chopped
225 g (8 oz) carrots, peeled and sliced
1 medium leek, washed and chopped
1 tbsp fresh sage, chopped

Salt and black pepper
About 600 ml (1 pint) light lager
6 thick cod fillets
*Crispy topping*
50 g (2 oz) fresh breadcrumbs
6 rashers streaky bacon, diced
25 g (1 oz) butter/oil

Mix together onion, carrots, leek, and sage, then layer with pota-toes in a shallow casserole dish, starting and finishing with pota-toes.

Heat the lager without boiling, season with salt and black pep-per, then pour over the vegetables. Cover with foil and bake in a hot oven (400°F, 200°C, gas mark 6) for around 1 hour, or until potatoes are tender when tested with a skewer.

Remove foil and lay cod fillets on top. Fry diced bacon in butter and mix with breadcrumbs, then scatter over the fish. Return to oven for 20 minutes until cod is cooked and the topping crispy. Serve with a green vegetable or salad.

*To drink: this is quite a strongly flavoured dish and I would go for a darker, more malty lager alongside.*

## Crab Cakes with Ginger and Spring Onions in a Black Bean and Stout Sauce (serves 6)

Stout is wonderful with shellfish – not just the classic stout and oysters. I like to drink a dry stout with oysters, but in this dish a slightly sweeter stout goes wonderfully with the sweetness of the crabmeat and takes the edge off the drier, saltier flavour of the black bean sauce.

Meat from a large crab or around 275 g (10 oz) dark and white crabmeat mixed
3 spring onions, peeled and chopped finely
1 tbsp root ginger, peeled and chopped finely
1 beaten egg
1 tsp mushroom soy sauce
1 tbsp fresh chervil, chopped

40 g (1½ oz) each fresh and toasted brown breadcrumbs
*Sauce*
Walnut oil for frying
3 spring onions, peeled and chopped
5 cloves pickled garlic, chopped
3 tbsps black bean sauce
3–4 tbsps sweet stout
½ tsp anchovy essence

Mix crabmeat, spring onions, ginger, egg, soy sauce and chervil in a large bowl. Add enough of the fresh and toasted brown breadcrumbs to bind and stiffen the mixture. Form into 12 small patties. Place on a grill pan lined with foil. Grill under a medium heat on both sides until cooked through and crispy (around 10 minutes). Keep warm.

To prepare the sauce, heat walnut oil in a wok and sauté spring onions until just soft. Then add pickled garlic (sweeter and gentler than fresh garlic, available in Chinese supermarkets) and black bean sauce. Heat gently to simmering point, stirring, and allow to bubble for a few minutes until thickened. Add stout and anchovy essence and simmer for a few more minutes, stirring throughout. Serve 2 crab cakes per person with 1 tablespoon sauce next to them; garnish simply with a couple of young crisp salad leaves topped with grated radish and a cherry tomato.

*To drink: a rounded stout, slightly drier than the one used in the sauce, or a dry porter such as Sam Smith's Taddy Porter, served in small, chunky tumblers.*

# Fillets of Red Gurnard with Wild Mushrooms, Saffron and Old Ale (serves 6)

Alistair Shaw, at the Froize, Chillesford, near Woodbridge in Suffolk, is a scintillating chef who prefers to cook in a pub. Above all, he is known for his fish dishes and the superb quality of the carefully sourced seafood which I have watched arriving in his kitchen. I think he is at his best when he cooks really fresh fish quite simply but accompanies it with clever sauces – as in this recipe, where he puts red gurnard with old ale, a strong, winey beer which used to be available mainly in winter but can now be found all year round, both draught and bottled. Gale's Prize Old Ale is a fine example and Alistair, who likes to use East Anglian beers, might well choose Greene King's superb bottled Strong Suffolk Ale. This recipe also uses wild mushrooms, which are abundant near the Froize, as I found on a fungal foray last year.

| | |
|---|---|
| 6 whole red gurnard | 4 bay leaves |
| 450 g (1 lb) mixed wild mushrooms, chopped | 6 sprigs rosemary |
| | 4 sprigs tarragon |
| 225 g (8 oz) unsalted butter | 5 tomatoes, de-seeded and chopped finely |
| 6 shallots, chopped finely | |
| 6 cloves garlic, sliced thinly | Heaped dstsp tomato purée |
| 600 ml (1 pint) old ale* | 10 strands saffron |

Fillet the red gurnard (or get your fishmonger to do it for you). Pour the pint of old ale into a saucepan, add tomatoes, tarragon, rosemary, bay leaves, garlic and shallots and cook rapidly to reduce by half. Pan-fry red gurnard fillets with a little butter and the saffron for a few minutes until cooked through; remove.

Add the rest of the butter to pan and heat until it goes brown, then add mushrooms and stir for around 3 minutes until cooked through. Add reduced liquor with herbs and tomato purée and simmer for 2 minutes.

*Alistair keeps the old ale for at least six months to undergo further fermentation, which gives it a nuttier flavour. If you use a bottle-conditioned old ale, buy a few bottles and leave them to mature before you try the recipe again!

To serve: place gurnard fillets on a plate and pour over sauce; garnish with red lettuce leaves dressed with walnut oil.

*To drink: this is a strongly flavoured dish that can take some of the full-bodied old ale used in the cooking; or try corn-coloured American beer Golden Gate from the Golden Pacific Brewing Co, with its malt and puff of smoke.*

# Fish in Beer Batter (serves 6)

One of the grossest items you will find on pub menus is 'cod in crispy batter' or, even more expressively, 'battered cod'. Generally it has arrived there as a portion of frozen fish in a thick, soggy batter, to be finished off in the oven or deep-fat fryer and emerge with all the flavour of blotting paper set in concrete, but without the charisma. Yet publicans, of all people, have the means to make the best fish and chips in the world – real ale. Living cask or bottle-conditioned beer is essential for this dish because the yeast, still fermenting, helps to produce a wonderfully light, hoppy – or happy – batter, which bears no relation to the aforesaid. Choose a light, savoury beer with a little sweetness and not too much hop bitterness, such as straw-coloured Hopback Summer Lightning.

6 medium-thick pieces skinned cod fillet, around 175 g (6 oz) each
100 g (4 oz) self-raising flour
½ tsp salt
Pinch turmeric
1 medium egg, beaten

150 ml (¼ pint) light real ale (including any yeast sediment)
Cold water
50 g (2 oz) seasoned flour
Oil (or pure fat) for deep frying

Mix together self-raising flour, salt and turmeric (to guarantee a lovely golden colour). Add egg, and stir in most of the beer, adding the rest little by little until you have a smooth coating batter with a texture somewhere between single and double cream. If it still seems a little thick when you've added all the beer, thin slightly with a drop of very cold water. Give it a good whisk with a balloon whisk, then rest for about an hour.

Wash cod, dry thoroughly with kitchen paper and dredge lightly in the seasoned flour. Heat deep fat (where I come from in Yorkshire they always use beef dripping for fish and chips) or oil to 350–375°F, 180–190°C, or until a cube of bread goes crisp and brown in about a minute. It is important to get the temperature right – if it is too hot the batter will go hard and dark; too cool and it will be soggy. Give the batter a final stir and dip in a piece of cod, making sure it is well coated all over but letting excess drip off. Lower gently into the deep fat or oil and cook for about 10 minutes until crisp and golden, turning once with a slotted spoon. Do not cook more than 2 pieces at once. Drain on kitchen paper and keep warm while you cook the rest.

Serve with freshly cut chips, salt, real malt vinegar and a couple of pickled gherkins in best fish and chip shop manner. (You can use haddock or hake, or even plaice fillets instead if you prefer.)

*To drink: a pint of best – a good, quenching bitter with a hint of yeast of the kind you'll find in many a public bar; bottled choices could include Shepherd Neame's bronze Master Brew with its citrus echo or the Hopback Summer Lightning.*

## Kedgeree with India Pale Ale (serves 4–6)

Kedgeree has the Colonel Blimp image of a middle-aged, fiery-faced army grandee sitting on an Indian veranda when we still had an Empire. The colonials developed a taste for spicy food and perhaps that is how kedgeree, a combination of smoked haddock, rice and curry, reached the Edwardian table; though why the breakfast table still puzzles me! On the same humid verandas they would have slaked their thirst with beer sent out from Britain – India Pale Ale, highly hopped to withstand the long sea journey. Today this fine style of brewing has been revived with plenty of varieties now available – both draught and bottled, including bottle-conditioned. For this dish I've created a subtler version of kedgeree, relying on the gentler curry spices, fresh coriander and the spices in the strong-tasting beer which stands up to the powerful smoked fish. And it's best eaten at suppertime in my view – or lunch, at the earliest.

550 g (1¼ lb) naturally smoked haddock
300 ml (½ pint) IPA
1 bay leaf
2 sprigs fresh parsley
3 peppercorns
3–4 saffron strands
2 rashers smoked streaky bacon, de-rinded and diced
50 g (2 oz) unsalted butter
1 small red onion, diced
2 cloves garlic, crushed
1 stick celery, sliced finely
1 tsp cumin

2 tsps garam masala
½ tsp powdered ginger
225 g (8 oz) best Basmati rice washed and soaked in hot water for 30 minutes, then drained
3 cardamoms
12 quails' eggs, hardboiled and shelled
100 g (4 oz) cooked shell-on prawns
3 tbsps fresh coriander, chopped
1 fresh lemon cut in wedges

Place haddock in a single layer in a large frying pan. Pour over IPA and add bay leaf, fresh parsley and peppercorns. Cover with a lid or plate and simmer gently for 5 minutes, then leave the fish to cool in the liquor.

Remove fish and flake roughly in large chunks, discarding skin and bones. Strain beer liquor into a measuring jug, add saffron strands and, if necessary, make up to 30 ml (½ pint) with hot water.

In a heavy-bottomed frying pan sweat bacon until fat runs out. Add the butter and gently fry onion, garlic and celery for 2 minutes without browning. Stir in cumin, garam masala and ginger and continue to fry gently, stirring, for another minute. Add drained rice and stir gently until all the grains are coated with the spiced butter. Add cardamoms and strain on the IPA/fish stock, stir once and cover closely, then simmer on as low a heat as possible for 5 minutes. Remove from heat and, without lifting lid, leave to stand for another 5 minutes until the rice is tender and virtually all the stock absorbed.

Meanwhile shell 9 of the hardboiled quails' eggs and halve lengthways. Shell all but 3 of the prawns and cut in half. Gently fork the smoked haddock chunks into the rice over a low heat, followed by the halved eggs, shelled prawns and fresh coriander; the mixture should be moist but not mushy. Pile on a large, warm salver decorating the top with the remaining quails' eggs and prawns still in their shells, and place lemon wedges round the dish.

*To drink: an Indian lager such as Kingfisher, or even one of the growing number of English wheat beers, draught or bottled.*

# King Prawns and Scallops with Chilli and Witbier
## (serves 4)

Here's a dish where seafood and chilli mix with wheat beer to produce quite a fiery dish, good for eating with your fingers, licking
off the hot sauce as you peel the prawns. It was devised by chef
Helen Hayward when she worked at a great beer cellar in Chich-
ester, sadly now closed.

15 g (½ oz) unsalted butter
½ tbsp light oil
2 spring onions, chopped
1 red chilli, chopped very
  finely
1 fat clove garlic, crushed
12 raw king prawns

16 large scallops
300 ml (½ pint) wheat beer
*To serve*
Mixed salad leaves
Roast tomatoes
Pitta bread
Lime quarters

Heat butter and oil in large, heavy frying pan. Add spring onions,
chilli and garlic and sauté for 1 minute.

Carefully peel off legs and body shell from the king prawns,
leaving on the head and tail, then add to the pan with the scallops
and cook for around 1 minute. Turn over and cook for another
minute, until the prawns are just pink and the scallops barely
cooked. Add wheat beer and turn heat up high for 1 minute to
bring to the boil and infuse all the flavours.

To serve: pile mixed leaves in the centre of each plate. Arrange 3
king prawns and 4 scallops on the leaves, drizzle sauce over, top
with thin slices of roast tomato. Garnish with lime quarters and
use warm pitta bread to mop up the juices.

*To drink: you could go the whole hog and have a Mexican chilli
beer with a hot chilli pepper in the bottle, but it's probably best to
have a chilled, spicy wheat beer, perhaps the scrumptious lime-
scented Sparkling Wit from Fenland Brewery in Cambridgeshire.*

# Monkfish, Mussel and Asparagus in Beechwood Hop Leaf Mustard (serves 6)

In this dish the beer is extremely subtle because it is confined to the beer mustard flavouring – Chiltern Brewery's Beechwood Hop Leaf Mustard. There are various beer mustards on the market (and a recipe for one in this book, see page 266), but Chiltern, at Terrick near Aylesbury, stock two using their own beers. This is the stronger of the two – a mustard to put hairs on your chest! Brewer Richard Jenkinson dreamed it up using his Beechwood Bitter with added Fuggles hop leaves for extra bite because he felt they needed a more macho mustard than their original jar of coarse ground with Chiltern Ale. The recipe comes from Mark Cartwright, chef at the Olde Coach House in Ashby St Ledgers.

| | |
|---|---|
| 4 shallots, chopped | 2 tbsps Beechwood Hop Leaf |
| 50 g (2 oz) unsalted butter | Mustard (or beer mustard) |
| 2 tbsps grapeseed oil | 600 ml (1 pint) double cream |
| 1.5 kg (3 lb) monkfish, | 1 tbsp fresh dill, chopped |
| skinned, boned and cut into | 24 green-lip mussels |
| 0.5 cm (¼ inch) slices | 6 tomato roses |
| 450 g (1 lb) asparagus, freshly | 2 sprigs dill |
| prepared | |

In a large, heavy pan sauté shallots and monkfish slices in butter and oil. Cook for 1 minute, then add asparagus, cut into 7.5 cm (3 inch) pieces, beer mustard and cream. Simmer on a low heat until the cream thickens to coating consistency, then add mussels and heat through by simmering for a further minute.

Pile high in the centre of 6 plates and garnish each with a tomato rose and sprig of dill. Accompany with buttered noodles.

*To drink: Chiltern's own light bitter, Chiltern Ale, with its spritzy finish would be nice, or a drop of real ginger beer, chilled, in a stemmed glass, or even a cold, smooth dry stout to complement the mussels and cream.*

## Pan-fried Monkfish Medallions on Date, Apricot and Ale Compôte with Plum Tomato Concassé (serves 6)

Phillip Buswell is an up-and-coming young chef, food writer and broadcaster who embarked on his career when he was just sixteen. He is now head chef of the Tollemache Arms, a thatched sixteenth-century inn in the village of Harrington, Northants, but has worked at various well-known pubs. He is especially keen on fish cookery and sometimes puts on a gourmet seafood night with treats like smoked trout and peach terrine or fresh grilled marlin . . . or maybe this exotic offering.

1 kg (2 lb) monkfish tail, filleted, skinned and sliced thinly
6 plum tomatoes
Olive oil for frying
*Compôte*
450 g (1 lb) dates

450 g (1 lb) apricots
175 g (6 oz) caster sugar
2 cloves
1 stick cinnamon
175 g (6 oz) unsalted butter
300 ml (½ pint) fruity bitter*

Soak dates and apricots in beer for at least 6 hours. Place all compôte ingredients in a pan and simmer gently for 20 minutes, then remove from heat.

Soak plum tomatoes in boiling water for 2 minutes then remove, skin, de-seed and finely dice the flesh to make a concassé. Pan-fry monkfish slices in olive oil for 2 minutes on each side, then divide compôte between 6 dinner plates, place monkfish pieces on top, and decorate with the plum tomato concassé.

*To drink: you can certainly drink a medium-strength ale like Bombardier, well balanced between fruit and hops, or even a dark lager such as Staropramen from Prague, which is widely available here.*

* Since this is a Charles Wells pub, Phillip can use their strong and fruity Bombardier with its blackcurrant finish – robust enough to go with the monkfish and complement the fruit in the compôte.

# Rick Stein's Cod with Beer, Bacon and Cabbage
## (serves 4)

I thought a man who appreciated real fish must also appreciate real beer, but I didn't realize to what extent, until TV chef Rick Stein of the Seafood Restaurant in Padstow, Devon, told me he had once been an enthusiastic member of the Campaign for Real Ale. He sent me this recipe with a note: 'Funnily enough, I've only just started cooking fish with beer and only in one dish, which was an idea given to me by Jason Fretwell, the chef at our second restaurant, St Petroc's. It's called Cod with Beer, Cabbage and Bacon and I think it's fantastic.' So do I.

4 175 g (6 oz) pieces thick cod fillet, skin on
50 g (2 oz) butter
1 small Savoy cabbage (around 750 g/1½ lb)
1 tbsp sunflower oil
75 g (3 oz) rindless smoked streaky bacon, cut into thin strips

1 onion, chopped finely
1 clove garlic, chopped very finely
300 ml (½ pint) chicken stock
300 ml (½ pint) pale ale
Salt and freshly ground black pepper
2 tbsps fresh parsley, chopped

Place the pieces of cod, skin-side up, on a greased baking tray. Melt 25 g (1 oz) butter in a small pan. Brush skin of cod with a little of the butter and sprinkle well with salt and pepper. Preheat grill to high.

Cut cabbage into quarters, remove and discard the core and slice thinly. Drop into a large pan of boiling salted water and bring back to the boil. Drain and refresh under running cold water.

Heat the oil in a large heavy-based pan. Add bacon and fry over a high heat until crisp and lightly golden. Add the rest of the butter, onion and garlic to the pan and fry for 5 minutes until the onion is soft and lightly browned. Add cabbage to the pan with chicken stock and beer. Cook over a medium heat for 10–15 minutes, stirring now and then, until just tender. Stir in the rest of the butter and some parsley. Season to taste with salt and pepper and keep warm.

Grill the cod for 8 minutes on one side only, until the skin is crisp and the cod is cooked through. Spoon the cabbage into 4 large, warmed soup plates. Sprinkle the skin of the cod with a little rock salt, coarsely ground black pepper and parsley, place on top of the cabbage and serve.

*To drink: either a delicate draught bitter with a citrus note, such as Mansfield Riding Bitter, cellar cool, in a wine glass, or echo the recipe with a fine bottled pale ale such as the spiffing Sam Smith's Old Brewery Pale Ale.*

# Roast Haddock in Beer and Garlic Crust (serves 6)

Just as I don't go along with the notion that fish must be accompanied by dry white wine, likewise I do not believe that it automatically needs a pale, dry pilsner. Like meat, fish has a variety of flavours, ranging from delicate sole fillets through to strong-tasting bass and mackerel. Haddock has a distinctive flavour, which is well matched by a medium-strength ale with a dry, citrus fruit astringency but not too heavy on the hops, because this high-heat cooking concentrates the flavour and could create a bitter edge, or even an English wheat beer – the choice is growing all the time, and you'll find them both draught and bottle-conditioned. As you blast the fish quickly in the oven it draws in the beer, leaving the garlic to flavour the crisp crumb crust.

6 thick fillets really fresh haddock

100 g (4 oz) wholemeal bread, processed into crumbs with 2 cloves garlic, salt and freshly ground black pepper to season

Approx 85 ml (3 fl oz) medium beer

2 tbsps fresh parsley, chopped finely

Lemon chunks to garnish

3 large parsnips, peeled and cut into chip shapes

Shredded carrot and cabbage mixed with a few scrapings of lemon peel

Home-made watercress sauce

Preheat oven to very hot – 450°F, 230°C, gas mark 8. Butter a large, rectangular, shallow ovenproof dish or baking tray and arrange the fish fillets on it skin side down. Put the seasoned crumbs and garlic into a bowl and lightly fork in the beer a little at a time until the crumbs are moist but still separate, not mushy. Press the crumb mixture over the fish to cover the top surface and sides completely, then place in the top of the oven for around 10 minutes, until the fish is just cooked and the crumbs are crisp.

Deep-fry the parsnip 'chips' until crisp, then briefly deep-fry the shredded carrot, cabbage and lemon-peel mixture until very crisp (like deep-fried seaweed).

To serve: place a haddock portion on a pool of home-made

watercress sauce. Top with the crispy cabbage mix and place a portion of parsnip chips and a chunk of lemon alongside.

*To drink: the beer used in the crust, especially if it was a pithy English wheat beer.*

# Salmon in Hoegaarden Aspic (serves 8–10)

Poached salmon is a classic, of course, but just a trifle dull? Or is it the blander taste of farmed salmon which makes it so now? This recipe offers the best of both worlds: cheap and accessible farmed salmon taking on the flavour of a another classic, Belgian weiss – or wheat – beer, Hoegaarden. One of the world's truly great beers, this cloudy 'white' beer is brewed in Hoegaarden village close to Brussels. I have supped it foaming in the brewery's vast beer hall, where much of the menu is cooked with beer – including their darkly sensual Forbidden Fruit – the brews all correctly served in their own special glasses. Flavoured with coriander and dried orange pith, Hoegaarden's subtle, complex spiciness with a touch of citrus makes it perfect for cooking the more delicate fish – and for drinking with it. In the splendour of Brussels's Hotel Metropole bar they even serve it with a slice of lemon perched on the rim of the glass.

| | |
|---|---|
| 1 fresh salmon (3 kg/6 lb) | *To garnish* |
| 2 bottles Hoegaarden | Cucumber slices |
| Cold water | Lemon slices |
| 1 lemon | Prawns |
| Fresh parsley | Parsley |
| | Samphire |
| | Lettuce |

Gut the fish or get fishmonger to do it for you, but keep the head and tail on for effect. If the fish is very large you may have to cut it in half for marinating and cooking. With a sharp knife make a few slits on both sides of the salmon. Place slices of lemon and a handful of parsley inside the cavity. Put salmon in a large dish and pour over the Hoegaarden, making sure the beer gets into the slits. Cover with clingfilm and marinate for at least 3 hours, turning once.

Put the whole fish in a fish kettle or both halves in a large pan (or 2 pans if necessary) and pour over the marinade. Cover and bring slowly to simmering point. Simmer for 10–15 minutes, depending on the size of the fish, then turn off the heat and leave the salmon to cool in the liquor. Remove salmon, retaining liquor, and carefully peel off skin and external fins/bones. Put fish back into the liquor and leave in fridge overnight while the stock turns gelatinous.

Place salmon on a large silver-effect platter and glaze all over with the Hoegaarden-flavoured 'aspic'. Decorate the top with translucently thin slices of peeled cucumber (using a few to disguise the 'join' if you cooked the fish in 2 halves) and equally thin lemon slices, with just a few slices of cucumber on the sides to create 'scales' on the glittering aspic. Surround with prawns, parsley, samphire and lettuce to make a spectacular centrepiece to a formal buffet.

*To drink: has to be chilled Hoegaarden, but not served in its usual chunky glass. Choose a wide-bowled, stemmed wineglass and slot a lemon slice on the rim à la Hotel Metropole.*

*Mussels with Beer and Bacon, see p. 23.*

# Seaweed-wrapped King Scallops in Beer Batter
## (serves 6)

The Talbot at Knightwick in Worcestershire is a most unusual inn, run by the multi-talented Clift family. The fourteenth-century hostelry on the River Teme has its own fishing rights, and the family also has a farm where hops are grown – I went hop-picking there one September. The cooking Clifts are sisters Annie and Wiz, who create an irresistible mix of the traditional (pea and home-grown lovage soup) and the modern, as in their little tartlets filled with olives, tomato and cream. Here is the delicious starter they devised for a beer banquet to open their pub's very own micro-brewery, brewing with hops grown on their farm. For the batter they used This (their other home brews are That and T'Other), a light golden, gently hopped beer.

225 g (8 oz) self-raising flour
Salt and pepper
Light ale

2 nori seaweed sheets, each cut into 4
6 king scallops

Sift flour into a large bowl. Mix in the seasoning and gradually stir in enough beer to make a thick and sticky batter. Wrap each scallop in a strip of seaweed and dip it into the batter, then deep-fry for around 4–5 minutes in oil or fat – don't let the fat get too hot or the batter will brown too quickly without cooking the scallops.

Annie likes to serve these cut in half on dressed lettuce with a slice of lemon and her beer and seed bread (see page 251), spread with home-made butter. The contrasting colours of fat white scallop, bright green seaweed and golden batter are gorgeous.

*To drink: you probably won't find their Teme Valley Brewery's draught This, so perhaps a pale ale such as Adnams' Broadside (bottled and draught) with a tang of the sea air from where it's brewed in Southwold, Suffolk, to go with the scallops.*

*Crab Cakes with Ginger and Spring Onions, see p. 51.*

## Skate Wing in Black-beer Sauce (serves 6)

You wouldn't normally cook a white fish such as skate in a dark beer. And you wouldn't normally put vinegar and beer in a stock together. In fact, I know a pub landlord in the Lake District who bans vinegar from his pub altogether on the grounds that the fumes affect the real ale. But this is a dish of contrasts that works through discord. Skate in black butter inevitably has a slightly burnt taste which is sometimes too raw. Instead, I used an unusual brown malt ale brewed by King and Barnes, a full-bodied bottle-conditioned beer with 10 per cent brown malt in the mix. The brown malt is produced by roasting pale malt to give a sweet, smoky aroma with burnt butterscotch in the taste. It also goes well with the malt vinegar. Other malty, roast brews include several of the Scottish beers, such as Caledonian's 80/-, or even a porter for a really black sauce.

| | |
|---|---|
| 6 portions middle skate wing | 3 peppercorns |
| Approx 300 ml (½ pint) | 10 preserved capers |
| Brown Malt ale | 1 tbsp malt vinegar |
| 150 ml (¼ pint) water | 25 g (1 oz) unsalted butter |
| 3–4 sprigs parsley | |

Place skate wings in a large frying pan. Cover with 150 ml (¼ pint) of the beer and all the water and bring to simmering point, skimming off any scum. Add parsley, peppercorns, 4 of the capers and the vinegar. Cover with a large plate or lid and simmer for 5 minutes, then leave to stand in the hot liquor for 5 minutes. Discard cooking liquor, keeping the skate wings warm on a serving dish.

Bubble the rest of the beer briskly in the pan with the remaining 6 capers until it has reduced and thickened. Drop in butter and, when it sizzles, whisk it in. Pour sauce over skate wings and serve with roast red shallots and fondant potatoes.

*To drink: a fairly strong India Pale Ale with enough spice and body to stand up to all those flavours; alternatively, echo them with a dark wheat beer such as Salopian Brewing Co's black wheat beer Jigsaw.*

# Smoked Halibut (or Haddock) Fish Cakes in Pilsner and Parsley Batter (serves 6)

This is not your wimpish fish cake of mashed potato and flaked fish all mushed up together. It is an altogether more robust affair – a piece of smoked haddock slapped sandwich-like between two slices of potato, based on the ones my mother and grandmothers used to make with fresh cod in Yorkshire, where they are still to be found in the deep-fat fryers of good old-fashioned fish and chip shops. Once you've made your 'sandwich', you dip it in batter and fry it in deep fat or oil. Beer is a revelation in coating batter – you'll never go back to using milk. Pilsner and lager are clean-tasting beers that go well with fish, creating a crisp, light, golden batter – and with enough hop character to match the less delicate, chunky fish such as haddock, cod and halibut, either smoked or unsmoked. Germany has some superb examples, but I chose one from Czechoslovakia, the original Budweiser Budvar, lagered for up to three months.

450 g (1 lb) medium-thick
  skinless fillet smoked
  haddock, halibut or cod
2–3 large potatoes
Oil for deep frying

*Batter*
100 g (4 oz) self-raising flour
Pinch salt
1 medium egg
150 ml (5 fl oz) pilsner
2 tbsps fresh parsley, chopped
  finely

Make batter by liquidizing all the ingredients except parsley. Rest in the fridge while you prepare the 'cakes'.

Cut fish into 6 pieces, peel potatoes and cut into slices slightly thinner than the fish, as the potato takes longer to cook. Keep the irregular end bits to use for chips, and sandwich the fish pieces between the potato slices, trying to match the fish to the potato slices for shape and size.

Heat deep fat or oil to medium hot. Take batter out of the fridge and stir in parsley. Spear fish cakes one at a time on a long-pronged carving fork, then dip each into the batter, making sure all of it is well coated, especially any gaps between fish and potato. Still on the fork, hold it in the hot fat for a few seconds until the batter sets just enough to hold it all together, then carefully push the fish cake off the fork with a spoon.

Turn down the heat to very low and add 1–2 more fish cakes. Cover and cook gently for about 20 minutes. Remove and cook the rest. Then turn the heat up until oil is very hot and return fish-cakes to crisp the batter to golden brown, 2 at a time. Remove with a slotted spoon and drain on kitchen paper, then keep warm while you crisp the other fish cakes.

These are great with mushy peas seasoned with a drop of vine-gar, but alternatively you could serve a green salad with a lemon dressing.

*To drink: Czech Budweiser Budvar, one of the world's classic bottle-conditioned beers, will be delicious.*

# Swordfish Steak with Lager and Lovage Sauce
## (serves 6)

Mark Prescott worked with the Roux brothers for fifteen years, at the famous Waterside Inn and then as head chef at Le Gavroche in London for eight years. He is now chef/proprietor of his own pub, the White Hart at Nayland in Suffolk, with the support of Michel Roux. He has put the White Hart on the map for serving 'restaurant' food in the more informal setting of a country pub and shows the originality which earned him his reputation in this dish, created for this book.

6 swordfish steaks
*Sauce*
75 g (3 oz) shallots, chopped finely
1 bouquet garni
6 juniper berries, crushed

600 ml (1 pint) medium, rounded lager
300 ml (½ pint) double cream
75 g (3 oz) unsalted butter
40 g (1½ oz) lovage, shredded
Salt and pepper to taste

Place shallots, juniper berries and bouquet garni in a heavy saucepan; add beer and reduce over a high heat by two-thirds. Stir in cream and continue reducing until sauce coats a wooden spoon. Pass through a chinois (conical strainer) and blend in butter with a hand mixer. Season to taste, stir in the lovage at the last minute, and serve with the swordfish steaks, grilled for 4 minutes each side.

*To drink: a clean, crisp beer with a hint of lemon to cut through the cream – try a chilled Belgian wheat beer which would be lovely with the lovage.*

# Turbot with Puy Lentils in Wine and Stout Sauce
## (serves 6)

OK. The hop and the grape don't mix. Mostly. But they do in this recipe by hobby cook Chris Ralph, who devised it for a competition at his local pub. He used brill, but for a special occasion I have pushed out the boat and bought the dearer flat fish, turbot. Here you poach fillets of brill or turbot in white wine and finish off with a drop of fairly dry dark stout, or one for the connoisseur, Highgate Dark Mild, brewed not in that haunt of London's smart art set but in the Midlands by Highgate Brewery. The result is unexpectedly good.

Approx 700 g (1½ lb) brill or turbot fillets
100 g (4 oz) puy lentils
300 ml (½ pint) fish stock
150 ml (¼ pint) water
100 g (4 oz) unsalted butter
40 g (1½ oz) spring onions, chopped finely
150 ml (¼ pint) dry white wine
110 ml (4 fl oz) dark stout
Slice lemon
Salt; freshly ground black pepper

Simmer lentils in half the fish stock (made from the fish trimmings) and the water for about 20 minutes until the stock is absorbed and the lentils are just soft.

Meanwhile, in a wide shallow pan, soften the onion in half the butter without allowing it to colour. Add turbot fillets, wine and remaining fish stock to only just cover – top up with a little water if necessary. Bring back to simmering point and cook for around 4 minutes. Remove fillets from pan carefully and keep hot.

Reduce stock by about a third, add dark stout or mild and reduce by about a third again. Whisk in remaining butter bit by bit, season to taste with salt and pepper and a touch of lemon juice. Serve the fish fillets on a bed of puy lentils, masked with the wine and stout sauce.

*To drink: do try the Highgate Dark Mild – it is getting easier to find on draught and is quite a classic, with far more body than its 3.25 per cent suggests. Perfect here with the combination of fish and puy lentils. Or echo the wine with a French blonde bière de garde with wired cork, served chilled.*

# POULTRY AND GAME

Jug a hare in porter, create the definitive game pie with barley wine, have coq à la biere instead of coq au vin – there are so many stunning ways to cook poultry and game in all the different styles of beer now flowing into Britain. If meat is improved by a beer marinade, so too is game. The toughest old game birds and sinewy venison can be tamed in a 48-hour marinade of a vinous, high-alcohol beer – a barley wine, one of the incredibly strong and complex Belgian beers, a sexy Christmas Ale from England, or a wonderful malty, spirited beer from Scotland. And with Christmas in mind Delia Smith has donated her stunning recipe for venison with port, Guinness and pickled walnuts. A fine way to get pickled for the Christmas season.

Game-bird dishes in this chapter range from Guinea Fowl Orval, a recipe using Trappist Orval beer from the monastery's own cookbook, to my own recipe for pheasant stuffed with wild figs and a real ginger beer and the Scottish brewer of the heather beer Fraoch's recipe for grouse – with due deference to the Chinese!

Cheap meats such as rabbit and pigeon also come into their own cooked in beer, as you will see.

Poultry, of course, embraces both the delicate white chicken breast and strong-tasting turkey. Chicken can be pot-roasted with herbs and vegetables in one of the fruitier beers, just as it is in cider. Keith Floyd's slurpy recipe for chicken cooked with both pale ale and spirits is here. I'm also very keen on the recipe from a Cumbrian pub producing damson beer, which they used to create a recipe for me.

Beers to drink with poultry and game are numerous, and some are detailed here. With these strong meats I love the beers that fill your wine glass with a claret hue or impenetrable blackness. In winter in our house in Hertfordshire I like nothing better than to draw the curtains, cut through the crust of a game pie and release that intoxicating barley-wine steam.

# Chicken Flamed with Gin in Damson Beer (serves 6)

At juicy-sounding Strawberry Bank near Lake Windermere in Cumbria is the Masons Arms with stunning views over Cartmel Fell. The pub is also home to a micro brewery, which produces an unusual dark-russet damson beer made from fruit grown near the pub, a strong 7 per cent as a draught ale and even stronger 9 per cent bottled. Helen Stephenson, the landlady, is a sassy cook with a grand repertoire of vegetarian dishes but here she uses their damson beer to cook a powerful chicken dish. The beer is available at the pub, where they also have a 'museum' of rare and old ales, and at some specialist beer shops. You could also use a Belgian plum beer or perhaps another Cumbrian brew, Jennings's Sneck Lifter, tawny-port hued with toasted caramel and fruit, available bottled in supermarkets and wine/beer chains. (By the by, up north a sneck is a door catch and its lifter someone on their way into a welcoming public bar on a grim, snowy night.)

1 large fresh chicken (around 2.7 kg or 6 lb)
3 tbsps oil
40 g (1½ oz) butter
3 shallots, chopped
85 ml (3 fl oz) gin
20 g (¾ oz) flour
450 ml (¾ pint) damson beer
350 g (12 oz) button chestnut mushrooms
Bouquet garni
Salt and freshly ground black pepper
85 ml (3 fl oz) crème fraîche
1 tbsp parsley, chopped

Chop chicken into 12 serving portions (or use 12 chicken thighs). Heat oil and butter in a heavy, shallow casserole. Add chicken pieces a few at a time and brown well on all sides. Remove from the pan, add shallots and cook for 2 minutes until soft.

Return chicken pieces to the pan, pour over the gin, and flame. Sprinkle chicken with flour, turn over and cook for 1 minute. Add beer, mushrooms (whole if very small, or else halved), bouquet garni, salt and pepper and bring to simmering point.

Cover and cook gently for 45–60 minutes until the chicken is tender. Discard the bouquet garni and skim off excess fat. (You could leave the dish to cool to make it easier to remove the fat, then reheat gently.) Add the crème fraîche, bring to a brisk simmer and taste for seasoning.

Serve sprinkled with fresh parsley, accompanied by spinach pasta and a tossed green salad.

*To drink: the damson beer if you can get it – or there is a luscious Belgian plum beer, though that's not easy to locate either! Jennings's Sneck Lifter, brewed in Cockermouth, is a lot easier to track down (in supermarkets) – and an absolute blinder.*

## Coq à la Bière (serves 6)

Coq au vin is one of those classic French dishes that often gets abused in translation – instead of strongly flavoured joints of quality poultry with a roast patina in a concentrated sauce, you end up with portions of bland chicken drowned in a thick sauce of cheap red wine with tinned tomatoes and even green peppers. I think the dish tastes much better cooked with beer rather than wine, a slightly vinous and yeasty French bière de garde – it wants to be quite strong and spicy, but not overpowering. I used Jenlain, a classic cut-and-come-again example brewed in northern France near Valenciennes and readily available. But there are several choices – the main supermarkets here now sell their own brand of bière de garde; look for the wire-corked bottles. Having taken the liberty of swapping beer for wine, I've taken another by boning and stuffing the chicken joints to give a more robust flavour to meet the beer.

12 free-range chicken thighs, boned
Lard and butter for frying
100 g (4 oz) fresh chicken livers
50 g (2 oz) pale part of leek, shredded and chopped finely
100 g (4 oz) smoked back bacon (with some fat) cut into strips
4 fat cloves garlic
24 shallots, skinned
50 g (2 oz) seasoned flour
100 g (4 oz) small button mushrooms
1 measure brandy
Around ½ pint (or 330 ml bottle) bière de garde
1 tbsp light brown sugar
Fresh sage leaves
Salt and freshly ground black pepper

First make a very simple pâté by sautéing fresh livers gently in butter with the leek and 2 crushed cloves garlic in a covered frying pan. When soft and cooked through (3–4 minutes), season with salt and pepper, then mash up the livers and leek in their juices and put in the fridge to firm up.

In the same frying pan melt a little lard and butter, then scatter in bacon strips, followed by the shallots and fry gently for a few minutes until browned and slightly caramelized. Remove bacon and shallots with a slotted spoon and place in a flat-bottomed casserole. Take about 1 tsp of the 'pâté' and roll it in your palms to a small ball, then gently use to stuff a chicken thigh, pulling the loose edges together so that the stuffing is enclosed.

Coat thighs in the seasoned flour, being careful not to let the filling fall out. Brown on all sides in the bacon fat, again carefully. Warm brandy gently, pour over chicken pieces, and flame. Place chicken thighs gently among the onions in the casserole, 'edges' side down, then deglaze the pan with a little of the beer, bringing it to the bubble. Remove frying pan from the heat and stir in the rest of the bière de garde and sugar, then pour over the chicken. Tuck 3 sage leaves among the chicken pieces and distribute mushrooms in any gaps. Cover with foil or a lid and cook in the middle of a moderate oven (350°F, 180°C, gas mark 4) until the chicken is tender (about 1½ hours).

Discard sage leaves and arrange chicken pieces, shallots, bacon and mushrooms on a large platter.

Pour stock into a pan, season to taste, then reduce by about a third; pour over the chicken pieces and serve.

*To drink: just as you drink red wine with coq au vin, so you can enjoy coq à la biere with a full-flavoured beer. Amber-hued Jenlain with malts from Burgundy and Champagne is ideal – another on sale here is Ch'ti (meaning 'it suits you'). Blonde, paler but strong (6.5 per cent) and characterful with wine notes.*

# Keith Floyd's Chicken in Beer (serves 6)

When I was writing the first *Good Pub Food* guide for the Campaign for Real Ale the Chair of their books committee asked who I thought should pen the foreword. For me there was only one person: Keith Floyd. A passionate advocate for some of our best British dishes and ingredients, his brilliant TV series on Britain and Ireland had found him not infrequently in a hostelry. 'You'll be lucky,' said the Chair. But I wrote to Keith, who phoned to say he supported the work of CAMRA and produced a vigorous foreword. Later he opened his own pub in Devon, where I have enjoyed his ability to 'put sunshine on a plate', and where he also supported the small brewers in his area. Floyd does not cook only with wine, he has also originated several delicious beer recipes – and this one is a true Floydian sip; not one beer but two, plus a measure of spirits, all in one dish from his *Floyd on France* collection. His own introduction says it all: 'Remember, the better the beer, the better the dish. At the very last minute before finishing the sauce, whisk in 2 tablespoons of Guinness – it transforms the taste dramatically.'

1 1.5 kg (3 lb) corn-fed chicken, quartered
125 g (4 oz) butter
Oil
4 shallots, chopped finely
200 g (7 oz) mushrooms, sliced
350 ml (12 fl oz) pale ale or lager
1 small glass Marc d'Alsace (gin will do)
Salt and pepper
300 ml (10 fl oz) single cream
2 tbsps Guinness
Fresh parsley, chopped finely

Sauté the chicken pieces in 50 g (2 oz) butter and a little oil. Add shallots and mushrooms and continue to cook. When they are well browned, pour over the beer and the Marc d'Alsace or gin. Season with salt and pepper and simmer on a gentle heat for about 1 hour, or until chicken is tender.

Shortly before serving, arrange chicken pieces in a deep dish and keep hot. On a high heat reduce the sauce by half. Add the cream to thicken the sauce, and the rest of the butter, whisking all the while. Whisk in the Guinness. Pour the sauce over the chicken and sprinkle with the parsley. Serve with fresh pasta.

*To drink: I would serve this with French beer Ch'ti Blonde, available in some supermarkets and beer shops, at a strong 6.5 per cent, or a rounded, bronze-tinted lager. Serve only just chilled in a large wine glass.*

# Sesame Chicken Gingersnap (serves 6)

Martin Barry is what you might call a Chef and Brewer – a brewer, that is, who originally trained as a chef and came to the art of beer creation via cooking in his own pub. Ex-chefs make some of the best brewers; beer formulas are, after all, known as 'recipes'. Perhaps that is why the unusual beers he originated at the Salopian Brewing Company, Shrewsbury (try saying that when you've had a few!), work extremely well in cooking, especially Gingersnap, a genuine ginger beer produced with traditional ingredients but flavoured with freshly ground root ginger, which makes it extremely appropriate for an oriental-style dish, as in this recipe devised by Martin.

3 chicken breasts
1 egg, beaten
Sesame seeds to coat
½ tsp garlic salt
25 g (1 oz) unsalted butter
25 g (1 oz) light brown sugar
50 ml fresh orange juice
150 ml (¼ pint) Gingersnap or
  ginger beer

1 dstsp cornflour
Light oil and butter for frying
To serve
Stir-fry of mangetout, baby
  corn on the cob and bamboo
  shoots
Plain boiled Chinese noodles
  or rice

Slice the chicken breasts into strips about 5 cm (2 inches) long and 0.5 cm (¼ inch) wide, dip in egg and toss in sesame seeds mixed with garlic salt; set aside until needed.

In a heavy frying pan melt the unsalted butter and brown sugar, stirring until it bubbles, then add orange juice, stir in and remove from the heat. Add the cornflour to the ginger beer and blend well to remove all lumps. Stir into the orange mixture and return the pan to the heat, bringing it slowly to simmering point and stirring all the time until it thickens. If it looks too thick, add a little more orange juice and beer to taste (drinking the rest as you cook, says Martin). By now the sauce should be an attractive orange/brown and smell delicious – set aside while you cook the chicken.

Heat the light oil and butter in another frying pan and cook the chicken strips until crisp on all sides (around 5 minutes). Remove with a slotted spoon and keep warm while you stir-fry the vegetables in the same pan. Meanwhile cook the rice or noodles. Serve the chicken strips on the rice or noodles with the reheated sauce poured over, garnishing the plate with the stir-fry mix.

*To drink: Martin produced a five-spice beer brewed as a one-off, which made an interesting accompaniment but not, I think, a beer for posterity. Ideally choose a clean, dry pilsner, which always goes well with Eastern-style dishes.*

# Roast Duck Breasts with Artichokes on a Cherry Beer Sauce (serves 6)

A classic beer dish, inspired by the traditional roast duck with cherries. Some cherry beers have a russet, winey colour, but in this recipe I used Lindemans bright crimson Belgian cherry beer (kriek), still fermenting in the bottle – a double-sealed bottle with fat cork hiding under a metal cap. It makes a wonderful deep pink sauce, just sweet enough, but with that lambic tartness from the wild yeast in the beer to cut straight through rich duck with its fat, crisp skin. The flavour is infinitely better than the glutinous cherry syrup or tinned cherries we often get with duck.

6 Barbary duck breasts (not too large, this is very rich)
2 shallots, peeled and chopped finely
50 g (2 oz) button mushrooms, sliced thinly (reserve stalks)
25 g (1 oz) flour
300 ml (½ pint) cherry beer
150 ml (¼ pint) chicken or vegetable stock
Salt and pepper to season
12 Jerusalem artichokes
12 fresh, dark-red cherries in links
Watercress

Place duck breasts skin side up in a grill pan. Grill under a fierce heat until the skins are crisp and fat runs out. Place them in an ovenproof dish towards the top of a very hot oven (450°F, 230°C, gas mark 8) until the breasts are cooked to your liking – up to 10 minutes for quite pink, 15 minutes for medium. Remove from the oven and keep warm, draining off the fat.

Use a little of the fat to sweat the shallots and mushroom stalks until tender, then stir in flour and cook gently for 2 minutes. Add half the cherry beer and the stock, bring to a brisk simmer and cook to a thick sauce, reducing by almost half. Strain through a fine sieve and reheat gently in a clean pan. Add the rest of the cherry beer and again cook briskly to reduce, seasoning to taste.

Meanwhile, cook the artichokes in their skins like new potatoes until tender.

To serve, pour a pool of cherry-beer sauce on to each plate and

carve the duck breasts on top. Decorate with a garnish of watercress topped by a pair of fresh cherries and accompany with the
Jerusalem artichokes, deliciously nutty when boiled, split open and
anointed with a knob of butter.

*To drink: cherry beer by all means, but go for the tarter Belle-Vue
Kriek from Belgium, which truly marries beer with wine in a tall
bottle under a wired champagne cork, or the extraordinary Liefmans dry and slightly sour kriek, at a hefty 7.1 per cent, in its tissue-wrapped bottle, 300 years of brewing taking a bow in its complexity.*

# Summer Madness Brie, Watercress and Turkey Pie
## (serves 6)

When my first *Good Pub Food* guidebook was launched, I asked cooks from some of the listed hostelries to come along and bring a doggy bag for the press to taste. The impromptu buffet ranged from griddled lavabread pancakes to home-made Scotch eggs using eggs from the pub's free-range hens. But I asked Heather Humphreys to do a game pie because she is anything but a simple pie person. Now that she is landlady of the Rising Sun at Woodland near Ashburton in Devon she has raised pies to an art form, with pie nights when diners can choose from steak and pigeon pie, fidget pie, duck and cherry pie, smoked haddock lattice pie and many more. She even sends them out mail order. But this pie she has created especially for this book, a turkey pie flavoured with a light summer ale – more and more breweries are creating seasonal brews with lovely, delicate straw-hued beers in summer. Heather used Ushers' Summer Madness, a wheat beer with a hint of honey. You can get bottled and draught summer ales for a couple of months in season, or choose an English wheat beer.

450 g (1 lb) turkey breast, diced
2 tbsps seasoned flour
1 medium onion, chopped
2 tbsps grapeseed oil
300 ml (½ pint) summer ale

1 bunch (approx 75 g, 3 oz) watercress
225 g (8 oz) Brie, cubed
450 g (1 lb) flaky pastry (bought puff or shortcrust can be substituted)
Egg/milk to glaze

Dredge turkey breast in seasoned flour. Sauté chopped onion in the oil until soft but not coloured, then add turkey breast and seal on all sides until lightly coloured. Gradually stir in the ale and bring gently to the bubble, then simmer gently until the turkey is cooked – 15–20 minutes.

Wash watercress well, then roughly chop the leaves. When turkey is cooked, stir in the chopped watercress and cubed Brie. Check seasoning and leave to cool. Roll out half the pastry and line a greased flan tin. Spoon in filling and top with remaining pastry. Use the pastry trimmings to decorate. Brush with the egg/milk wash and bake towards the top of a hot oven pre-heated to 425°F, 220°C, gas mark 7, for 25–30 minutes until the pastry is cooked and golden brown.

Serve hot with fresh summer peas and new potatoes or cold with a green leaf and tomato salad.

*To drink: although turkey breast is a light meat, it is stronger tasting than chicken breast and the dominant flavours of Brie and watercress make this a challenge. A bouncy summer ale or pale but strong wheat beer are certainly acceptable – and also consider linking that touch of peppery bitterness in the watercress with the tongue-tip sulphur characteristic of some Midlands bitters.*

# Bodger's Game Pie (serves 6)

The legend above the door of Chiltern Brewery reads, 'Fear God and give him the glory' . . . and well it might. For inside they brew, and then bottle-condition, Bodger's Barley Wine at a heftily alcoholic 8.5 per cent, a truly heavenly nectar. Powerful, dark, vinous, it is verily a hop wine and, in my view, one of the great classic beers. This is really a beer for sipping slowly from a brandy balloon at the end of a meal – and cooking with it might well incur the wrath of the gods, but I'll risk it for this definitive game pie; nothing fancy, just strong gamey flavours with a hint of root vegetables in a stunning barley-wine stock. I have known Richard and Lesley Jenkinson of Chiltern Brewery for a long time; the explanation for the religious tract, also on some of their bottle labels, is that they attribute the success of their brewery to divine providence. About once a month they hold a prayer meeting in the brewery – at other times visitors can view the brewing process, their tiny beer museum and the shop, filled with goodies from beer cheese and beer pickle to beer shampoo.

*Pastry*
125 g (8 oz) self raising flour
Pinch salt
75 g (3 oz) good-quality cooking fat
25 g (1 oz) unsalted butter
1 medium egg
A little chilled milk
*Filling*
550 g (1¼ lb) mixed game – venison, rabbit, hare, and pigeon or pheasant – cubed roughly
1 bottle (½ pint) Bodgers or a strong barley wine
25 g (1 oz) seasoned flour

2 fine-quality pork sausages
50 g (2 oz) dry cured smoked streaky bacon, diced
25 g (1 oz) dripping for cooking
100 g (4 oz) chicken thighs, boned and cubed
1 large onion, chopped
1 large carrot, diced
1 stick celery, sliced
6 juniper berries
Good meat or game stock (I simmer a pigeon carcass after removing the breasts for the game mix)

Place game in a glass dish, pour over the barley wine, and marinate in the fridge overnight.

Next day, place a sieve over a bowl and drain the game through it; blot the cubed game and toss lightly in seasoned flour.

Heat dripping in a frying pan and add diced bacon and sausages, frying briefly to brown on all sides and release fat. Remove to a heavy pan or casserole with a slotted spoon, cutting the sausages into chunks. Fry the game a little at a time to seal quickly on all sides, then also add to the pan or casserole. Add chicken, onion, carrot, celery and juniper berries to the pan, then pour over the barley wine marinade, adding around ½ pint stock, to cover all the ingredients. Simmer very slowly in the oven or on top of the stove for 2 hours until the meat is tender but still has a little bite.

As soon as the filling starts cooking, make pastry by sieving flour and salt into a large mixing bowl, then rubbing in the fat and butter very lightly, lifting your hands above the bowl to incorporate as much air as possible, till it resembles crumbs. Whisk the egg and stir in a very little milk, then make a well in the centre of the mixing bowl and pour it in, reserving around 1 tbsp to glaze the pie. Mix together, adding enough cold milk to make a soft but not sloppy pastry. Wrap in clingfilm and chill for 2 hours.

Remove from the fridge and bring back to room temperature. Pour game mixture into a pie bowl and allow to cool slightly while the oven heats to 425°F, 220°C, gas mark 7. Roll out the pastry on a floured board and cover the pie, crimping the edges and brushing with retained egg/milk. Bake towards the top of the oven for 30 minutes until the filling is bubbling and the pastry crisp and golden brown.

I like to serve this with traditional vegetables such as mashed potato and swede or braised red cabbage.

*To drink: Bodgers or one of our other big barley wines, fortunately growing in number – London's two main brewers both produce one, Golden Pride from Fuller's and Old Nick from Young's or winkle out Harvey's Elizabethan. Serve in a deep-bowled wine glass. But beware – these are very strong. If you want to lower the alcohol content slightly, try a dark characterful porter such as Nethergate's Old Growler or Samuel Smith's Taddy Porter, at room temperature.*

# Grouse Seared in Heather Beer and Honey (serves 2)

Fraoch Heather Ale is flavoured with ling and bell heads of heather in full bloom – 12 litres in every barrel to produce this distinctive floral and herbal, delicate beer, wonderful for both cooking and sipping. I met brewer Bruce Williams swinging round the Great British Beer Festival in full kilt when the Heather Ale Brewery from Scotland made its triumphant debut. Bruce first re-created the ale in 1993 after getting hold of a recipe translated from the Gaelic, which had been passed down verbally from the Picts. He named his beer Fraoch (pronounced frooch), which is Celtic for heather and, although a seasonal beer in draught form made when the heather is in bloom, it is now available bottled all year round in High Street chains and supermarkets. I asked him if he had ever used it in cooking and he told me that Fraoch comes into its own on the Glorious Twelfth when the grouse season starts. Grouse simmered in heather beer then glazed in heather honey are 'the Celtic answer to Peking Duck', says Bruce.

1–2 grouse (serve either 1 grouse per person, if small, or ½ grouse per person with accompanying vegetables)
1 bottle Fraoch Heather Ale
Few stalks parsley (or sprig heather!)
Heather honey
Around 4 small turnips and 4 same-sized new potatoes, peeled and par-boiled
Butter
1 dstsp plain flour

Place grouse in large, heavy pan. Pour over heather ale, cover and simmer for 1 hour, then leave in pan until cool. Pre-heat oven to very hot (425°F, 220°C, gas mark 7), remove grouse from stock and dry; strain liquor and reserve. Spread heather honey thinly all over the grouse, put parsley (or heather) in the body cavity and place breast down in a roasting tin. Cook towards the top of the oven for around 20–25 minutes, turning the grouse the right way up and basting well halfway through. They are ready when sizzling hot with a marvellous dark brown patina; set aside in a warm place.

Add a little unsalted butter to the roasting tin and heat on top of the stove, then add parboiled vegetables and toss until caramelized; remove and keep warm. Stir plain flour into remaining fat/juices in the roasting tin and cook for a minute. Slowly stir in about ½ pint reserved beer stock to make a smooth, slightly thickened gravy. Strain into a clean pan and reheat gently, adding a little heather honey, just enough to flavour the gravy without smothering the gamey taste. Either serve the grouse whole per person or a half per person, accompanied by the caramelized turnips and potatoes, with the gravy in a sauceboat.

*To drink: fragrant Fraoch of course, with its unique floral flavour and delicacy; you might also put a bottle of honey beer on the table, such as bottled Pitfield or Vaux Waggledance.*

# Guinea Fowl in Orval Trappist Beer with Onion Preserve and Honey (serves 4)

The Trappist monks of the Orval monastery in southern Belgium near the French border can truly be said to produce manna from heaven. They make their own cheese, bread and honey – and brew their own beer; just the one, but it's quite enough to have gained respect worldwide. Its triple fermentation process, the third fermentation in the bottle, and dry hopping produce a strong amber beer with a frothy head and complex, unmistakable palate – the yeast sediments are a rich source of vitamin B. A fish with a golden ring is the brewery's symbol because legend has it that the Countess Mathilda of Tuscany lost a gold ring in the lake in the adjoining valley. When a fish recovered the ring for her, she was so grateful she gave the land to God for the foundation of the monastery. Orval is so good to cook with that the monastery has its own recipe book by Nicole Darchambeau, which has been translated into English. Here is one of her recipes, in which Orval makes a gutsy accompaniment to game.

2 bottles Orval
1 guinea fowl
Liver from guinea fowl
200 g (7 oz) onion preserve*
1 tbsp dark clear honey
1 tbsp sour cream
2 slices Orval bread (use a
  dark German-style rye bread)

Unsalted butter
2 whole matured goat's
  cheeses
Salt and pepper

*To serve*
Game chips and spiced red
  cabbage

Arrange guinea fowl in a flameproof casserole. Season with salt and pepper. Add 1 bottle Orval beer. Bring to the boil, then leave to simmer covered on a low heat for 20 minutes. Add onion preserve and other bottle of beer. Bring to the boil and continue cooking, covered, at a brisk simmer for 30 minutes.

* The monks make their own – it is more mellow and less sharp than onion chutney, so if using chutney cut the quantity by half.

Remove the bird and keep warm.

Reduce sauce over a high heat, add honey and sour cream, then continue to reduce until sauce is thick and creamy. Sauté liver in butter for a few minutes until just cooked, then mash. Toast the bread, butter one slice, then spread it with mashed liver and cut into quarters. Spread the other slice with a little honey and also quarter. Cut goat's cheeses in half and place a piece on each honeyed quarter, then brown under the grill.

Arrange a piece of liver-topped toast and cheese-topped toast on each plate along with a few slices of carved guinea fowl, pour the sauce over the meat and serve with game chips and cranberry sauce.

*To drink: Orval actually presents a contrast to the dish itself as it is quite dry, but with a spiciness to match the sauce. Sold here in 33 cl skittle-shaped bottles, it is readily available in both specialist beer shops and High Street chains.*

# Pigeon Breasts with Porter Sauce (serves 6)

A sophisticated winter supper-party dish, simultaneously elegant and sustaining. The porter is strong enough to tenderize a pigeon then make a spicy sauce, setting it off to perfection. Use a dry black porter combining the flavours of roast malt, nuts and raisins. The style has made a come-back and is now hugely popular – available both draught and in many bottled varieties. Classic Taddy Porter brewed by Samuel Smith's and available bottled (named after their Tadcaster brewery, but in this house after my son Taddy short for Tadeusz), a cross between a stout and a porter, is absolutely glorious – and an utterly appropriate accompaniment to the meal.

3 pigeons
Stock made by simmering car-
  casses with 1 onion, 1 carrot,
  1 tsp fresh parsley and seasoning
600 ml (1 pint) dry porter
1 tsp powdered mace
Unsalted butter for frying

100 g (4 oz) chestnut
  mushrooms, sliced
1 tbsp redcurrant jelly
50 ml (2 fl oz) double cream
Salt and freshly ground black
  pepper
*To garnish*
Fresh redcurrants and watercress

Remove pigeon breasts with a very sharp knife and use the car-casses to make stock as above. Place breasts in a dish and rub in mace, then cover with porter and marinate overnight. Remove pigeon breasts, retaining marinade, and fry them in butter for 2 minutes on each side until still pink in the middle; remove and keep warm.

In the same pan, gently fry mushrooms, then pour in around 150 ml (¼ pint) stock and reduce rapidly until quite concentrated. Add marinade, bring to the boil and reduce again until thickened and glossy. Stir in redcurrant jelly. Season to taste, remove from heat and stir in double cream; return to low heat and bubble for a few minutes, stirring, until coating consistency.

To serve: carve one breast per person and fan on to a pool of the sauce; garnish with fresh redcurrants and watercress. Parsnip and celeriac rosti makes a good accompaniment (see page 135).

*To drink: the Taddy Porter is grand in flavour, strength and colour; King and Barnes produce a bottle-conditioned porter which is also a treat; St Peter's brewery now has a bottled porter with honey; or find a full porter with a hint of port.*

# Pot-roast Pheasant Stuffed with Wild Figs and Ginger Beer (serves 2)

Ginger beer is usually a non-alcoholic fizzy drink with little allure, generally sold, for a reason that escapes me, in fish and chip shops. As I've previously mentioned, two years ago the imaginative Salopian Brewing Co. in Shropshire came up with Gingersnap, a real beer brewed with root ginger. Since then other beers flavoured with ginger have been produced both draught and bottled, so it is now quite easy to find. It really lends itself to the almost Elizabethan flavours of this recipe, making a spicy filling for the pheasant and, just as important, helping to tenderize and flavour what can be a tough old bird.

1 pheasant, weighing around
 750 g (1½ lb)*
25 g (1 oz) butter
1 600 ml (1 pint) bottle Gingersnap or other real ginger beer
25 g (1 oz) plain flour
Salt and freshly ground black
 pepper

*Stuffing ingredients*
50 g (2 oz) wild figs, rinsed
 and chopped
25 g (1 oz) walnuts, chopped
25 g (1 oz) sultanas, washed
*To Garnish*
Fresh figs

Mix stuffing ingredients in a bowl and pour over ginger beer to cover by about 4 cms or 1½ inches. Soak overnight and next day drain off the ginger beer and reserve.

Rinse pheasant inside and out with cold water, wipe dry, upend and fill the cavity with the stuffing mix, pressing down loosely, and truss. Place pheasant breast-side down in a heavy casserole, pouring in enough ginger beer to come about a third of the way up. Cover and place in the middle of a pre-heated medium oven (350°F, 180°C, gas mark 4) and cook for 90 minutes. Increase heat to 425°F, 220°C, gas mark 7, turn the pheasant over, blot the

* One plump pheasant up to 1 kg (2 lb) will serve 2–3 people, or you can double the ingredients and cook a brace for a dinner party. You can use the same stuffing to roast a pheasant, basting it with ginger beer, but only if you are sure the bird is very young and tender.

breast dry with kitchen paper, baste with half the butter and return to the oven, uncovered, for 20 minutes until the pheasant is tender, crisp and golden. Remove pheasant from the casserole and keep warm.

In a roasting pan melt the rest of the butter. Sprinkle on the flour and cook gently for 1 minute to make a roux; stir in ginger-beer stock from the casserole and cook gently while it thickens and reduces by about a third. Stir in the reserved ginger beer used to soak the stuffing (try a sip, it tastes gorgeous) and continue to simmer for another 2 minutes. Taste for seasoning and strain into a gravy boat.

Serve half each, garnished with fresh sliced figs and a spoonful of stuffing, with the gravy separate.

*To drink: Harvey's Elizabethan Ale at over 8 per cent is suitably warming and medieval; the ginger beer is an interesting contrast – quite dry and with a wheat beer prickle.*

# Oregon Amber Ale and Cider Rabbit (serves 6)

One of the very best recent developments on the brewing scene has been the production of seasonal or 'one-off' beers either to reflect the time of year or try out an experimental brew. Young's Brewery in south London is among those carrying out an increasing amount of research in this direction. Summer sees their version of Oregon Amber Ale, brewed in Wandsworth using Fuggles hops grown in Oregon, lighter and fruitier than the US version and with a citrus tang that goes well with rabbit – especially when combined with scrumpy cider and a few exotic spices to produce an offbeat bunny stew. The recipe was sent by Denise Thwaites, formerly a Young's landlady in Richmond, Surrey. Now she serves it to her regulars at Keith Floyd's former pub, the Maltsters' Arms free-house, on Bow Creek at Tuckenhay in Devon, where she regularly serves Young's ales and has several real ciders to choose from.

1 kg (2 lb) boneless rabbit, diced
1 large onion, chopped finely
3 sticks celery, chopped finely
3 cloves garlic, crushed
3 whole star anise
3 medium pieces cassia bark
Few strands saffron
1 medium red chilli, chopped finely
150 ml (¼ pint) decent stock
150 ml (¼ pint) real cider ('the cloudier and drier the better!' – Denise)
300 ml (½ pint) Young's Oregon Amber ale*
2 large potatoes, peeled and chopped into medium- sized dice
Salt and freshly ground black pepper

Place all the ingredients except potatoes and seasoning in a large casserole dish. Cover and marinate overnight. Add potatoes and stir well. Cover and cook in a moderate oven (350°F, 180°C, gas mark 4) until almost all the liquid has been absorbed and the potatoes are cooked through – about 1 hour. Halfway through, season to taste.

*Available in Young's pubs on draught in late spring/early summer, but also bottled in leading supermarkets. Amber ales from America are making their appearance here in specialist beer shops.

Serve with 2 green vegetables such as French beans and broccoli. 'It should turn out a lovely golden amber colour,' says Denise.

*To drink: this is a dish full of zingy flavours, so serve a strong hopped and spicy IPA alongside; Young's Oregon Amber can certainly be drunk as well or try actual amber beers from the USA, Stan's Whistle Stop Ale or Roscoe's Red are available here and have a malty sweetness which is succulent with rabbit.*

*Grouse Seared in Heather Beer and Honey, see p. 89.*

# Rabbit with Mustard and 1845 Overture (serves 6)

In 1995, London brewers Fuller's decided to brew a bottle-conditioned ale to commemorate the 150th anniversary of their birth in 1845. The result is a towering beer – strong, malty and vinous. It's almost a barley wine, but not quite – Fuller's do a splendid example of that in their smaller bottles of Golden Pride. The new beer is perfect with the strong flavour of wild rabbit, that hint of burnt malt bringing out the sweetness in the meat; long, gentle cooking is essential for the beer stock to mellow. Alternative beers could be a malty Scottish ale or even a dark mild, which stands up well in casseroles despite its relatively low strength. Bottled 1845 is readily available in supermarkets, off-licences and Fuller's pubs.

1 wild rabbit, jointed (or 6 portions wild rabbit)
4 green peppercorns
7 fl oz (200 ml) dark malty ale or dark mild
1 tbsp plain flour
1 tbsp mustard powder
1 small onion, diced
1 small leek, washed and shredded
2 rashers smoked streaky bacon, chopped
Fat for frying

1 stick celery, chopped
1 carrot, diced
50 g (2oz) chestnut mushrooms, sliced
25 g (1 oz) dried ceps soaked in a little hot water
7 fl oz (200 ml) water (or water left from boiling potatoes)
1 tbsp dried thyme
Grating of nutmeg
Salt and freshly ground black pepper

Put the pieces of rabbit in a glass dish with the peppercorns and pour over the beer. Marinate for 6 hours or overnight, turning twice.

Remove rabbit from beer and blot dry. Mix flour and mustard, and use to dust the rabbit portions.

Heat fat in a frying pan, add the bacon and fry for 1 minute, then add onion and leek and sauté gently until soft. Transfer to a casserole, using a slotted spoon. Add a little more fat to the pan and quickly fry the coated rabbit portions on all sides till golden

*Gigot of Lamb with Rosemary, see p. 123.*

brown. Place them in the casserole and scatter over the celery, carrot and chestnut mushrooms, then add the ceps and their soaking water. Pour over the beer marinade and the water; add dried thyme and a good pinch of freshly grated nutmeg.

Cover the casserole and place in the middle of a medium oven (350°F, 180°C, gas mark 4) and leave to cook for around 3 hours, until the rabbit is really tender. Season to taste.

Serve with potatoes and parsnips mashed together with a knob of butter and seasoning.

*To drink: you can't do better than large-bowled wine glasses filled with carefully poured 1845 or another classic, Marston's incomparable, big and complex Pedigree Bitter from the home of brewing, Burton upon Trent.*

# Rodenbach Rabbit with Prunes (serves 6)

Rodenbach is a red ale from west Flanders with the distinctive sour taste of the region, which results from their own strain of top-fermenting yeast and from long maturation in raw oak vessels, where the beer gains more character from cultures in the wood. It is a big beer which is at its best in hearty peasant cooking, as in this dish popular in Brussels bars – and in London at the Wheatsheaf in Rathbone Place, where mother and daughter Irene and Maureen Van Der Meersch sometimes put it on the menu in their Belgian restaurant upstairs. Rodenbach is available here bottled both as a blend of old and young, or the fuller, aged Grand Cru.

| | |
|---|---|
| 1 rabbit | 100 g (4 oz) no-soak stoneless |
| Butter for frying | semi-dried prunes |
| 1 large onion, chopped finely | Cornflour to thicken |
| 1 bottle Rodenbach | Salt; freshly ground black pepper |

Cut the rabbit into pieces (or use about 1 kg/2 lb jointed rabbit portions). In a large pan or casserole fry the rabbit pieces in butter until golden brown, then remove and fry the chopped onion in the same pan. Replace rabbit and add enough Rodenbach to cover, then put the lid on and either simmer gently on top of the cooker or in the oven until the rabbit is tender (at least 1 hour), making sure the meat is always covered by the beer. Add prunes and continue cooking for a further 10 minutes.

Remove rabbit and prunes. Keep warm while you thicken the beer stock with cornflour; season to taste, then serve the rabbit with the prunes and sauce poured over. 'This is particularly nice served with French beans sautéed with shallots, and apple sauce,' says Maureen.

*To drink: oaky like a good wine, Rodenbach's big brother, bottled Grand Cru, its neck wrapped in gold foil, is a sour red beer which gains flavour from ageing in wooden casks. It is an afficionado's beer, too acerbic for some – an alternative could be a rather different Belgian beer, Belle-Vue Kriek, a brown cherry beer with some of the character of claret.*

# Delia Smith's Venison (or beef) with Port, Guinness and Pickled Walnuts (serves 10–12)

Here is a sumptuous festive recipe from *Delia Smith's Christmas*. To me it's the perfect Boxing Day dinner, to be left simmering in the oven whilst the cook and all the guests go for a long, crisp walk. As Delia says, it is a very special braised dish, which is wonderful for a party since it demands no last-minute attention or fuss.

6 lb (2.75kg) venison or beef* cut into 1-inch (2.5 cm) squares
2 pints (1.2 litres) Guinness
10 fl oz (275 ml) port
2 bayleaves
4 sprigs thyme
8 oz (225 g) onions, chopped
2 cloves garlic, crushed
2 x 14 oz (400 g) jars pickled walnuts
3 tbsps butter
3 tbsps olive oil
2 level tbsps flour
Salt and freshly milled black pepper

Begin this the night before by placing the meat in a large bowl along with the bayleaves and thyme. Pour the Guinness and port all over it, place a plate on top of the meat (to keep it pushed down into the marinade as much as possible), and leave in a cool place overnight. The next day, stir everything well.

When you're ready to cook the meat, pre-heat the oven to gas mark 1, 275°F, 140°C. Take a large flameproof casserole, add half the butter and oil to it and heat gently. Drain the meat (reserving the liquid and herbs), and dry a few pieces at a time with kitchen paper. Turn the heat up high, then add these few pieces to the pan to brown them (if you add too much meat in one go, it will release too much steam and not brown sufficiently). As soon as they're browned, remove them and continue until all the meat is browned.

Now add the rest of the butter and oil to the pan and as soon as it foams and bubbles add the onions and garlic to brown these for about 10 minutes. Meanwhile drain all the liquid off the walnuts

---

*Delia recommends shoulder of venison for a 'richer, more gamey flavour' or, alternatively, a well-flavoured cut of beef, such as brisket.

and cut them into quarters. Return all the meat to the casserole to join the onions. Stir in the flour to soak up all the juices, then pour in the marinade (including the bayleaves and thyme), add the walnut quarters, and season well with salt and pepper.

As soon as it reaches a gentle simmer, put a lid on, transfer the casserole to the middle shelf of the oven and forget all about it for 3 hours – by which time the meat will be tender and the sauce marvellously dark and rich

Delia suggests serving this with Traditional Braised Red Cabbage with Apples, and Purée of Potato and Celeriac with Garlic – both recipes to be found in *Delia Smith's Christmas*.

*To drink: I would lean to the port side with bottle-conditioned King and Barnes Festive Ale, which has a gorgeous hint of Amontillado – in the colour, too; port-coloured Gale's Prize Old Ale in a corked bottle or Ushers' Tawny Ale, also bottled, and one of three Ushers' Vintage Ales designed to accompany food – the others are White Ale and Ruby Ale.*

## Heritage Venison Cobbler (serves 6–8)

A cobbler is a hearty, old-fashioned winter dish with a rich scone topping which makes it as filling as a pie. For this recipe Roger Payne, head chef at the Rattlebone Inn at Sherston in Wiltshire, chose to slowly simmer a cheap cut of venison in the beer they serve in their bar – ripely sweet Smiles' Heritage Ale, brewed not too far away in Bristol. Smiles was originally set up there in 1977 to supply a restaurant, but has since grown apace to vittle increasing numbers of both tied and free pubs with a growing beer range.

1 kg (2 lb) diced casserole venison
25 g (1 oz) seasoned flour
Oil and butter for sealing
2 large onions, chopped
2 cloves of garlic, crushed
2 sticks celery, cleaned and chopped
25 g (1 oz) brown sugar
250 ml (8 fl oz or almost ½ pint) Smiles' Heritage Ale, available bottled
150 ml (¼ pint) strong beef stock
Salt and freshly ground black pepper
*For cobbler topping*
225 g (8 oz) self-raising flour
25 g (1 oz) butter
50 g (2 oz) Double Gloucester cheese, grated
Pinch each cayenne pepper, mustard powder and salt
Approx 150 ml (¼ pint) milk

Toss the venison in seasoned flour, then seal and brown on all sides in the oil and butter to give it a good colour. Remove with a slotted spoon to a heavy pan or casserole. Adding a little oil to the frying pan if necessary, sauté the onions, garlic and celery briefly until lightly browned, then stir in the sugar and add to the venison.

In a separate pan, simmer the Smiles' Heritage uncovered until reduced by half, then pour over the venison and vegetables together with the beef stock.

Cover and either cook in a low oven or simmer on top of the stove until the venison is tender – about 2 hours, adding a little stock or water if it seems to be getting too thick.

Make the cobbler by sifting the self-raising flour into a bowl, then lightly rub in the butter and stir in the grated cheese and seasonings.

Make a well in the middle and add enough milk to make a soft dough. Rest for 1 hour, then roll out on a lightly floured surface to 1 cm (½ inch) thick and cut out into rounds with a 3.5 cm (1½ inch) fluted cutter.

Taste venison for seasoning and transfer to a large, rectangular pie dish. Arrange scone rounds overlapping all round the dish to leave a gap in the centre. Brush with milk and bake towards the top of the oven (400°F, 200°C, gas mark 6) for around 15 minutes until the scones are risen and golden.

*To drink: a robust English cask beer with some sweetness – gorgeous Jennings' Sneck Lifter with its smooth burnt caramel and toast flavours (available bottled) is marvellous with venison; Ringwood Old Thumper, delivering bitter-sweetness, and Badger's Tanglefoot also spring to mind.*

# Venison in Scotch Ale with Caramelized Root Vegetables and Crystallized Ginger (serves 6)

Red wine is the classic tenderizer and sauce for venison. But a high-strength, malty beer is big enough to do both jobs and add a roundness I don't find in wine. You could use most strong barley wines – some of them have almost as high an alcohol level as grape wine – but I chose a Scottish ale because Scotland is where you still find most wild venison, and you don't want the meeker, 'domestic' variety for this dish – the strong beer marinade and long simmering will tame it. I used Old Jock brewed by Broughton in the Borders, not actually a barley wine but, at 6.7 per cent alcohol, damned near there; it's a gorgeous dark vinous beer with Scotch whisky somewhere in the background. Produced both as a cask ale and bottled, you find it in some chains and in beer stores.

6 venison shoulder steaks
1 bottle (275 ml) Old Jock or a barley wine
6 juniper berries
1 medium onion, chopped
2 cloves garlic, chopped finely
50 g (2 oz) dried ceps, soaked in a little hot water
12 shallots, peeled

1 large carrot, 1 medium parsnip and 1 thick slice swede all peeled and cut in julienne sticks
25 g (1 oz) crystallized ginger, in small cubes
Unsalted butter for frying, plus 25 g (1 oz) extra butter
Salt and freshly ground black pepper

Place steaks in a shallow dish and pour over beer, then dot the juniper berries among steaks. Cover and marinate for at least 14 hours or overnight.

Remove steaks from marinade, dry on kitchen paper, then fry quickly on all sides – including edges – in hot butter in a frying pan to brown and seal in the beer. Place steaks in an ovenproof dish. In the same butter fry the onion and garlic, then add the marinade, stir, and pour over the venison, stirring in the ceps with their hot water. Cover and casserole below the centre of a low oven (325°F, 160°C, gas mark 3) for around 3 hours until the steaks are tender (farmed venison will take less time).

Meanwhile, caramelize the shallots in butter. Remove, then toss the julienne sticks of root vegetables in the same butter until slightly browned and add onions and vegetables to the casserole 30 minutes before the end of cooking time together with the crystallized ginger. When cooked, remove venison and vegetables with a slotted spoon and keep warm.

Strain stock into a pan and cook briskly to reduce by almost half; taste and add salt and pepper, then whisk in the extra 25 g (1 oz) unsalted butter to make a glossy sauce of coating consistency. Place a venison steak on each serving plate on a pool of sauce and arrange the vegetables alongside.

*To drink: this is a rich dish with dark flavours. Sip a wine glass of barley wine; a Scottish 'wee heavy' malt character beer also drinks well, such as Maclay 80/-, St Andrew's Ale with its cobnut middle note or, to match the strength of the barley wine, bottled Traquair House Ale brewed in a Scottish stately home.*

# MEAT DISHES

Meat has always been the obvious partner to beer in a dish, as everyone who's had the landlord's beef and beer stew or steak and ale pie will tell you. And there's nothing wrong with these traditional pub dishes. But the lack of imagination involved in pouring a drop of 'cooking bitter' into the pot started me thinking constructively about cooking with beer, and all the different styles apart from bitter or lager that might complement food.

So it is with meat. A delicate pork escalope can be partnered by a pilsner and mild mustard sauce, while stronger pork can be casseroled with an apple-edged ale or varnished with the spectacular dark wheat beer Aventinus (see page 136). Lamb is luscious with one of our fruity bitters or with a geniune fruit beer, such as raspberry beer, making a special dinner-party dish. Or get hold of a bottle of Belgian mint beer to make a sauce for grilled chops!

The pub landlord was quite right in one respect, though; beef and beer are a marriage made in heaven. But don't stick to bitter; try beef with a crafted old ale as the master, Albert Roux, does in boeuf aiguillette, or a vinous Trappist ale brewed by Belgian monks in a classic carbonnade, or steak collops with porter sauce, or combined with smoked oysters in the oyster stout suet pudding you will find here. A beer marinade both tenderizes and adds flavour before and during cooking.

Dark mild is a lovely beer to use in slow cooking and you will forgive me for sharing with you my recipe for oxtail richly casseroled in mild – I am relying on my cookbook outliving the ban on this under-appreciated cut.

You will also note the terrific combination of a rounded,

savoury bitter with gammon, both in Barry's famous bacon roly-poly, created by a brewer turned chef, and in my recipe for cooking a whole gammon in ale then finishing it with a mash tun marmalade glaze.

As I have said earlier, beer is brilliant in batters, and in this chapter you will find another kind – Yorkshire pudding batter, here in a sophisticated toad-in-the-hole made with venison and pork sausages.

Needless to say, the fuller and more mature beers are an ideal accompaniment to meat, helping to bring out its flavour even if you don't use them in the cooking, and you will find suggestions for what to drink throughout the chapter.

# Albert Roux's Boeuf Aiguillette Braised with Ale
## (serves 8)

When Albert Roux went to the home of brewing, Burton upon Trent, to present a beer banquet he certainly produced beer dishes with panache. Cooking at the Bass Museum, he used craft ales made by the museum's own in-house brewery, the oldest micro-brewery in the world, where they keep archive beer recipes alive. M. Roux proved not to be one of those elitist chefs who dismiss our honest ales in favour of the grape, but showed that he appreciated the complexity of a well-crafted ale and its potential in the kitchen. He gave us a 'Welsh rarebit' of scallops and Dublin bay prawns in a cheese sauce flavoured with stout served on shredded leeks as a starter, and ended with light apple fritters in beer batter dusted with cinnamon and accompanied by the brewery's bottle-conditioned barley wine, thick enough to stir with a spoon. Or, as he said to me, 'strong enough to knock your socks off'. His main course was beef in ale; albeit the Roux version – meltingly tender rump steak cooked whole in the museum's Masterpiece Ale, and then carved on to plates with a beautifully balanced beer gravy accompanied by braised chicory and mash. Here it is.

| | |
|---|---|
| 3 kg (6 lb) 'aiguillette' or top rump, in one piece | 200 g (7 oz) small mushrooms, halved |
| 100 ml (3 fl oz) oil | 3 bottles (3 pints) Bass Masterpiece or a good IPA |
| 3 medium onions, peeled and cubed | 1 litre (1¾ pints) veal stock |
| 4 cloves garlic, crushed | 1 litre (1 ¾ pints) water |
| 3 medium carrots, peeled and cubed | 1 bouquet garni |
| 2 stalks celery, chopped | Salt and pepper to taste |
| | 50 g (2 oz) brown roux |

Trim any fat off the rump, and season well. Heat oil in a frying pan, place meat in hot oil and seal all over until the sides have caramelized, then remove from pan. In the same pan sweat the onions until soft; add the garlic, carrots, celery and mushrooms and cook for 5 minutes. Deglaze vegetables with the beer and simmer for a further 5 minutes.

Place meat in a braising pan together with vegetables and beer, add veal stock, water and bouquet garni; place over heated hob and bring gently to the boil. Cut a round of waxed paper to fit and cover the top of the pan, then cover with a well-fitting lid. Put the pan into a pre-heated oven (250°F, 130°C, gas mark ½) and braise for 3 hours, checking the meat from time to time.

Once cooked, remove from oven and leave the meat in the pan to cool for 30 minutes. Remove meat from the pan, strain the sauce through a fine sieve and return to a saucepan. Add brown roux and reduce to the right consistency; check the seasoning. Return the meat to the sauce and keep hot.

To serve: slice the meat into thin slices, place on the plates and pour over the sauce. Serve with mashed potato and braised endives.

*To drink: it is not easy to get the limited edition bottle-conditioned Bass Masterpiece, named after one of their Shire horses, who occupies a stable in the Bass Museum yard. But it is now easy to get a fine draught or bottled high-hopped India Pale Ale which will drink well with this.*

# Beef Medallions with Wild Mushroom, Truffle and Porter Sauce (serves 6)

Beer not sophisticated? Not classy? Not *haut*? Well, here a humble glass of porter shines in the company of some very superior ingredients. It is an example of a dish where restraint is the key word – the main ingredient is plainly cooked best fillet steak, the beer a muted background to the extremely rich mix in the accompanying sauce. I used the dangerous Old Growler, brewed by Nethergate in Suffolk, a deep, smooth beer you can drown in at an unusually high strength (5.5 per cent) for a porter; available draught and bottled.

6 75 g (3 oz) beef fillet medallions
6 herbed bread slices, same size and shape, for croûtons
15 g (½ oz) dried ceps or boletus slices
50 ml (2 fl oz) boiling water
25 g (1 oz) unsalted butter
1 shallot, chopped finely
1 clove garlic, crushed
1 dstsp truffle flour or 1 tsp truffle oil
50 g (2 oz) small chestnut mushrooms, sliced
225 g (8 oz) mixed wild mushrooms, chopped (I found some wonderful horse mushrooms when I was devising this dish, but you can now buy all sorts of wild mushrooms; try to include dark chanterelles for their sumptuous flavour)
50 ml (2 fl oz) beef or vegetable stock
150 ml (¼ pint) dark dry porter
Salt, pepper, nutmeg to season
1 oz chilled unsalted butter, cut into small dice and tossed in flour

Place dried cep or boletus slices in a small bowl and add the boiling water; leave to soak for 15 minutes, remove and chop. Strain the soaking liquor and reserve.

Sweat the shallot and garlic in the unsalted butter, then add chestnut mushrooms, wild mushroom mix, and soaked ceps or boletus. Cook gently until mushrooms begin to soften, then stir in truffle flour or oil, add the soaking liquor and the beef or vegetable stock and cook for a few minutes until the liquid starts to reduce; pour in the porter slowly, stirring, and cook gently for a few more minutes until the sauce is reduced, then whisk in the diced butter to thicken and add gloss; season to taste with salt, pepper and nutmeg.

Meanwhile, fry the beef medallions in butter on both sides either rare or medium, as wished; remove from the pan and keep warm, stirring the juices into the mushroom sauce. Fry the croûtons in butter and set one on each plate, top with mushroom sauce and place a beef medallion on each. Serve with baked tomatoes still on the vine and a green salad dressed with walnut oil and a little chopped red basil.

*To drink: yes, the Old Growler will rise to the occasion, served in a balloon wine glass. Otherwise drink an expensive Belgian Trappist beer with as much character as a fine wine – Chimay White, the second-strength Chimay, or fox-red Rochefort 6.*

# Classic Carbonnade with Trappist Ale (serves 6)

Only five breweries in Belgium and one in the Netherlands are allowed by law to call their beers Trappist because they are brewed by Trappist monks. Not to be irreverent they are, quite simply, heavenly. Perhaps the most famous and widely available is Chimay, its intense, mellow palate as soft in the mouth as a long-matured Burgundy, flavours unfurling like the petals of a rose. You can get Chimay Red, White and Blue, ascending in alcoholic content. The Blue is also available as Chimay Grande Reserve, at 9 per cent strength in champagne-size wire-corked bottles, to be drunk and savoured reverently; it even has a chunky, stemmed glass. Traditionally in Belgium carbonnade flamande is made with one of the Flemish sour brown beers of east Flanders – Liefmans' is one which can be bought over here – but I find Chimay gives a rich, vinous hint and is more readily available. OK, this dish is basically braised beef; so it's either the Trappist beer or divine intervention that makes it taste out of this world!

6 portions good braising steak
1 bottle Chimay Red (just over 300 ml or ½ pint)
6 peppercorns
1 bay leaf
Lard for frying
3 small red onions, sliced thinly
3 cloves garlic, crushed
2 rashers smoked fat streaky bacon, diced
1 small celeriac, peeled and cubed
1 leek, cleaned and sliced
1 medium carrot, peeled and sliced thinly
1 small raw beetroot, peeled and cubed
1 tbsp tomato purée
1 heaped tbsp seasoned plain flour
85 ml (3 fl oz) beef stock
1 bouquet garni
Salt and pepper

Place steaks in a dish and pour over the Chimay Red, add peppercorns and bay leaf and marinate overnight. Next day fry onions, bacon and garlic in lard over a medium heat for around 30 seconds, then add celeriac, leek and carrot and fry for another 2 minutes, stirring, until lightly browned. Remove with a slotted spoon to the bottom of a heavy casserole.

Take steak from marinade, pat dry with kitchen paper and quickly brown on all sides in the fat left in the pan to seal in the beer, then place on top of the vegetables and put in the beetroot and tomato purée. Add a little more lard to the pan, if necessary, heat and sprinkle in the flour, stirring it in briskly and cooking for 1–2 minutes. Pour in the beef stock and bring slowly to simmering point while it thickens.

Remove from heat, stir in the rest of the marinade, pour over the steak in the casserole, add the bouquet garni, cover and cook very slowly towards the bottom of a low oven (325°F, 160°C, gas mark 3) for 3 hours, or until the meat is tender and the gravy slightly thickened. Taste and season if necessary (the beer adds a good deal of spiciness), remove the bay leaf and bouquet garni and serve with mashed potatoes and a green vegetable – Brussels sprouts, even!

*To drink: you can opt for a large wine glass half full of Chimay Red because it's always a joy, though perhaps more suited to game; or find a strong, spicy IPA such as Ushers' (on draught in some of their pubs or widely available bottled).*

## Nun's Steak Out! (serves 6)

Since taking over the Froize at Chillesford near Woodbridge in Suffolk, Alistair Shaw has nailed his colours to the mast as a real ale chef. And not just any real ale – he specializes in East Anglian beers, including Adnams, Greene King, Tolly Cobbold, Nethergate (with its coriander Umbel Ale), multi-award winning Woodforde, Elgood, and micros such as Brett Vale, Iceni, Reepham and Greene Dragon. But he goes one further – outstanding Mauldons Brewery, which in 1991 won Champion Beer of Britain with its strong dark stout Black Adder, now brews four house beers for the pub including the Nun's range (the pub's formal name is Friar's Inn). For this recipe you need a dark, full-bodied beer with a strength of around 6 per cent. Alistair uses Nun's Revenge.

| | |
|---|---|
| 6 225 g (8 oz) fillet steaks | 1½ tbsps cornflour |
| 6 medium potatoes, peeled and chopped | 225 g (8 oz) Blue Stilton |
| 1.2 litres (2 pints) Nun's Revenge | 100 g (4 oz) butter |
| | Milk |
| | Salt and pepper |

Pour the Nun's Revenge into a heavy saucepan and reduce down to about two-thirds, then thicken with the cornflour, simmering until it is slightly thicker than gravy. Boil and mash the potatoes with butter and milk, seasoning to taste, then divide between 6 medium-sized round cutters and place under a hot grill to brown.

Pan-fry the fillet steaks in butter until cooked to taste – around 15 minutes for medium, turning halfway through, and seasoning with salt and pepper.

To serve: place a potato galette on each plate and place a steak on top; surround with the boozy jus and finish by crumbling a little Stilton over the top. Garnish with watercress and cherry plum tomatoes, with beer mustard on the table.

*To drink: any of those just mentioned, or Nethergate's other famous beer, a deep and dark porter aptly named Old Growler, available bottled.*

# Steak and Smoked Oyster Pudding with Oyster Stout
## (serves 4–6)

Marston, Thompson and Evershed sound like a partnership of dusty accountants, but not a bit of it. More usually known as Marston's, this is one of the country's finest brewers – and the only brewery still using the Burton Union method, dating back to the Middle Ages, in Burton upon Trent. The method uses vast oak casks, each holding 144 gallons, with troughs above them where the yeast foams up – a quite amazing sight as you stand on one of the raised walkways looking across the union room. The brewing equipment and the building have both been listed to protect them.

   This dish also dates back to the middle of the last century when Marston's began brewing and uses their award-winning Marston's Oyster Stout (winner best bottle-conditioned beer, Great British Beer Festival 1996; I was a judge). It is a subtle, complex, dark stout with just a hint of sweetness, making it ideal with molluscs. The pudding takes hours to cook, but is one of those sterling dishes you associate with gentlemen's clubs, and the substitution of smoked oysters for the usual kidney takes it from the pub to the dinner table. You can use a substitute full-bodied stout, but Marston's Oyster Stout is widely available.

*Suet-crust pastry*
225 g (8 oz) self-raising flour
100 g (4 oz) shredded beef suet
150 ml (¼ pint) very cold
   water (approx)
1 tsp salt

*Filling*
450 g (1 lb) blade steak

1 tbsp seasoned flour
10 smoked oysters*
6–8 small shallots, peeled
50 g (2 oz) small whole button
   mushrooms, wiped
1 tsp fresh sage, chopped
½ tsp dried thyme
1 bottle Marston's Oyster
   Stout

Make suet-crust pastry by mixing the dry ingredients and stirring

*Instead of oysters you could use 75–100 g (3–4 oz) lamb's kidneys, halved, or extra mushrooms.

in enough water to make a soft dough, with only a brief kneading at the end – too much handling and it will be rubbery. Roll out the dough to a 12-inch diameter round, cut out a little less than a quarter, and use the rest to line a greased 1.2 litre (2 pint) pudding basin, sealing the joint firmly.

Cube the blade steak – the ideal cut for this dish, cooking to a fall-apart tenderness – and toss in the seasoned flour. Mix in oysters (tinned smoked oysters or mussels can be used if you can't get fresh smoked), shallots, mushrooms and herbs, then fill the pudding basin almost to the top. Pour over enough oyster stout to come about three-quarters of the way up the meat mixture.

Roll out the remaining pastry into a round to fit the top of the bowl and place on top, using cold water to seal the edges firmly. Cover with buttered foil with a fold in the middle to allow for expansion, securing with string or a strong rubber band. Steam for at least 5 hours in gently simmering water in a large, covered pan, or in a steamer. The water should come about one-third of the way up the bowl; top up as necessary with hot water so that it does not boil dry.

*To drink: the Marston's Oyster Stout is a great bottle-conditioned beer, which drinks superbly with this classic pudding – you could substitute a draught porter.*

# Oxtail Casseroled in Dark Mild (serves 6)

A mild ale is a distinctly English ale, lightly hopped and lower in alcohol than other styles of beer. It is generally draught – and better as a real cask ale, in my view, though you can find bottled styles. Some are chestnut hued or even lighter, but most are dark with a creamy head – which is the sort you want for this dish. Since it never reaches more than a gentle simmer, this low-alcohol beer, often with more body than its strength suggests, is ideal for slowly tenderizing an underestimated meat and mingling with its juices to produce a richly glutinous stock. This is a simple, cheap and exceedingly cheerful dish – or was until they banned oxtail. It may be back on sale by now or buy it on your next French hypermarket trip; at a pinch use stewing lamb.

1 kg (2 lb) oxtail – try to get it from a butcher who will chop whole tails and give the little bits as well as the big lumps
Beef dripping (or fat) for frying
25 g (1 oz) seasoned flour, mixed with 1 tsp English mustard powder
1 large onion, chopped roughly
1 medium carrot, sliced
2 inner sticks celery, sliced
1 medium parsnip, diced roughly
1 bay leaf
About 6 dried chestnuts
3 fresh sprigs thyme
600 ml (1 pint) dark mild
Salt and freshly ground black pepper

Coat oxtail pieces in seasoned flour, brown quickly on all sides in hot fat, remove with a slotted spoon to a casserole. Adding a little more fat if necessary, fry the vegetables for 2 minutes and distribute them in the gaps between the meat. Add bay leaf, chestnuts, thyme and mild, cover and cook in the bottom of a very slow oven (300°F, 150°C, gas mark 2) for 4–5 hours or even longer, until the meat is utterly tender and the stock has a marvellous dark sheen and spicy aroma, with a hint of hops. About 30 minutes before the end of cooking, season with salt and black pepper.

This is a dish to eat informally with friends because you will need to use your fingers and suck the bones to flush out every scrap of meat. Make sure you have plenty of bread to mop up the gravy – and you can serve mashed potato if you want.

*To drink: mild though mild is, this dish is quite powerful and it needs a stronger beer. Copper-coloured Rooster, a symphony of malt and hops with bitter peel orchestrated in Harrogate by internationally renowned brewer Sean Franklin, springs to mind, also available bottled. Or choose a big fruity bitter.*

# Sautéed Calves' Liver with Hot Mustard and Light Ale Sauce (serves 6)

Liver, bacon and onions are a robust contribution to many bar blackboards, generally with a thick, strongly flavoured gravy served with lashings of mash. And nothing wrong with that. This is a more elegant version with a delicate flavour, using a mustard sauce suggested by chef Helen Hayward, a cooking-with-beer enthusiast.

12 thin slices calves' liver
12 rashers smoked streaky
  bacon
50 g (2 oz) unsalted butter
2 shallots, chopped finely
100 g (4 oz) small firm button
  mushrooms, sliced thinly

100 ml (4 fl oz) chicken stock
100 ml (4 fl oz) light ale
450 ml (¾ pint) double cream
4 tbsps Dijon mustard
Salt and freshly ground black
  pepper

Sauté liver quickly in half the butter until brown on the outside and still pink inside; remove from the pan and keep warm.

Roll up streaky bacon rashers, thread them on 2 skewers and grill until crisp; keep warm.

Add remaining butter to the pan and sweat the shallots until soft and transparent, then add the mushrooms and sauté until just tender – about 2 minutes. Add stock and beer and reduce by about one-third; add cream, stir in mustard and simmer, stirring, until coating consistency; season to taste.

Serve 2 slices of liver per person on a pool of mustard sauce with a little trickled over and top each with a bacon roll. You can still accompany with mashed potatoes: make it a garlic mash piped in swirls on a baking sheet and browned under the grill or in the oven.

*To drink: a fruity bitter that develops a hint of woodsmoke – Brakspear's Oh Be Joyful, commonly known as OBJ; for bottled, seek out a toasty tasting wheat beer called Grozet imbued with gooseberry skins and made by Heather Brewery in Strathclyde.*

# Gigot of Lamb with Rosemary on a Raspberry Beer and Redcurrant Gravy (serves 4)

For this dish I used the Scottish gigot cut – the fillet end of a leg of lamb, which provides a small roasting joint. Weighing about 1 kg or 2 lb, it's just enough to serve 4 people. You could use the English cut, which is thick steaks across the leg, or roast a whole leg of lamb if you want to feed more people. However, I wanted a piece big enough to roast yet with the tenderness and flavour of the fillet. The lamb is roasted until just pink with a delicate hint of garlic and rosemary; the gravy is a port-like pink with the raspberry beer and redcurrants cutting through the richness of the meat. I think it's a classic combination. Keep the accompaniments simple – plain boiled tiny new potatoes, shredded leeks steamed for about 10 minutes. The raspberry beer is Lindemans Framboise in a half-pint bottle.

Gigot of lamb (about 1 kg or 2 lb)
Few sprigs fresh rosemary
1 small clove garlic, cut into thin slivers
A little fat for roasting
300 ml (½ pint) raspberry beer

100 g (4 oz) redcurrants, prepared and washed
1 rounded dstsp plain flour
300 ml (½ pint) stock from cooking potatoes
Pinch salt

Pre-heat oven to 375°F, 190°C, gas mark 5. Make a few shallow slits in the lamb and push in 2–3 sprigs of fresh rosemary and a few slivers of garlic, just enough to add a little flavour without being overbearing. Place in a roasting tin, spread a very little fat over the top and roast in the centre of the oven for 90 minutes, basting occasionally, until the lamb is tender and still pink but not bloody. Immediately remove the rosemary and garlic, and rest the lamb somewhere warm for about 20 minutes while you make the gravy.

Pour the raspberry beer into a small pan, set aside a few stalks of redcurrants and add the rest to the pan, then bring slowly to simmering point and cook uncovered until reduced by about one-third, by which time the redcurrants will be tender. Strain beer into a jug, retaining the redcurrants.

Pour off most of the fat from the roasting tin – lamb is a fatty meat and you don't want greasy gravy – then heat on top of the stove, stirring in the plain flour to make a smooth roux, and cook it out until brown. Slowly stir in the potato water, then simmer briskly until reduced by half to a thick gravy. Stir in the strained raspberry beer a little at a time until it reaches pouring consistency and is a deep crimson, then season with a pinch of salt to bring out the fruit and finally add the cooked redcurrants.

To serve: carve the lamb in thick slices around the bone and set each slice on a pool of raspberry beer gravy, filling the 'bone hole' with hot redcurrants. Garnish the edge of the plate with 2–3 redcurrants on the stalk.

*To drink: I would serve the Lindemans Framboise used in cooking chilled as an aperitif; its delicate champagne fizz makes it the perfect alternative to a kir royale. It is too sweet to drink with the meal. My choice would be something more wine-like – one of the stunningly complex sour Flemish beers. Easiest to get here is Rodenbach matured in Polish oak, which you will find in a tissue-wrapped bottle.*

# Most Peculier Lamb (serves 6)

Robert Lyons, award-winning chef-proprietor of the Bay Horse Inn at Ulverston, Cumbria, has gone for a very famous ale – Theakston's Old Peculier, a rich, strong ale majoring on malts with a touch of licorice and enough fruitiness to make a good accompaniment to lamb.

| | |
|---|---|
| 1 kg (2 lb) shoulder of lamb | curry powder |
| 50 g (2 oz) dried apricots | salt and pepper |
| 3 large onions | 100 g (4 oz) apricot jam |
| 2 cloves garlic | 6 tbsps tomato purée |
| 1 tbsp olive oil | 600 ml (1 pint) Theakston's |
| 1 level teaspoon mild Madras | Old Peculier |

Mince together lamb, onion, apricots and garlic (or get your butcher to mince the lamb, and mix with the chopped onion, apricot and garlic).

In a large, heavy-bottomed saucepan heat the olive oil and add the minced ingredients. Cook for 5 minutes, stirring from time to time to prevent sticking. Add curry powder, salt and pepper, mix well and cook for a further 5 minutes. Add remaining ingredients and simmer for 30 minutes. Ideal with perfectly cooked Basmati rice.

*To drink: there's so much going on in this dish that I feel it wants a clean, dry beer with enough hop character not to be vanquished – try Batham's light gold best bitter, which progresses through fruit to a truly hoppy finish, or a bottled crisp, cool pilsner.*

## Mutton with Beer and Rhubarb (serves 6)

Saffron is now often associated with Indian dishes, but it was also a prized spice in Elizabethan times when it was as rare and expensive relatively as it is now. This dish has a medieval feel to it, using good old-fashioned mutton and rhubarb. Annie Clift cooks it at the Talbot Inn, Knightwick, where her family also farms, raising cattle and sheep, so she is probably better placed than many of us to get the right sort of meat. 'Genuine mutton', she says, 'is not always easily obtainable; an alternative is to use teg or wether, which are yearling animals and should be readily available in May when the rhubarb is about.' At the dinner to celebrate the opening of the pub's own small brewery, she cooked it with their beer named T'Other (the other two being This and That), a ruby-tinted ale, full flavoured with their own home-grown Northdown hops. When fresh rhubarb is not available she uses pickled kumquats.

300 ml (½ pint) real ale (choose a well-balanced quite hoppy bitter such as Shepherd Neame's Spitfire)
Pinch saffron threads
1 kg (2 lb) boned mutton shoulder, cubed and trimmed of excess fat
1 large onion, chopped
Fat for frying

2 tbsps orange juice
Salt and freshly ground black pepper
300 ml (½ pint) beef stock
2 tbsps parsley, chopped
1 tbsp mint, chopped
6 stalks rhubarb (de-stringed if necessary), cut in 1-inch chunks

Warm the beer gently and add the saffron threads, leaving them to infuse for around 15 minutes while you cut up the mutton and chop the onion.

Soften onion in fat and set aside, then get the pan hot and quickly seal the mutton cubes on all sides. Place in a large saucepan or casserole with onions, add orange juice, saffron beer, seasoning and about two-thirds of the stock.

Cover and cook very gently either in the oven or on top for around 2 hours until the meat is tender; when just cooked add parsley, mint and rhubarb and simmer for a further 20–25 minutes. Remove the meat with a slotted spoon and keep warm; skim the fat from the surface and simmer more briskly, uncovered, to reduce by about one-third, checking the seasoning.

I would serve this with creamed potatoes, just-cooked carrots and spring greens.

*To drink: at the Talbot's banquet this was perfect with their full-bodied and nutty-flavoured That, described as a beer from the past. Another beer from the past which would be nice is Elizabethan spiced Morocco Ale from the Daleside brewery near Harrogate.*

# Rack of Lamb in Highgate Mild with Chestnut and Horseradish Mash (serves 6)

My friend Mark Dorber is a pub landlord extraordinaire. Licensee of the famous White Horse in Parson's Green, west London, he keeps one of the finest beer (and wine) cellars you will ever find in a pub. He's consistently been first in this country to introduce new character beers from overseas, holding many noble beer events from single varietal hop brews to tutored tastings on all sorts of beer styles. He lectures about beer both here and in the USA, is a noted expert on the history of beer styles and on the exacting art of cellarmanship – caring for cask ale and serving it in top condition. Mark is my co-conspirator in devising the annual beer banquet for the British Guild of Beer Writers; every year we spend a pleasurable couple of evenings in the White Horse matching beers to ingredients as we put together a five-course feast – our deliberations invariably aided by a drop of excellent ale and stimulating food from their innovative kitchen. This dish was created by chef Liam Reddy during a spell at the White Horse. It uses malty, nutty Highgate dark mild.

3 8-cutlet racks of lamb
1 litre (1¾ pints) lamb stock
600 ml (1 pint) Highgate Mild
1 generous tbsp black treacle
4 stalks fresh rosemary
12 black peppercorns
6–7 large Desirée potatoes

60 g (2 oz) fresh horseradish, grated finely
250 g (9 oz) chestnuts, peeled
500 g (1 lb 2oz) mangetouts
100 g (4oz) butter
Salt and pepper
Olive oil

Marinate the lamb for 6–24 hours in the Highgate Mild with the chestnuts, peppercorns and rosemary stalks (retain leaves).

Heat a little olive oil in a roasting dish until gently smoking, brown racks of lamb evenly, lay fat side down in the dish and place above the centre of a pre-heated oven (350°F, 180°C, gas mark 4) for approx 15–20 minutes, or a little longer if you want the meat well done.

To prepare the sauce, bring the lamb stock to a rapid boil, add half the Highgate marinade along with the chestnuts and peppercorns, then skim. Add treacle, stir and simmer for 45 minutes, then remove chestnuts and mash them; continue to simmer for a further 20–30 minutes until sauce is a syrupy consistency, then season to taste.

Meanwhile, peel and wash the potatoes and cut into quarters. Boil in salted water until tender, then mash with butter, salt and pepper to taste, mashed chestnuts and horseradish.

To serve: place a scoop of piping hot mash in the centre of the plate, surround with mangetouts which have been plunged into boiling water for 30–45 seconds and drained, then circle with the sauce. Finally, arrange 4 cutlets in a criss-cross pattern and decorate with a few rosemary leaves.

*To drink: draught Highgate Mild is a fine beer everyone should experience and wonderful with the hint of sweetness in this savoury dish. For something stronger, pour a large bowled glass of Trappist Chimay Bleu as carefully as Mark's bar staff pour it in the pub.*

## St Peter's Jerusalem Pie (serves 6)

Beer in a gin bottle! St Peter's Golden Ale is sold in a most unusual flat flask that looks for all the world like a half-bottle of spirits.
But the taste is totally different. This aromatic golden ale has a
gorgeous whiff of the farmyard and when you sip it there is just a
bit of straw and manure – in the nicest possible way. Its sweet
earthiness is perfect with lamb and leeks, pepped up with the nuttiness of Jerusalem artichokes, under a suet-crust pastry topping.
The beer is brewed at thirteenth-century St Peter's Hall near Bungay in Suffolk. For an alternative, use a light-hued, well-rounded
fruity ale.

*Suet-crust pastry*
225 g (8 oz) self-raising flour
Pinch salt
100 g (4 oz) shredded suet
Very cold water

*Filling*
750 g (1½ lb) cubed leg of
  lamb
25 g (1 oz) seasoned flour
1 medium onion, diced

Fat for frying
350 g (12 oz) leeks (white and
  green parts), washed and
  sliced
175 g (6 oz) Jerusalem artichokes, peeled and diced
2 tbsps fresh parsley, chopped
2 sprigs rosemary
450 ml (15 fl oz) golden, fruity
  ale
Salt and pepper

First make pastry by sieving flour into a large bowl, adding salt,
and mixing in the suet with a knife. Mix in enough cold water to
make quite a sloppy dough – so that it is almost difficult to roll
out. This helps give a softer pie crust; suet pastry can dry out during cooking and go hard, so it helps to get more moisture in before
you start. Cover with clingfilm and chill.

For the filling: dredge lamb cubes in flour, sauté onion in fat
until soft, then add lamb to the pan and seal on all sides. Remove
from heat and mix in leeks, artichokes and parsley; tuck in sprigs
of rosemary and add beer. Simmer in covered pan for around 45
minutes until the lamb is almost tender then season to taste. Transfer to pie dish.

Take pastry out of fridge 30 minutes before baking time, roll out to about ½ cm (¼ inch) thick, and cover pie dish, decorating with leftover pastry cuttings. Glaze with egg and milk mix and bake towards the top of a hot oven (425°F, 220°C, gas mark 7) for 30 minutes until the pastry is risen and as golden as the ale!

*To drink: St Peter's Golden Ale, whose nostril-filling ripeness is lovely with the lamb and the earthiness perfect with the artichokes. If you want a flagon of draught beer, choose one of the juicy Kentish beers so good with lamb like Larkins Best Bitter or Shepherd Neame's Spitfire (also bottle-conditioned).*

## Roast Pork Fillet Filled with Cream Cheese and Apple in Fruity Ale Jus (serves 6)

Pork is traditionally cooked in cider, creating a rustic sort of meal. But there are plenty of fruity beers which complement the sweetness of the meat and create a slightly more savoury, sophisticated dish. I prefer to use a draught ale straight from the pub handpump in this, such as easily available Bass – a rounded beer with some malt and apple, or Thomas Hardy's Country Bitter, ripely fruity, available both draught and bottled. Anyway, a mellow beer sparing of hop bitterness.

2 450 g (1 lb) pork fillets
200 g (7 oz) cream cheese
1 eating apple, peeled, cored
  and grated
Small knob unsalted butter

4 sage leaves
225 ml (8 fl oz) draught fruity
  bitter
1 dstsp clear honey (optional)

With a sharp knife, cut a pocket along the side of each pork fillet, not quite reaching the ends. In a bowl mix together the cream cheese and grated apple, then use to stuff the pork without overfilling; you should be able to pull the edges of the meat together. Wrap both fillets separately in clingfilm, then chill for around 8 hours or overnight.

To cook: remove film and truss each fillet with fine string or cotton. Melt butter in a heavy pan and brown fillets quickly on all sides, then transfer to a shallow oven dish and put 2 sage leaves on top of each. Place towards the top of a hot pre-heated oven (425°F, 220°C, gas mark 7) and cook for 20–25 minutes, depending on thickness.

Remove from oven and keep warm, pouring any juices into the pan used to brown the fillets. Heat juices in the pan until they start to sizzle, then add the beer, simmering briskly to reduce until thickened and reduced by about one-third; taste and, if you would like to sweeten it, add the honey.

Remove the string. Using a sharp knife, slice the pork fillets fairly thickly on to 6 serving plates; dribble over some of the pan jus.

To accompany, you could serve braised, caramelized shallots and small mashed potato 'nests' filled with a fairly sharp apple sauce, then baked in the hot oven on a shelf below the pork.

*To drink: something with a bit of malt and a bit of cheese, such as Chiltern Brewery's singular Three Hundreds Old Ale, both draught and bottled, with a slight lactic tang which I love.*

# Sage and Garlic Pork with Plum Pilsner Sauce
## (serves 6)

Pilsner works wonderfully well with the pork dishes of northern Europe – but pilsner does not automatically mean the light-coloured lagers we associate with Germany. Their style is fine for the more delicate flavoured pork cuts such as escalopes; dark pork is more robust and you can still choose pilsner for it, but go for a darker, richer brew such as malty Staropramen. Brewed in Prague, it is a silky drink with a hint of pepper and a sweetness perfect to bring out the sweetness in the pork and plums. You don't always have to cook meat in beer; sometimes it is best to put it in the accompanying sauce, as in this dish, where it ends up almost as a variation on sweet and sour pork.

| | |
|---|---|
| 350 g (12 oz) plums (the sort that look OK but are slightly too hard and sour for eating raw) | 2 cloves |
| | 6 pork leg steaks |
| | 50 g (2 oz) unsalted butter |
| 200 ml (8 fl oz) dark pilsner | 2 cloves garlic |
| 1 dstsp dark brown sugar | 2 tbsps fresh sage, chopped |

Wash the plums, place in a saucepan and just cover with pilsner. Cover and simmer gently for around 30 minutes until the plums are soft. Cool enough to remove the stones, then liquidize plums and beer. Return sauce to the pan and cook over a high heat to reduce by half; sweeten to taste with the sugar – it should still be slightly tart – add cloves and allow to simmer, covered, over a very low heat while you cook the pork.

Meanwhile, crush the garlic and mix into the butter with the sage. Heat the grill to very hot, spread one side of the pork steaks with the butter mix and grill for 2 minutes to seal; turn, spread the butter over the other sides and again grill for 2 minutes. Reduce the heat to medium and cook for a total of around 15 minutes, depending on thickness, turning once. Finish with a quick blast of high heat to brown.

To serve: remove cloves from the sauce, which should now be a deep burgundy colour and pour a pool on to each plate. Place a pork steak on the sauce and top with remaining blobs of sage and garlic butter.

You could serve this with a parsnip and celeriac rosti, made by grating the vegetables on the largest side of the grater, then pressing them into hot butter in a frying pan. Season, cover with a plate and cook for 10 minutes on a low heat until the bottom is crisp, then turn and cook for a further 5 minutes or so until the mix is tender and crisp on both sides.

*To drink: the dark pilsner is a snug fit between the plums and the pork, or, if you would like a draught bitter, serve Wadworth 6X, with its harvest taste of ripe corn and fruit. Use a tall, slim tumbler.*

## Twice-cooked Pork in Aventinus (serves 2–4)

Bock is the German word for strong beer, so it's not hard to deduce that doppelbock is doubly strong. And when you drink Aventinus, it's not hard to guess that this is indeed a doppelbock. Brewed by Schneider in Bavaria, creators of the even more famous golden wheat beer Schneider Weisse, this is a dark ale brewed to a hefty 8 per cent. It has enormous stature and is full of mouth-watering complexity – soft spice and fruit, a hint of aniseed, touch of spirits, the classic Bavarian wheat-beer characteristics of cloves, aniseed and boiled sweets woven in. A sip tells you that here is a beer which has cost at least as much knowledge and skill to perfect as a vintage wine. I once asked the current Georg Schneider what made Aventinus so distinctive and he replied, 'It has more than three centuries behind it.' Every year is there in the bottle. When the Weisse and Aventinus were launched in the UK, a German chef showed me how to turn and turn pork hock in Aventinus until it is mahogany hued and tender. This is my adaptation of the dish.

2 pork hocks  
300 ml (½ pint) water  
1 bottle Aventinus  

½ tsp caraway seeds  
Seasoning  

Skin the pork hocks (or get the butcher to do it) without removing the fat. Place in a heavy pan with the water and 300 ml (½ pint) of the Aventinus, caraway seeds and seasoning, and bring slowly to simmering point. Cover and cook for about 1 hour, then remove; strain and reserve the cooking liquor.

Pre-heat the oven to 375°F, 190°C, gas mark 5, place the hocks in a roasting tin, and pour over a little neat Aventinus. Place on a high shelf and cook for around 1 hour, turning, basting and pouring over a drop more beer about every 15 minutes until the outside of the meat is crisp and as dark as the beer, the inside fall-off-the-bone tender. Use the cooking liquor to de-glaze the roasting tin and make a gravy.

Although there is enough meat on one cheap hock (I paid £1 each) to feed 2 people I like to serve 1 hock per person – it looks great to put a whole hock on a plate and let people carve this mini-roast themselves. The German chef who showed me this dish served it with bread dumplings (which I found a bit solid), boiled potatoes and sauerkraut. I like it with roast parsnips, lightly cooked dark-green cabbage tossed with pepper and butter, mashed potatoes (flavoured with horseradish) and the dark gravy.

*To drink: definitely the Aventinus, in its own distinctive glass, which holds a whole bottle. It makes an unexpected contrast, since the meat has a savoury roast flavour and the beer an underlying sweetness – though that sweetness is also there on the glazed crisp pork. Between them, the beer and the hock are so substantial that this is definitely a one-course meal!*

## Barry's Famous Bacon and Beer Roly-poly (serves 6)

The very first pub I ever wrote about was the Elsted Inn near Mid-hurst in West Sussex. Lured there by the 'pub food with a bit of glitz' served by ex-Ronay inspector Tweazle Jones and her partner, ex-brewer Barry Horton, I was riveted by the combination of fine local produce – the home-made faggots and sausages of pensioner Ron Puttock, local game, braised oxtail, Alresford trout – and the brilliant Ballard beers, such as Trotton Bitter, with its beautifully balanced finish, my favourite malt and fruit Wassail at a respectable 5.7 and their incredibly strong barley-wine-style vintage ale. Their beers were once brewed in a barn behind the pub by Barry himself, and occasionally he still plays hooky from the kitchen to go and give a hand in the brewery, which is now at Nye-wood on the West Sussex/Hampshire border. And I nearly forgot. The other attraction is Barry's to-die-for Sussex bacon pudding flavoured with Ron's bangers and Ballard's ale.

275 g (10 oz) self-raising flour*
150 g (5 oz) shredded beef suet
1 tsp salt
Approx 150 ml (¼ pint) Bal-lard's best bitter (or a medi-um-strength bitter savoury rather than sweet)

Freshly ground black pepper
1 large onion, chopped very finely
350 g (12 oz) best back bacon
175 g (6 oz) meaty butcher-made sausagemeat
1 tsp fresh sage
1 tsp fresh thyme

Make a suet-crust pastry by sifting the self-raising flour into a large bowl, then lightly mix in the suet and salt and add enough beer to make a soft dough.

On a floured surface, roll out to a rectangle approx 30 cm x 20 cm (12 inches x 8 inches) and cover all but a 5 cm (2-inch) strip along a narrow side on the right with the sausagemeat. Then sprinkle on the chopped onion and lay the bacon rashers on top, followed by the

* Barry uses stoneground plain flour from Weald and Down museum – if using stoneground plain flour, add 1 heaped tsp baking powder.

herbs, adding a good seasoning of freshly ground black pepper. Roll from the left towards the uncovered edge, damp that edge with cold water, and seal.

Wrap in greased foil or baking paper and steam for 3 hours. Serve with mashed potato and hot onion and mustard sauce.

*To drink: draught Ballard's is wonderful, but this is the sort of traditional British dish that goes so well with many mid-strength bitters on handpump. Or buy a bottle-conditioned premium ale.*

## Gammon Cooked in Ale then Caramelized in Mash Tun Marmalade (serves around 20 as a buffet centrepiece)

1996 saw the twenty-fifth anniversary of the Campaign for Real Ale, the organization which single-handedly saved cask beer in the UK. I created a menu for the occasion (served in the only board-room in town with beer on handpump!) and this handsome joint formed the centrepiece – gammon slow-simmered in local brewer McMullen of Hertford's full-flavoured, well-rounded Gladstone Bitter, then spread with Mash Tun Marmalade from Chiltern Brewery near Aylesbury, which contains their Beechwood Bitter, (literally a 'bitter' marmalade!) and finished in a very hot oven to emerge with a deep varnish.

2.25–4.50 kg (5–10 lb) gammon joint, green or smoked
1 medium onion and 1 large carrot, peeled and left whole
About 1.2 litres (2 pints) full-bodied bitter, preferably draught
  (you can buy it direct from the pub)
Water
Mash Tun Marmalade (or a bitter Seville)

Place gammon in large pan or casserole. Pour over between 600 ml and 1.2 litres (1–2 pints) beer, depending on size, and top up with water to three-quarters cover. Add onion and carrot, then bring very slowly to simmering point; skim off any scum. Cover and sim-mer very gently for 45 minutes to 1 hour for smaller joints, 90 minutes to 2 hours for larger, then remove from heat and leave to cool in the liquor.

Remove joint, discarding onion and carrot, but not the stock (it makes the best pea soup in the world), and leave to dry naturally; remove rind and score fat.

Heat oven to very hot (450°F, 230°C, gas mark 8), place gam-mon in roasting tray and spread sparingly with marmalade, including the bits of peel. Place in oven for up to 30 minutes, depending on size, until the marmalade caramelizes to a dark, glossy veneer.

Leave overnight to go cold and firm enough to carve into thin slices, each with the lovely contrast of the bitter/sweet crisp edge. (Gammon on the bone looks impressive, but boneless is easier to carve in round slices.)

*To drink: the draught Gladstone's used for cooking drinks well with this, or enjoy Shepherd Neame's well-balanced, bottle-conditioned Spitfire Ale.*

## Gammon Grilled with Smoked Beer (serves 6)

German smoked beer is quite extraordinary. As a drink it has a throat-catching aroma and flavour, like kippers hanging in a chimney. The most widely available brand of rauchbier in the UK is bottle-conditioned Schlenkerla Rauchbier from Bamberg in northern Bavaria, which is made entirely from barley malt smoked over beechwood. As a drink it is a taste worth acquiring and bullish alongside barbecued ribs, German sausages and ham or big cheeses. It is just as strong in cooking – and excellent with the sweet, salty taste of gammon, turning it to the same smoke-darkened hue as the ceiling of a public bar!

6 gammon steaks
2 bottles Schlenkerla Rauchbier
3 medium red onions
2 fat cloves garlic, crushed
1 dstsp walnut oil
Light brown sugar

*To accompany*
½ French stick cut into 6
  rounds
Mustard powder
Mixed green and red leaf salad
Clear honey
Freshly squeezed orange juice
Fresh dill

Place gammon steaks in a dish and pour over enough smoked beer to cover. Reseal the rest of the beer. Marinate for at least 2 hours, turning once.

Meanwhile, peel red onions and quarter from the top, separating out the layers. In a frying pan sauté garlic and onions gently in walnut oil until just softened, then pour in enough beer to barely cover. Place a lid or glass plate over the pan and simmer gently for 5 minutes until the onions start to soften. Remove the lid and continue to cook uncovered until the mixture thickens and the onions caramelize in the beer.

Heat the grill to very hot; remove gammon from the marinade and place on the grill rack. Grill for 4 minutes each side, brushing frequently with the marinade, until the gammon is cooked and crisp – when almost ready sprinkle a little brown sugar on each steak and replace under the grill until melted and bubbling.

Meanwhile mix runny honey and freshly squeezed orange juice in equal quantities to make a salad dressing for the mixed red and green leaves. Use some of the remaining smoked beer to make a mustard with the mustard powder, spread on rounds of French stick and toast briefly.

To serve: divide the caramelized beer and onion between 6 plates and place a gammon steak on each. Garnish with dressed salad and the rounds of mustard toast each topped with a dill frond.

*To drink: chill the Schlenkerla and sip out of small tumblers, or choose a beer with a little honey sweetness to offset the saltiness and mustard, such as Vaux's Waggledance, named after the courtship dance of honey bees.*

## Sausage and Sauerkraut in Smoked Ale (serves 6)

I guess I was about the first to taste Salopian Brewing Company's smoked beer within days of beer 'designer' Martin Barry first brewing it, and my instant response was, Wow! Without the throat-catching harshness of the German smoked beers, his is rounded, mellow and with a hint of sweetness, like the lazy smoke from a peat fire; indeed, the malt is smoked over peat. Martin was a chef before he became a brewer and gave me a recipe for his new beer with a Germanic feel in keeping with its style. There is an evocative, smoky aroma as it simmers away and the taste of the smoked beer is quite distinct in the finished dish. When I tasted it he hadn't thought of a name (he turned down my husband's suggestion of Smokin' Barrel!) and it finally emerged as Firefly.

750 g (1½ lb) meaty pork
  sausages*
1 large onion, chopped
2 cloves garlic, crushed
15 g (1 oz) butter
15 g (1 oz) flour
1 tsp tomato purée

350 g (12 oz) sauerkraut
300 ml (½ pint) water
Last third of bottle (i.e. with
  the yeast sediment) of
  Salopian's Firefly †
1 dstsp paprika
salt and pepper

In a heavy pan, fry sausages in butter briefly to brown on all sides, then remove from the pan. Add onion and garlic and sweat slowly until softened, then stir in the flour and cook gently for 1 minute before mixing in tomato purée. Pour in the beer and bring to simmering point.

Meanwhile, rinse sauerkraut and cook for 20 minutes in a separate pan, then add it to the main pan and stir well. Cover and cook for 5 minutes, then add a little more water if it seems too thick. Stir in the paprika. Return sausages, halved, and cook for another 15 minutes; taste and adjust seasoning if necessary,

*Martin: 'The sort you like best – you know, the fat ones with herbs.'

† If you can't get Firefly, look for another English smoked beer. If using the more powerful German Rauchbier, don't add the extra drop at the end.

adding a little of the beer just before the end to bring back the flavour.

Martin suggests you serve the sausages with mushy peas and mashed potato enriched with cream; I added caraway seeds to the mash. His alternative suggestion is hot beetroot in sweet and sour sauce and trenchers of dark rye bread.

*To drink: Firefly, if it's still being produced; otherwise choose a German beer but not a smoked one, a dark-gold rounded lager with discernible hops.*

## Smoked Beer Cassoulet (serves 6)

A classic French cassoulet has a smoky tang from smoked meats, and maybe a drop of red wine to enrich what is basically a warming peasant dish. But use a smoked beer, such as Schlenkerla Rauchbier, and you get the smokiness, the alcohol and the richness all in one.

450 g (1 lb) dried haricot beans, soaked in cold water overnight
50 g (2 oz) fatty bacon, cut in strips
Pork fat or dripping for frying
1 medium onion, sliced finely
1 medium leek, sliced thinly
550 g (1¼ lb) pork, cubed
4 cloves garlic, crushed
100 g (4 oz) cooked gammon, diced
50 g (2 oz) garlic sausage, sliced
75 g (3 oz) button mushrooms, sliced
4 large plum tomatoes, chopped roughly
1 tbsp tomato purée
1 bay leaf
1 dstsp fresh thyme, chopped
1 tbsp fresh parsley, chopped
300 ml (½ pint) water
350 ml (12 fl oz) smoked beer
½ tsp cayenne pepper
Freshly milled black pepper
3 smoked pork or venison sausages

After soaking, drain the haricot beans, put in a pan and cover with fresh water. Bring to the boil and continue boiling for 10 minutes. Drain and refresh.

In a large casserole fry the bacon strips in the pork fat or dripping for 2 minutes, then add onion and leek and cook gently until soft. Remove with a slotted spoon. In the same pan seal the cubed pork on all sides. Remove pan from the heat and return the bacon/onion/leek mix; add garlic, gammon, haricot beans, garlic sausage, mushrooms, plum tomatoes, tomato purée, bay leaf, herbs, water and 300 ml (10 fl oz) of the smoked beer. Cover and cook just below the centre of a medium oven (350°F, 180°C, gas mark 4) for at least 2 hours.

Remove from the oven, add cayenne pepper, stir and add a little water if the cassoulet needs more liquid. Cook for another hour and meanwhile part-cook smoked pork or venison sausages, browning the skin. Add another drop of beer to the casserole to thin the stock slightly and bring up the flavour, season with black pepper (it is probably salty enough). Halve the sausages lengthways, place on top and cook in the oven uncovered for another 30 minutes. Serve with malted grain bread and a really crisp green salad, ensuring everyone gets a piece of sausage. The beans will have soaked up the gorgeous juices and this raucous, tarry beer will have softened to a smouldering hint.

*To drink: the Schlenkerla is a little overpowering as a main-course drink. On draught you could try Brakspear's Oh Be Joyful with a tongue-tip smoke tang or Salopian Brewing Company's bottle-conditioned Firefly, more gently smoked than the German brew. Or leave the smoked flavour in the cassoulet and balance with a malty draught bitter.*

# Toad-in-the-barrel (serves 6)

Toad-in-the-hole is a popular pub dish – though why landlords rarely use the good ale they have on handpump in the batter beats me. It is also a dish people tend to eat as a cheap filler using rather ordinary bangers; yet with the extraordinary combination of flavours now filling sausage skins, from lamb with apricot to pigeon with redcurrant, you can turn it into something much more alluring. You can even buy sausages containing beer, such as Irish beef with stout, or pork with ale and mustard, and you could use some to make this dish. I decided to go for a slightly gamey flavour, mixing my butcher's meaty home-made porkies with smoked venison sausages. For the batter choose a savoury, hoppy beer.

6 pork sausages
6 smoked venison sausages
Dripping
*Batter*
175 g (6 oz) plain flour
1 tsp salt
2 medium eggs
175 ml (6 fl oz) milk
175 ml (6 fl oz) dry, hoppy
  bitter (slightly chilled)

*Gravy*
1 large onion, chopped finely
A little dripping to fry
1 tbsp flour
About 1 cup water
1 heaped tbsp fresh sage,
  chopped
Brown ale

Put all batter ingredients in a blender and liquidize to make a batter with a consistency somewhere between single and double cream. Preheat the oven to 425°F, 220°C, gas mark 7.

Place a little dripping and the sausages – arranged alternately, pork then venison – in a large meat roasting tin and place toward the top of the oven for 15 minutes until the fat is sizzling and the sausages slightly browned. Take out the roasting dish, pour over the batter, return to the oven, and cook for about 30 minutes until the pudding is risen, crisp and brown. Slice up so that everybody gets half a pork and half a smoked venison sausage and serve with sage, onion and brown ale gravy.

Make the gravy by sautéeing the onion gently in dripping until soft and golden, then stir in the flour. Add the water - preferably from boiling potatoes which can accompany this meal – and bring slowly to simmering point until the mixture thickens. Scatter on the sage and stir in enough dark, sweet brown ale (such as Manns) to make a fairly thick gravy, cooking for a few minutes to bring out the flavour of the sage. Season to taste and serve with mustard mash, made by adding wholegrain mustard to taste to mashed potatoes.

*To drink: a frothing tankard of good draught bitter with a savoury, yeasty bent.*

# VEGETARIAN

At the Guild of Beer Writers annual dinner, we tend to be a load of unreconstructed carnivores. Nonetheless, I invest as much anxiety in creating a special vegetarian beer dish for the half dozen or so who order it as I do for the other hundred fish and meat eaters. More, in fact, because I try to create a vegetarian dish flavoured with real ale that non-vegetarians would also enjoy, which has also been my philosophy here.

The recipes in this chapter are a bit of a mixture, really. Some are vegetable side dishes which can be served with a main course or on their own, such as beer bubble and squeak or roast vegetables in stout; some are purely vegetarian main dishes, including my special Winter Warmer Wellington, dark-gilled large mushrooms stuffed with chestnuts puréed in spicy Christmas ale, which meat eaters always eye enviously; and other are almost vegetarian but have meat input as an option like black peas with Guinness, which can contain bacon or not, as you wish.

Vegetable fritters in a light beer batter using lager or pilsner are superb with hot, spicy dips, and some vegetarian recipes are delicious accompanied by fruit beers.

But don't assume that because you are cooking with vegetables you will only use the lighter ales. Some vegetables, such as swede, wild mushrooms, Brussels sprouts, parsnips, sweet potatoes, beetroot and onions, have big flavours which can be cooked in – or accompanied by – big beers; as can dishes containing full-flavoured nuts.

# Beer Bubble and Squeak (serves 6)

You'd think that bubble and squeak is as British as fish and chips. Not so. The Belgians have their own version, which might stump you when you spot it on bar menus because they call it *stoemp* – it's wonderful with their wild boar sausages. For this recipe, though, I'm staying thoroughly British – to the extent of using cabbage instead of Brussels sprouts! This is another dish which beer transforms from simple mash into a luscious vegetable accompaniment for everything from bangers to cold roast beef or cold ham and pickles. By swiftly sealing both sides of the 'patty' in hot fat you trap all the beer inside; you don't need an expensive beer for this, simply a medium-strength savoury bitter either draught or bottled. Since it's a London favourite, Fuller's hoppy and fruity London Pride brewed in Chiswick will do fine. Quantities are elastic, but roughly speaking you need two-thirds the amount of cabbage to potatoes (weights before cooking).

| | |
|---|---|
| 750 g (1½ lb) potatoes | Knob butter |
| 450 g (1 lb) cabbage | Salt, pepper and nutmeg |
| Small amount of bitter | Fat for frying |

Peel the potatoes and cook them in lightly salted water until tender. Drain and mash roughly. Either steam the cabbage leaves over the potatoes or cook separately, drain and chop fairly small, adding a knob of butter. Stir enough beer into the mashed potatoes to moisten and soften – just as if you were adding milk to them – then season with salt, pepper and a grating of nutmeg. Mix in the cabbage quite gently with a fork.

Heat fat (I use meat dripping, but vegetarians can use a non-meat cooking fat or oil) until smoking hot and drop in large dollops of the mixture to seal swiftly. Flatten slightly with a fish slice, and quickly turn to seal the other side. Turn down the heat and cook for about 3 minutes each side until piping hot and golden brown on both sides. (You can, or course, use left-over cooked potatoes and cabbage, for which the dish was originally intended.) Another way to make beer bubble and squeak is to dice a small onion and fry it in a heavy frying pan for 2 minutes, then add thinly sliced raw potatoes and start to brown on both sides. Almost cover with beer, place a plate or lid over the pan and simmer very gently until the potatoes are half cooked and have absorbed most of the beer. Add shredded raw – or cooked – cabbage and either more beer or just water to almost cover again, then put the plate or lid back and allow to cook very gently for at least 30 minutes until the vegetables are soft and the liquid almost gone. Remove the lid or plate and cook until all the liquid has been assimilated, turning frequently to brown all over. This method produces a stronger beer flavour – you can add chopped sausages or left-over Sunday roast if you wish.

*To drink: If eaten with cold roast meat, ham and pickles, or sausages, accompany with a tankard of well-hopped bitter, such as award-winning Oakham Ales' JHB.*

# Beery Tomato and Fennel Gratin (serves 6)

Just as they reached the 1997 finals of the *London Evening Standard* 'Pub of the Year', Denise and Tristan Thwaites upped and left the famed White Cross Hotel near Kew Bridge in Richmond for deepest Devon. All the country produce has given landlady Denise even freer rein for her creative cooking, not least her imaginative vegetarian dishes. While she was at the White Cross, a Young's house, this was a favourite with locals. It's made with Young's ordinary (or cooking!) bitter at a lightish 3.7 per cent, best described by Roger Protz in *The Real Ale Drinker's Almanac* as 'Cockney ale with stunning hoppy edge'. And due to the hop strength, you don't need very much of it.

3 large fennel bulbs, prepared and sliced

3 large tomatoes, peeled and chopped

1 medium onion, chopped finely

1 large clove of garlic, crushed and chopped finely

25 ml (1 fl oz) good olive oil

½ small bunch fresh parsley (approx 250 g or 1 oz), chopped finely

3 slices granary bread, grated coarsely

50 g (2 oz) grated cheese (Mozzarella, Gruyère or Emmenthal – vegetarian if you like)

25 g (1 oz) unsalted butter

50 ml (2 fl oz) vegetable stock

85 ml (3 fl oz) light bitter

Salt and freshly ground black pepper

Sauté fennel, tomatoes, onion and garlic in oil for 10 minutes; add vegetable stock and beer and simmer uncovered for 5 minutes to reduce; season. Pour cooked mixture into a buttered ovenproof dish.

Mix breadcrumbs, cheese and parsley with a little freshly ground black pepper and spread evenly over the top of the fennel and tomato mix; dot with tiny blobs of butter. Cook in a pre-heated hot oven (400°F, 200°C, gas mark 6) for about 10 minutes – or place under the grill – until the gratin top is brown and crispy. Serve with a bowl of crisp mixed salad including slivers of young carrot and a few raisins.

*To drink: I might choose Bavarian Schneider Weisse, which now has a real following in this country and is readily available bottled, for its spritzy sweet spice with discernible aniseed to go with the fennel; or Young's own beautifully crafted Special Bitter with rounded malt and dash of orange.*

# Black Peas with Guinness and Garlic (serves 6)

This is one of those simple dishes with a regional flavour, which seems to survive in old-fashioned pubs where it's easy to eat, scooped up from a bowl with a hunk of bread. In the Midlands they call it 'gray payes' and use peashooter peas (pigeon peas) to make it; further north they call them black peas. Use dried peas that keep their shape during cooking, not the marrowfat or yellow peas that disintegrate to a thick purée. The recipe was given to me by Sue Burrell, a pub landlady near Bury, where they definitely call them black peas. She used Guinness, but you can substitute one of the dryish porters now being brewed.

| | |
|---|---|
| 450 g (1lb) dried, black or pigeon peas | Salt and pepper |
| 150 ml (¼ pint) malt vinegar | *To serve* |
| 4 fat cloves garlic, crushed | 350 g (12 oz) smoked, streaky bacon, or 225 g (8 oz) |
| 1 pint Guinness | smoked English cheese |

Soak the peas overnight in plenty of water. Next day, drain peas, rinse, place in a pan. Just cover with fresh water and malt vinegar, bring to the boil, turn down to simmering point, cover and cook gently for about 2 hours until soft and moist. Add garlic and season with salt and pepper, then pour on the Guinness, cover and continue to simmer on a low heat until the peas have drunk most of the Guinness.

De-rind the bacon and cut into 5 cm (2 inch) pieces; fry in a frying pan until crisp, then remove with a slotted spoon.

Serve the peas piping hot in bowls with a generous spoonful of bacon pieces on top, accompanied by doorsteps of warm, wholemeal bread. (Vegetarians can top with a spoonful of grated, smoked cheese – or copy Sue Burrell's regulars: 'Instead of bacon some prefer mint sauce or onion rings soaked in vinegar, hot water and sugar.') Whatever way, her description is: 'A delicious, satisfying, inexpensive meal ideal for supper parties after a night at the pub!'

*To drink: this thick, dark potage with its malt sweetness from the vinegar and salt from the bacon is at home with the Guinness or porter used in cooking. Mackeson Stout is fine, too.*

## Carrots in Honey Beer and Tarragon (serves 6)

This is for really sweet young spring carrots – and one of the growing number of beers brewed with honey. Which is not to say they
are sickly sweet; they are actually quite deep and hoppy, but with
a definite honeycomb undertone. I used Pitfield's Honey Ale, a live
bottle-conditioned beer produced by the micro Pitfield Brewery at
the Beer Shop in Pitfield Street, north London, where the retail side
stocks some simply amazing beers (here you can get a whole magnum of Belgian Chimay Reserve and Pitfield's own Millennium
Ale, to be laid down for the year 2000, not to mention banana
beer). Other honey beers include Vaux of Sunderland's bottled
Waggledance, named after the strange courtship dance of the
honey bee. It is delicious with the new season's lamb.

| | |
|---|---|
| 1 spring onion, chopped | 1 tbsp fresh tarragon, chopped |
| 25 g (1 oz) unsalted butter | Salt and pepper to season |
| 450 g (1 lb) young, slim | ½ tsp dark clear honey |
|   carrots, scraped | Squeeze of lemon |
| Approx 150 ml (¼ pint) honey | |
|   beer | |

Sauté the spring onion briefly in butter, then add carrots and turn
for around 1 minute to coat all over with butter. Pour in enough
honey beer to half-cover the carrots, sprinkle over tarragon, cover
with a close-fitting lid, and simmer gently for 5 minutes until the
carrots are half-cooked. Remove lid, season to taste with salt and
freshly ground black pepper, increase heat, and simmer more
briskly until the beer is well reduced. Stir in honey and caramelize
to a dark glaze.

# Red Cabbage Steamed in Raspberry Beer (serves 6)

Uncap a bottle of Lindemans Framboise (raspberry beer) and get a noseful of sheer sarsaparilla. It's an extraordinary drink – a blast of sherbet sweetness followed by the sour wild yeast tang of the Belgian lambic beers. Just gorgeous. It is produced in a Brabant farmhouse brewery near Brussels, then fermented in oak casks for up to two years, before being flavoured with both raspberries and raspberry juice. The makers liken it to champagne – I think it's the kir royale of the beer world. It certainly adds sparkle to red cabbage, served in a haze of raspberry steam.

1 tbsp hazelnut oil
15 g (½ oz) butter
½ small onion, chopped finely
1 clove garlic, crushed
1 tsp cinnamon
¼ tsp fresh ginger, chopped
450 g (1 lb) red cabbage,
  shredded

3 cloves
1 tsp pink peppercorns
2 tbsps sultanas
Grating fresh nutmeg
250 ml (8 fl oz) Framboise

Heat oil and butter in a large, deep pan, then sauté onion and garlic until they start to soften; stir in cinnamon and ginger and continue to cook gently for 1 minute. Tip in red cabbage, turning over and over until it is well coated with the oil and spices, then add cloves and pink peppercorns, cover the pan and cook on a very low heat for 5 minutes, turning the cabbage a couple of times, until it starts to soften and cook in its own steam.

Add sultanas and nutmeg, then about one-third of the Framboise and cook uncovered for 15 minutes until most of the beer is soaked up. Then add another third, stir and cover and cook for another 30 minutes. Continue cooking until the beer has reduced to a glaze and the cabbage is just cooked, fragrant and glistening – much better than soggy, overspiced red cabbage braised for hours to a pink sludge. It will taste sweet with just that hint of sharpness from the beer's lambic pedigree.

# Red Onion Tart Glazed with IPA (serves 6)

Beer and red onions caramelized to sweetness fill a handsome veg-etarian tart. This filling works extremely well with India Pale Ale (IPA), not especially pale but a recently revived style harking back to the days of Empire. You will find several bottled IPAs on sale – I got good results with Ushers' spicy example, but equally appro-priate are Marston's and Deuchars brewed by Caledonian, and you can get a growing number of draught IPAs.

| | |
|---|---|
| 175 g (6 oz) wholemeal pastry made with half plain, half wholemeal flour | the layers separated 2 cloves garlic, crushed A little walnut oil and butter |
| 4 medium red onions, peeled, then quartered vertically and | for cooking 150 ml (¼ pint) IPA |

Roll out the pastry and use to line a greased 23 cm (9 inch) oven-proof plate or fairly flat dish, then bake blind for 10 minutes.

Sweat onions and garlic in walnut oil and butter until soft, but without breaking up the onions as the tart looks so pretty if the onion 'petals' keep their shape. Pour on the beer, bring to the boil, then swiftly turn down the heat to very low and simmer until the beer caramelizes to a glossy dark veneer.

Spread the onion mixture carefully over the pastry, leaving a narrow, fluted edge, and cook towards the top of a hot oven (425°F, 220°C, gas mark 7) for 15 minutes. Serve by the slice with a spinach and red-leaf salad, maybe with an orange and beer dressing.

*To drink: the IPA does drink with this – bottled Worthington White Shield is a wonderful example – or something French in the style of the dish, such as Duyck's bière de garde blonde Sebourg, a hop champagne under a wired cork.*

# Red Pepper and Dried Chestnuts in Beer Aspic with Blue Cheese and Spring Onion Crust (serves 6)

My friend Leon Lewis is a vegetarian chef *par excellence*, catering for diners from boardroom to Glastonbury Festival, as well as a broadcaster and author of cookbooks, his latest being *More Vegetarian Dinner Parties*. Apart from many convivial evenings at his home, I will be forever grateful to Leon for teaching me how to find, recognize and cook edible fungi – he phones every autumn to say he's found the first cep, and I'm off, work forgotten! He researched this recipe especially for my book and experimented on doctors at St George's Hospital in London, who were all delighted to be guinea pigs. The beer he used was Ruddles County, sulphurous and quite highly hopped; you can use a hoppy bitter for this as it offsets the sweetness of the chestnuts and sweetcorn.

*Pastry*
300 g (11 oz) wholemeal flour
1 tsp baking powder
Pinch salt
100 g (4 oz) unsalted butter
100 g (4 oz) blue cheese, grated
3 spring onions, chopped finely
Cold water to mix

*Filling*
250 g (8 oz) dried chestnuts
  (soaked overnight in bitter)
1 medium onion, chopped finely
Unsalted butter for frying
100 g (4 oz) firm mixed mushrooms, chopped roughly
(chestnut, field and wild such as ceps, boletus, shiitake)
1 medium red pepper, diced finely
1 medium can sweetcorn kernels, drained
1 dstsp vegetarian Worcestershire sauce
Salt and pepper
Pinch grated horseradish*
100 g (4oz) yellow and grey oyster mushrooms*
2 tsps (or 1 sachet) vegetarian gelatine
150 ml (¼ pint) Ruddles County or a hoppy bitter

* Leon uses a wonderful orange mushroom called chicken of the woods, but unless you've got someone like him to find it for you oyster mushrooms make a good alternative. His tip for horseradish is to find a wild root then freeze it; grate it while frozen and return it to the freezer to use in small quantities as needed.

Make the pastry by sifting the wholemeal flour with baking powder and salt into a mixing bowl, then lightly rubbing in the unsalted butter until the mix resembles fine crumbs. Stir in the grated blue cheese (Leon uses a French one) and onion, then mix in enough cold water to make a medium soft pastry. Wrap in clingfilm and chill for 1 hour, then bring back to room temperature while you make the filling.

Sauté onion in butter until translucent, then add the wild mushrooms, red pepper, sweetcorn, Worcestershire sauce, salt and pepper, grated horseradish and oyster mushrooms. Stir and cook gently for about 7 minutes, then add the chestnuts in their soaking beer and bring to simmering point, cooking for another 2 minutes to reduce the liquid slightly. Roll out half the pastry and line a 27 cm (11 inch) quiche dish, then pour in the filling. Roll out the rest of the pastry, and cover the pie, rolling over the edges to seal; make several holes over the surface about the size of your fingertip – you could use the big end of a chopstick. Glaze with beaten egg and cook towards the top of a preheated oven (375°F, 190°C, gas mark 5) for around 30–35 minutes until the filling is cooked through and the pastry crisp and brown.

Remove from the oven and mix the vegetarian gelatine with the ¼ pint beer, whisking well to dissolve. Using a very small funnel, pour it through the holes in the topping right down into the pie and leave it somewhere warm for around 20 minutes while the aspic sets enough to bind it all together. Serve warm – though you can leave it to go cold.

*To drink: this is a robust pie in a really dark, tobacco-brown pastry. Enjoy it with a full-bodied, dark malty beer, preferably draught.*

# Roast Plum Tomato and Pepper Sauce with Red Basil, Plum Beer and Penne (serves 6)

To be honest, I don't really believe beer goes in Mediterranean-style food; it's not an olive oil and peppers style of ingredient. Except in this recipe. I bought a nip-sized bottle of the 'spontaneous fermentation' (or wild yeast, lambic) plum beer from the Chapeau brewery in Belgium, expecting it to be a cloyingly sweet pudding beer. And yes it was sweet and rounded, but it also had the lambic tartness that came across like a plum just turning from sour to sweet – perhaps the green plum on the label (looking more like an apple) was a clue. The other surprising element of this beer is that its alcohol content is negligible, only 3 per cent, yet it tastes much stronger. Anyway, I made this sauce for pasta, and it was wonderful.

1.5 kg (3 lb) almost over-ripe plum tomatoes
2 large red peppers
2 red onions
2 fat cloves garlic, unpeeled
1 tbsp olive oil
2 tbsps fresh red basil, chopped
1 tsp sugar

1 small bottle plum beer
Pinch salt
Freshly ground black pepper
450 g (1 lb) penne
*To garnish*
Red and green basil leaves
Plenty of freshly grated good Parmesan

Wash and dry tomatoes and red peppers. Cut peppers in half lengthways, removing seeds and core; wrap garlic cloves in foil. Cut 'root base' from onions, but do not peel. Preheat oven to 400°F, 200°C, gas mark 6. Place tomatoes upright in a large, shallow ovenproof dish; add peppers, cut side down, and place in the oven along with onions and garlic; roast for about 45 minutes – the onions may take a further 15 minutes if they still feel a bit hard – then remove.

Put peppers in a plastic bag for a few minutes. When they are cool remove blackened skin; cut into strips. Peel onions when cool and chop small; peel garlic and slice very thinly, then sweat onions and garlic together in the olive oil in a heavy pan for a few minutes. Liquidize tomatoes with their cooking juices, then push through a sieve to remove pips and add to the pan; stir in the red pepper strips, red basil and sugar then cover and simmer gently for 15 minutes until thick. Add half the plum beer (approx 150 ml or 5 fl oz) and simmer gently, uncovered, until the mixture thickens again. Taste and add just a little salt and black pepper to balance the sweetness.

Meanwhile cook greedy amounts of penne in a large amount of boiling, salted water for about 10 minutes until *al dente*. Just before the pasta is ready, add a little more plum beer to thin down the sauce to pouring consistency and 'bring up' its beer taste. Immediately drain the penne, rinse it with boiling water, and pile on a huge white serving platter with the sauce poured over, the rim of the plate garnished with red and green basil leaves. Finish with the Parmesan and rush it to the table while piping hot.

*To drink: the vinous quality of a Trappist brewed beer is a fine substitute for red wine. A good example is Westmalle Dubbel (or double strength), brewed at an abbey to the north-east of Antwerp; it has the power and colour of clashing conkers – but is velvet on the tongue.*

# Root Vegetables Roasted with Sweet Stout (serves 6)

When my husband tried these he said he'd been hoping for years to taste a roast vegetable that seemed to have the gravy on the inside instead of on the outside, and I'd finally cracked it. As you simmer a selection of root vegetables in a little sweet stout, you can see the beer being drawn deep into the vegetables. When you finish them in a hot oven, the liquid is sealed inside, while the outside is seared to roast caramel. I serve them with the Sunday roast, but for a vegetarian they are strong-flavoured and substantial enough to *be* the Sunday roast.

225 g (8 oz) each peeled parsnips, swede and large carrots, cut
  into roasting size chunks, roughly equal in size
Approx 150 ml (¼ pint) sweet stout or brown ale
25 g (1 oz) butter for roasting

Place the vegetables in a large pan and pour in enough stout to half cover. Put on the lid and simmer gently until they start to soften, then remove from the heat, but leave in the pan to cool and draw in the beer, turning the vegetables in the stock from time to time. Remove vegetables from stock and place in an ovenproof dish.

Roast towards the top of a hot oven (400°F, 200°C, gas mark 6) for 10 minutes until the vegetables start to caramelize. Glaze with the butter and return to the oven to crisp for a further 20 minutes, basting twice, until soft on the inside and crisp on the outside with an intense sweetness. Simple but effective.

*To drink: contrast with a dry, hoppy bitter if eaten as a main course – if an accompaniment be guided by the meat.*

## Sam's Real Baked Beans (serves 6–8)

They never do anything by halves in the USA, and they have thrown themselves into producing craft beers with hoppy enthusiasm. Not only are they authentically recreating some of the classic British styles such as stout and porter, going back to the original concepts, but they are also adding their own ideas to give them a distinctive character. I have met American brewers whom I can only describe as obsessive. Perhaps Jim Koch comes into that category for his determination to restore the brewing tradition imported by his immigrant ancestors, at the Boston Brewing company under the Samuel Adams label. His amber-hued, triple-hopped Boston Ale, with its big spicy flavour, seemed the ideal brew for biting Boston baked beans. Available here bottled, or choose a mid-brown British brew like Hook Norton's Old Hooky or Morland's Old Speckled Hen, both draught as a real ale and bottled - though not bottle-conditioned. In traditional recipes they use black treacle, but I felt brewer's malt, available from chemists or wholefood stores, was more appropriate.

225 g (8 oz) haricot beans
300 ml (½ pint) Samuel
  Adams Boston Ale
1 medium onion, skinned and
  chopped
2 cloves garlic, crushed
1 tsp mustard powder
2 tbsps brewer's malt

1 fresh red chilli, de-seeded
  and chopped finely
Pinch mixed spice
1 clove
3 very ripe tomatoes, chopped
2 heaped tbsps tomato purée
1 tbsp brown sugar
Salt and pepper

Wash the beans, pour over enough beer to cover, and soak overnight. Drain, reserving the beer, and put the beans in a heavy casserole (preferably clay); add onion, garlic, mustard powder, brewer's malt, chilli, mixed spice and clove. Stir in the soaking beer.

Cover and cook in a low oven (300°F, 150°C, gas mark 2) for around 6 hours. Then stir in the tomatoes, tomato purée and brown sugar. Turn the oven up to 350°F, 180°C, gas mark 4, and cook the beans for another hour or so until really soft, dark and moist. Half an hour before the end of cooking taste and season with salt and, if wished, black pepper.

This is a wonderfully dark, aromatic dish, which can be served with rice and wedges of malt bread to soak up the juices, or as an accompaniment to grilled pork ribs.

*To drink: yes, Old Speckled Hen, or something chewy and malty such as Maclay Scotch Ale.*

## Spiced Onion Collops with IPA (serves 6)

East meets West in a dish that harks back to a traditional snack I used to tuck into as a child in the north, spiced up with flavours from the Indian restaurant revolution which came later. We used to call them collops, a slice of raw onion sandwiched between two slices of raw potato, coated in batter and deep-fried. Asian cuisine has its own 'collops' – pakoras, various vegetables coated in spicy batter then crisply fried. I've brought the two together by dipping the onion/potato collop in a batter coloured by turmeric, bursting with fresh coriander and, fittingly, enlivened by a hoppy India Pale Ale (IPA). It had almost died out, but is now being revived by any number of breweries – and you can even get supermarkets' own brands.

| | |
|---|---|
| 100 g (4 oz) self-raising flour | 2 tbsps fresh coriander, |
| 1 large egg | washed and chopped finely |
| Pinch salt | 3 large potatoes, peeled |
| ½ tsp turmeric | 2 large onions, peeled |
| 1 heaped tsp garam masala | Oil for deep-frying |
| 150 ml (5 fl oz) IPA | |

To make the batter put the first 6 ingredients in a food-processor goblet and liquidize to a smooth batter the texture of cream. Rest in the fridge for at least 1 hour, then add 1 tbsp very cold water and stir in (add a little more water if it seems a little too thick). Mix in chopped coriander.

Slice the potatoes lengthways, getting a dozen slices around 0.5 cm or ¼-inch thick flat on each side (set aside the irregular outer slices). Cut 6 slices of onion horizontally, the same thickness as the potato slices, then match up onion and potato slices to roughly the same sizes and sandwich 1 onion between 2 potato slices. Heat deep oil to medium hot. Using a long-pronged carving fork, spear a collop and dip in the batter, making sure it is well coated, especially around the onion. Place in the hot oil, allowing it to set for a few seconds before gently pushing it off the fork with a spoon; cook in batches of 3. Turn heat down very low, cover and cook for 20 minutes. Then turn collops over and the heat right up to finish cooking and crisp the batter, which will be a real yellow full of green flecks.

Drain first 3 collops on kitchen paper and keep warm in a very low oven while you cook the other 3. You can dip the left-over potato slices in any remaining batter and cook them as well.

Serve as a starter or snack on their own or with home-made tomato sauce, as an accompaniment to grilled lamb chops and fried chicken. (You can use smaller potatoes/onions to make little ones as a side dish in an Indian meal.)

*To drink: why not Nethergate brewery's Umbel Ale with its touch of coriander? Or spicy Belgian wheat beer Hoegaarden with cumin and dried orange pith woven in.*

## Stuffed Mushrooms in Beer Batter (serves 6)

Deep-fried mushrooms in batter or, more commonly, crumbs, have become staple starters on pub menus. Most of them are poor, soggy things, tasting of grease and blotting paper, bought in deep-frozen and slung in the deep-fat fryer. But when freshly made with a tangy filling and dipped in a crisp beer batter, they take on a whole new dimension. I first tried mushrooms in beer batter at the Mildmay Inn in Holbeton, South Devon, a pub brewing some excellent ales in an adjoining barn. They used their Mildmay Colours Best to create the batter, a light-tasting bitter giving a light-tasting crispy batter. For my version I've added a stuffing.

2 medium eggs
275 g (10 oz) plain flour
300 ml (½ pint) Mildmay
  Colours Best (or a lightly
  hopped bitter)
Salt and pepper
6 medium closed-cap mush-
  rooms
Oil for deep-frying

*Filling*
100 g (4 oz) garlic-flavoured
  cream cheese
50 g (2 oz) pine kernels
1 tbsp fresh chives, chopped

Beat the eggs, add flour and seasoning whilst continuing to beat, then add enough beer to make a fairly thick coating batter. Wipe mushrooms, making sure they are dry, and remove stalks. Mix together the filling ingredients and use to stuff the mushrooms. Dip them in the batter, making sure the filling is well covered.

Deep-fry in hot oil for about 5 minutes until golden brown and crisp. (An easy way to do this is to spear the stuffed mushroom on a large meat fork to dip it into the batter, shake off excess, and place in the hot oil until sealed, then slip fork out, leaving the mushroom cooking.)

Serve as a starter, possibly accompanied by sliced tomatoes with cider vinegar dressing, or use larger mushrooms and make extra filling to serve as a vegetarian main course on a bed of spinach with home-made tomato sauce (maybe the rich plum tomato and plum beer sauce on page 163).

*To drink: Mildmay's award-winning bottled pale ale Old Horse-whip slips down dangerously easily for a 5.7 per cent beer; or a draught beer with a bit of sweet nuttiness, like award-winning Highgate Mild.*

# Wild Fungi and Oyster Mushroom Pudding with Pickled Walnuts in Truffle and Oyster Stout Gravy
## (serves 6)

This is the vegetarian version of the steak and smoked oyster pudding (see page 118) – and since I'm using strong-flavoured mushrooms alongside the oyster mushrooms, I see no reason to deviate from Marston's Oyster Stout. You only use a drop, but it's a telling drop, producing a dark, thick, aromatic stock. This is the sort of deeply satisfying dish that makes anyone, vegetarian or not, know they've had a proper meal. In case any vegetarians are hesitant, this oyster stout is not flavoured with oysters, but the name harks back to Victorian times when stout and oysters were commonly consumed together by the working classes, although some oyster stouts actually had oysters and their shells added during the brewing process until as recently as the 1960s. Stout has continued to be regarded as an excellent partner for shellfish. This is a sustaining winter night dish with enough luxury in the ingredients to make for a festive dinner party. I was able to gather wild mushrooms and used ceps I had collected and dried, but both fresh and dried wild fungi are now readily available in supermarkets and oyster mushrooms are plentiful. (I go to an oyster mushroom log near a local golf course.)

*Vegetarian suet-crust pastry*
225 g (8 oz) self-raising flour
Pinch salt
115 g (4 oz) vegetarian suet
150 ml (¼ pint) very cold water
*Filling*
Few slices dried cep
50 ml (2 fl oz) hot water for soaking
1 small onion, chopped finely
225 g (8 oz) small, firm chestnut mushrooms

225 g (8 oz) mixed fresh 'wild' mushrooms, including yellow and grey oyster mushrooms, horse mushrooms, chanterelles, whatever else you can lay your hands on – make up with cubed strongly flavoured flat mushrooms
3 large pickled walnuts, quartered
1 tbsp fresh parsley, chopped finely
½ tbsp fresh chervil, chopped

50 ml (2 fl oz) Marston's
Oyster Stout (or dark, dry
stout)
½ tbsp fresh dill, chopped
2 tbsps plain flour
1 dstsp truffle flour or 1 tsp
truffle oil

2 tbsps plain flour
1 dstsp truffle flour or 1 tsp
truffle oil
50 ml (2 fl oz) Marston's
Oyster Stout (or dark, dry
stout)

First put the dried ceps into the hot water and leave to soak.

Make the suet-crust pastry by sifting the flour into a large bowl, stirring in salt and vegetarian suet, then adding enough very cold water to make a really soft dough. Grease a 1.2 litre (2 pint) pudding bowl, roll out the pastry into a circle about 30 cm (12 inches) in diameter and cut out a quarter. Use the larger piece to line the bowl, letting the edges hang over the top, firmly sealing the bottom and join – if the liquid seeps out during cooking it can spoil the pudding. Put onion in a large bowl and add the chestnut mushrooms (left whole if tiny, halved or quartered if larger) and the rest of the mushrooms, again cutting them up if they are too large, but try to leave the oyster mushrooms whole. Add pickled walnuts, herbs and soaked ceps, mixing well but gently to mingle without breaking up. Lightly stir in the flour, followed by the truffle flour or oil. Put the mixture into the pastry-lined pudding basin, then pour on the liquor from soaking the ceps and the oyster or dark stout.

Roll out the remaining quarter of pastry into a round to cover the bowl, sealing the edges well. Cover with a round of pleated foil, secure with a rubber band, and steam in a steamer or large pan with water to a depth of 5 cm (2 inches) up the pudding bowl for 3 hours.

Turn out and serve with fluffy mashed potatoes containing plenty of butter and cream and flavoured with chopped chives.

*To drink: Marston's Oyster Stout or something similar, draught or bottled, really is the best choice with this dark cocktail of mushrooms soaking into a suet crust.*

## Winter Warmer Wellington (serves 6)

If you want a special vegetarian dish for Christmas Dinner, look no further. This is the definitive meatless meal for the festive season. Chestnuts and a strong, spicy winter beer – fittingly called winter warmers – or Christmas ale make the perfect Yuletide combination. It is wonderful to see such a resurgence of Christmas ales – not least for names like Red Nose Reinbeer or Myrrhy Xmas! I've had excellent results using beers such as King and Barnes bottle-conditioned Christmas Ale, brewed annually though you can certainly lay down bottles for future years, or a draught ale such as Talisman Winter Warmer (4.8 per cent) brewed by Pilgrim in Surrey (Pilgrim also bottle a cherry-flavoured Christmas beer called Pudding at a muscle-flexing 7.3 per cent). The choice is huge, but go for a spicy, fruity kind rather than one with wine or spirit overtones.

| | |
|---|---|
| 6 large mushrooms | 1 tsp nutmeg, grated freshly |
| 1 medium onion, chopped small | 2 tbsps fresh parsley, chopped |
| 2 cloves garlic, crushed | 600 ml (1 pint) Winter or Christmas ale (about) |
| Walnut oil for frying | 2 packs (about 1 kg or 2 lb) puff pastry |
| 2 tins chestnuts (about 500 g or 1 lb), chopped roughly | Beaten egg to glaze |

Pre-heat oven to 425°F, 220°C, gas mark 7.

Wipe mushrooms and remove and chop the stalks. Sauté onion and garlic gently in walnut oil until translucent, then add chestnuts, mushroom stalks, nutmeg, parsley and enough ale to cover; stir. Cover and simmer gently, stirring occasionally, until chestnuts are soft and ale absorbed to make a thick – but not smooth – purée, adding a little more beer if it seems too dry.

Remove from heat and leave to stand while you roll out pastry into 6 pieces and stand a mushroom, gills up, on each. Fill each mushroom with chestnut and ale mix, then draw up the pastry to cover, sealing edges with beaten egg and decorating the join with a pastry holly leaf.

Brush the tops with beaten egg, stand on a greased baking tray and bake towards the top of the oven for 30 minutes until the pastry is golden brown and the mushrooms are cooked.

Serve with traditional accompaniments such as Brussels sprouts, roast potatoes and perhaps a hot cranberry sauce instead of gravy.

*To drink: I might be influenced by the occasion as much as the dish and choose a big bottle of Chimay Grand Reserve at 9 per cent (900 ml or 1½ pints, you can even get magnum-sized bottles if you hunt hard enough). Or buy copious quantities of draught winter or Christmas Ale from a local pub and serve it in large wine glasses.*

# CHEESE

## Cheese, Bread and Beer – the Holy Trinity, or Epicurean Ecstasy!

To prove that life's greatest pleasures are simple, set a really ripe farmhouse cheese – a well-matured fruity Cheddar or blue Stilton for preference – alongside freshly baked wholemeal bread, a spoonful of home-made chutney and a foaming pint of well-hopped, cask-conditioned English ale. In other words, the perfect ploughman's, the definitive pub grub from time immemorial. Best of all, cheese is equally splendid mixed with beer in cooking.

## Cheese in Beer Cookery

Both texture and taste make cheese a natural in a beer dish. Its savoury, sometimes sharp and tangy, sometimes rounded, flavours complement beer so well and it is also good for melting and thickening. Some beers have a slight lactic creaminess which, again, makes for great partnerships with cheese.

I suppose fondue is the dish which springs to mind and there are several cheese and beer fondue recipes readily available, but not here. I have a problem with fondues, probably springing from my wedding when I was given three fondue sets because they were *de rigueur* for supper parties at the time. Fondues always seemed to me high on hype and low on substance.

Cheese and beer soup, on the other hand, is wonderful; don't just stick to Cheddar, go for blue cheese, Emmental and Gruyère, too – but be very careful not to overheat or you'll end up with a stringy gunge in a sort of beer whey. Soft cheeses firm enough to flash-heat, such as goat's cheese or a small Camembert, are excellent for cooking – try goat's cheese marinated in beer then grilled. Grate full-flavoured cheese to add to pies and tarts with beer, or make a savoury cheesecake, such as the one in which Emmental is combined with a smooth, hoppy ale, pine nuts and dwarf plum tomatoes. Cream cheese can happily go in a sweet cheesecake, perhaps with an apricot or American blackberry beer and caramelized peel.

Put together beer, cheese and eggs for a great omelette; try my updated version. And I finally gave in and revived that hoary old chestnut, Welsh rarebit, traditionally made with a drop of ale – but I hope you'll agree mine is toasted cheese with attitude.

A cheese and beer sauce can be splendid: try mixing Stilton with porter to pour judiciously round fillet steak, or melt Sage Derby with an appley beer to go with a crisply grilled pork chop, or Gruyère with a wheat beer and touch of fresh dill and cream to accompany a perfectly grilled sole.

Soufflé buffs can blend a little beer into their cheese soufflé for added puff and golden crust. Or blend a little live draught bitter into your pastry for cheese straws to add air and flavour. Porter with Stilton makes a full-flavoured cheese straw – and do make a crock of the portered Stilton on page 190. It's very moreish.

## Beers to Drink with Cheese

Cheese and ale can be a whole meal. It's entertaining to have a beer and cheese tasting, collecting a dozen different cheeses and pairing each one with a beer. Work upwards in strength of both flavour and alcohol and provide interesting breads, mustards and chutneys.

Or beer can go at the end of the meal with the cheese course. A big beer is perfect with the heavyweight cheeses which are traditionally eaten with a heavyweight red wine, or port.

Mild, soft cheeses, such as young goat's cheese, cream cheese, Mascarpone, Taleggio, Neufchatel or young Brie, can be accompanied by a sparkling raspberry beer, sweet, creamy stout, or a Bavarian wheat beer with its hint of boiled sweets.

*Red Onion Tart Glazed with IPA, see p. 160.*

Full-flavoured soft cheeses such as mature, ripe Camembert, stronger goat's cheeses, or Caboc, might well look for a strong malty beer, perhaps a Scotch ale, lightly chilled (Gordon's Scotch Ale with its creaminess would be heavenly); also Ushers Tawny Ale, which is designed to go with desserts and cheese. Full-flavoured soft blue cheeses such as Bleu de Bresse, are more difficult – I like the slightly sour Flemish browns, especially one flavoured with cherries.

Mild hard cheeses such as white Stilton, Caerphilly, Lancashire, Wensleydale, Gouda, Port Salut – partner these with a sweetish English cask ale or a medium-bodied Belgian or English wheat beer. for those with a salty edge look for some sweetness in the beer.

'Hybrids' containing candied fruit and peel are good with British Festive and Winter beers.

Medium-hard British cheeses such as the milder Cheddars, single Gloucester, red Leicester and red Cheshire, or sage Derby are made for our well-hopped full-bodied bitters.

The big cheeses: the follow-your-nose most mature Cheddar, blue Stilton, double Gloucester, Esrom, Gorgonzola, Roquefort, Danish blue, blue Cheshire, Shropshire blue, Spanish Manchego, smoked cheeses, rich, squidgy cheese such as over-ripe Camembert, Forres – eat these with the big beers, especially the bottle-conditioned winey ones, such as any of the Belgian Trappist Chimays (7–9 per cent), another Belgian brew Duvel (means devil, magically golden and seductive at 8.5 per cent strength); sour Rodenbach Grand Cru; a dark, thick, bitter-edged porter such as Old Growler; smoked beer, especially a small glass of Schlenkerla Rauchbier; bières de gardes with wired corks from France; Germany's strongest dark lagers (dunkels); glorious Suffolk Old Ale from Greene King and Gale's extraordinarily complex Prize Old Ale.

*Winter Warmer Wellington, see p. 174.*

## Heavenly Harmonies

These are some of the perfect pairings I have tried.

**White Stilton** flavoured with crystallized ginger – a really sweet pudding cheese; extremely pleasant with a syrupy sweet sparkling raspberry beer and even better with Young's award-winning Double Chocolate Porter, containing both chocolate malts and real chocolate. Either way, this is a very rich combination.

**Taleggio** – luscious rich, slightly salty, soft dessert cheese – great with the full almost fatty sweetness and yeast flavours in a bottle of Duvel.

**Jarlsberg** – its mellow sweet-edged nutty taste goes beautifully with thick, dark, sweet Forbidden Fruit, from Hoegaarden in Belgium. Fruit and nut, I suppose!

**Camembert** – salty and full; enjoy with a smoked beer.

**Smoked Brie** – a strong smoky flavour makes this far more powerful than plain Brie. It is superb with Alba Scots Pine Ale, a malty, peaty beer almost Belgian in its strength (7.7 per cent) and character, but made in Scotland using Scots pines and spruce sprigs, by the Heather Ale brewery (producers of Fraoch heather beer).

**Gorgonzola** – gorgeous Gorgo, sweet, desperately rich, slightly salty – just amazing with a giant wine glass of Chimay Bleu, the strongest Chimay.

**Beer cheese.** Yes, beer is beaut *in* cheese as well. Richard and Lesley Jenkinson of Chiltern Brewery near Aylesbury turned me on to beer cheese with their black-rinded Chiltern Beer Cheese, a rounded, nutty cheese containing their Beechwood Bitter, and their superb Terrick Truckle in glowing green wax, containing their Chiltern Ale Mustard, a past champion cheese at the Bath and West Show.

At Richmond in North Yorkshire the tiny Swaledale Cheese Co.

saved this threatened cheese and now produces a dark crust variety with Theakston's Old Peculier marbled through it – quite delicious. So is Y Fenni from Wales, a sweetish, Cheddar-type cheese flavoured with wholegrain mustard and brown ale, which I often see in supermarkets. Hereford Hop is a superb smooth Cheddar with hops pressed into the rind, from Malvern Cheesewrights, and you might also spot Somerton – a blend of garlic, Cheddar, ale and herbs. All good for cooking, too – try finishing a pork steak under the grill with a topping of Somerton or using Terrick Truckle for an interesting Welsh rarebit.

## Grilled Goat's Cheese in Coriander Beer (serves 6)

Beers flavoured with coriander have long been available in Belgium, dating back to the pre-hop days when coriander was used to improve the bouquet and taste of the brew. More recently British brewers have been experimenting with all sorts of herbs and spices in their beer recipes, and coriander has been reintroduced as an ingredient nearly 200 years since it was last used here. The result is quite different from the Belgian tart and spicy wheat beers – a fuller, more rounded flavour with a drier character; more of the dried coriander seeds than the fresh leaf. A distinctively coriander-flavoured bitter from the Nethergate Brewery in Suffolk, called Umbel Ale, is available both draught and bottled. It is not only a pungent marinade for this goat's cheese salad, but drinks well with it.

6 thick slices rind-on goat's cheese
300 ml (½ pint) coriander-flavoured beer
1 tbsp fresh parsley
1 tbsp basil, chopped
1 tsp coriander powder

Salt and freshly ground black pepper
Green salad leaves including lamb's lettuce, young spinach, watercress and a small quantity of fresh coriander leaves
1–2 tbsps set honey

Mix beer, parsley, basil, coriander powder, salt and pepper and use to marinate the goat's cheese slices overnight. Drain and reserve the marinade.

Warm about half the marinade in a pan and simmer gently to reduce; stir in honey to taste and thicken, then leave in the pan on a very low heat. Get the grill very hot, then quickly grill the goat's cheese on both sides, until just warm and toasted with grill markings.

Dress the salad with the beer/honey mixture and divide between 6 dishes, then place a slice of goat's cheese on top of each, and serve with hot olive ciabatta either as a starter or a light main course for two.

*To drink: a bottle of golden, spritzy Umbel Ale, with its citrus aftertaste, served cellar cold; widely available.*

# La Chouffe Parmesan Omelette with Black Truffle
## (serves 4)

La Chouffe, available in wine-size bottles ideal for the table, is a spicy, light-tan cloudy beer from Belgium, made at a farmhouse micro brewery with bar restaurant at Achouffe in the Ardennes. Here it helps to make a fluffy omelette even fluffier, adding colour and flavour, and combining brilliantly with the Parmesan.

| | |
|---|---|
| 6 large free-range eggs | Good olive oil |
| 1 egg white | Black truffle shavings |
| Freshly ground black pepper | *Filling* |
| 2 tbsps La Chouffe (chilled) | Either fresh cooked spinach or |
| 100 g (4 oz) chunk quality | young garden peas puréed |
| Parmesan | with cream and a dash of nut- |
| 25 g (1 oz) parsley, chopped | meg, seasoned with salt |

Crack 4 eggs into a bowl plus the other 2 egg yolks. Put the 3 egg whites in a separate bowl. Whisk 4 eggs together but do not over-whisk; season with a grinding of black pepper and stir in La Chouffe.

With a large-hole grater take off some long shavings of Parmesan and set aside, then finely grate the rest and add it to the egg mix with the parsley. Whisk egg whites briskly until they form peaks.

Warm an omelette pan or heavy frying pan, then pour in a little olive oil. While it is heating, fold the egg whites into the omelette mix. Pour half into the pan. As soon as it starts to set, top with the spinach or pea purée, scatter over a few shavings of black truffle and pour over the rest of the egg mix. Place a plate over the top and cook for a few more minutes until the top starts to set, then place under a very hot grill to finish off and brown.

Scatter over the reserved shavings of Parmesan and a few more tiny flakes of black truffle. Cut into 4 wedges and serve with green salad and hot Italian spinach bread.

*To drink: the rest of the La Chouffe, which you have resealed (wine savers work equally well on beer bottles) and chilled, served in either the special La Chouffe glasses or large wine glasses.*

# Leek, Potato and Walnut Slice in Welsh Ale and Cheese Pastry (serves 6)

A fruity, slightly bitter beer is the magic ingredient that produces a really rich, short, crumbly pastry for this vegetarian dish. It emerges from the oven solid, golden and satisfying, with tiny cheese bubbles erupting on the surface. I used a medium-strength Welsh beer because it seemed appropriate with leeks, but any mid-strength ale which is equally hoppy and fruity will do – choose one with a bitter edge, and a tawny hue to help the colour of the crust. The one I used is Brain's SA (Skull Attack to its regulars) brewed in Cardiff, and available both draught and bottled. At the end of cooking time you pour a drop into the pie, followed by a trickle of thick cream.

*Pastry*
225 g (8 oz) self-raising flour
Pinch salt
50 g (2 oz) butter
50 g (2 oz) red Leicester, grated
150 ml (5 fl oz) medium fruity
  bitter
*Filling*
1 medium onion, chopped finely
2 cloves garlic, crushed
50 g (2 oz) butter for frying
225 g (8 oz) waxy potatoes,
  peeled and sliced very thinly

1 large leek, cleaned and sliced
  in rings (white and green
  parts)
2 tbsps flat-leaf parsley,
  chopped roughly
2 tbsps chives, chopped
Salt and freshly ground black
  pepper and nutmeg
1 heaped tbsp walnuts,
  chopped
50 g (2 oz) yellow oyster
  mushrooms, halved
Thick pouring cream

To make pastry: sieve flour and salt into a large bowl then lightly rub in butter, incorporating as much air as possible. Stir in grated red Leicester, then add the beer slowly, pouring from well above the bowl so that it froths, lightly kneading to make a soft, moist dough. Wrap in clingfilm and refrigerate for 1 hour then bring back to room temperature before use.

To make the filling: sweat onion and garlic in lots of butter until soft but not coloured, then add potatoes. Cover with a lid or large plate to cook over a very low heat for a few minutes until potatoes start to wilt. Stir in leeks and cook, covered, for another 2 minutes, then stir in the herbs, seasonings and chopped walnuts.

Grease a shallow, round, glass pie dish and roll out the pastry into a large circle. Line the dish so that the pastry overlaps all round, then spoon in the filling, carefully distributing the oyster mushrooms so they do not break. Fold excess pastry back over the filling, bringing the edges together, but leaving a hole in the middle – use a rounded knife blade to push the filling away from the edges of the hole, and glaze with egg, sealing the pastry joins as you do so.

Bake above the centre of a fairly hot oven (400°F, 200°C, gas mark 6) until the filling is cooked through and the pastry risen and shiny golden brown. Slowly pour 2 tbsps beer into the hole in the pastry, tipping the dish so it trickles all through, then repeat with around 2 tbsps cream. Leave in a warm place for around 20 minutes for all the flavours to mingle, and serve in wedges. (This is also delicious cold and ideal for a picnic.)

*To drink: Perhaps a sweet, dark mild with nutty undertones, or Daleside Brewery's spicy Crackshot (bottled and draught) made to a seventeenth-century recipe from Ripley Castle, with malted oats.*

## Savoury Cheesecake with Pine Nuts, Baby Plum Tomatoes and Ale in a Crumb and Almond Croustade (serves 6)

Cheese and beer are made for each other – there is nothing finer than a ripe Stilton or Cheddar ploughman's with a pint of good ale. This recipe is slightly more exotic, mixing continental cheese and miniature sweet plum tomatoes with pine nuts in a well-risen, golden-crusted cake lightened with a golden ale. I used Exmoor Gold from Wiveliscombe in Somerset, where a brewery was first set up at Golden Hill in 1807. Smooth with a touch of vanilla, it is best on handpump, and a prize-winner at festivals up and down the country, but is also available bottled and works wonderfully in this recipe. It is a dish for a straw-hued ale which can be quite hoppy since only a little is used.

| | |
|---|---|
| 25 g (1 oz) fine brown crumbs, toasted | 1 tsp ground almonds |
| 15 g (½ oz) crushed almonds | 1 tbsp fresh parsley, chopped |
| 25 g (1 oz) melted, unsalted butter | Salt and pepper to season |
| 4 egg yolks | 2 tbsps pine nuts |
| 3 egg whites | 10 baby plum or cherry tomatoes |
| 100 g (4 oz) curd cheese | 75 ml (just over 2 fl oz) Exmoor Gold |
| 100 g (4 oz) Jarlsberg or Gruyère, grated finely | 40 g (1½ oz) sifted self-raising flour |

Cover base and sides of 20 cm (8 inch) high-sided glass or soufflé dish with melted butter, then press on mixed crumbs and crushed almonds. Mix together the egg yolks, then cream them with the curd and grated cheeses, ground almonds and parsley and season with salt and pepper. Mix in the pine nuts and tiny tomatoes, followed by the Exmoor Gold or golden ale. Fold in the self-raising flour. Stiffly whisk the egg whites and fold them into the mixture.

Pour the mixture into the dish and bake in the centre of a hot oven (425°F, 220°C, gas mark 6) for 15 minutes, then turn the oven down to 350°F, 180°C, gas mark 4 for about 40–45 minutes until the cake is well risen and the centre set.

Serve quickly by the slice before it starts to deflate – though it is equally nice cold when it sinks back to a springy cream-cheese texture. Good with a green salad simply dressed with walnut oil and lemon, garnished with a few of the raw tomatoes.

*To drink: a full-bodied malty ale such as Mauldon's Suffolk Punch or luscious bottled Hobgoblin brewed by Wychwood in Oxfordshire.*

# Y Fenni Layered Rarebit with Leeks and Honey Porter on Onion Bread (serves 2)

You get a double dose of beer in a rich, layered Welsh rarebit which you can serve as a quick snack for two people, or on small rounds of flavoured bread as nibbles with drinks, or even as a starter for an informal supper party. The two helpings of beer come first in the luscious Y Fenni Welsh cheese, which contains ale and whole black mustard seeds with a hot kickback both encased in a lovely lemon-coloured wax rind, and second in the honey porter (or use porter and a little runny honey to taste).

Bottom half of a round onion loaf
1 young leek, white part cut into thin rings (save top)
Unsalted butter for frying
1 spring onion, peeled and chopped
275 g (10 oz) Y Fenni, a few thin slices removed, the rest grated roughly (or a mature cheese containing mustard seeds) – save the rind
50 ml (2 fl oz) honey porter
1 level dstsp plain flour
1 large egg yolk
1 preserved red pimento, cut into thin strips
Fresh chives, chopped
Balsamic vinegar

Sweat leek briefly in butter in a heavy-based saucepan until just softened; remove with a slotted spoon and set aside. In same pan sauté spring onion for 2 minutes. Add the grated cheese and most of the beer, very gently melting them together – add the rest of the beer if it seems too thick. Cook extremely gently until melted – too hot and the mixture will separate – then stir in flour.

Remove from heat, and cool for a few minutes. Stir in the egg yolk.

Under the hottest grill briefly toast the base of the bread. Place base-down in a heat-proof dish and pour over the cheese mix. Arrange leek rings on top and the uncooked retained slices of cheese on top of that, then cover with thin slices of pimento. Place under hot grill until the cheese is bubbling and lightly browned, then scatter chopped chives on top.

Meanwhile wash the green part of the leeks, steam briefly until just wilted. Form into 2 bundles held in place with a strip of the cheese rind. Cut the round rarebit in half, arranging each half on a hot plate; put a leek bundle on each plate and dribble over a little balsamic vinegar.

*To drink: the honey porter in a small, thick, glass mug. And sometimes available is a vegetarian bottle-conditioned beer by King and Barnes called Clementine's Venus Gift.*

# Portered Stilton

No doubt you've indulged in port with Stilton; perhaps you've had potted Stilton, where this rich beast of a cheese is mixed with a little port (to use up the Christmas aftermath of both) and left in the cellar or fridge to mature. This recipe is based on the same idea, but uses a full flavoured, bottle-conditioned porter with a depth and maturity to match the cheese. I chose Old Slug Dark Porter, from the small Wessex Craft Brewers Co-operative, with a rich, rounded flavour, but you will easily find a dark, full-flavoured porter, either bottled or draught. Pot it in a heavy china crock and it will keep for up to two weeks in the fridge; pass around at the end of the meal.

225 g (8 oz) mature blue Stilton

25 g (1 oz) tiny chestnut mushrooms, sliced thinly

25 g (1 oz) walnuts, chopped

50 g (2 oz) unsalted butter

About 2 tbsps porter

Roughly grate Stilton into a bowl and stir in walnuts. Gently sauté mushrooms in 25 g (1 oz) butter until just softened; add mushrooms with their butter to the bowl and stir in. Add 1 tbsp porter and stir in, then add a second a little at a time until there is just enough to soften the mixture, bind it together and give off a faint porter aroma.

Pack firmly into a heavy china pot. Melt the remaining butter in a clean pan to clarify and pour over the top of the cheese to seal.

As well as serving this cold, you can spread it on bread and crisp under the grill, or use to enrich a savoury pie filling or to make a sauce to accompany a good steak.

*To drink: there's no shame in drinking a good dry porter – one of the stronger ones. But since this is an end-of-the-meal course and you're feeling mellow, a brandy glass of barley wine would be glorious as you pass round the crock of portered Stilton. Although this is a convivial act, I rather like sitting with my toes to the fire on my own, self-indulgently spreading it on thin crisp toast while drinking an entire bottle of barley wine. It vanquishes the day . . .*

# SALADS

Beer salads? Or perhaps just ale and arty! Seriously, beer is great in salads, especially now we are all hooked on warm salads with ingredients such as chicken livers – in this chapter as a stir-fry with leaves and cherry beer.

Both beer mayonnaise, which adds hop bite to the normal bland variety, and beer vinaigrette, perhaps using one of the sour Belgian brown Gueuzes in place of vinegar, bring a new dimension to salad leaves. Look out, too, for the recipe in which chilli beer is used to make a tongue-tingling salsa.

# Chicory, Jambon and Walnut Salad with Beer Vinaigrette (serves 6)

Irene Van Der Meersch and her daughter Maureen are self-taught cooks in the traditional Flemish style. I first met them when they demonstrated cooking with Hoegaarden beer in the kitchen above the London shop, Books for Cooks. Maureen is married to the landlord of The Wheatsheaf in Rathbone Place (a Tudor inn where Dylan Thomas met his wife) – and with her mother now runs the Belgian Restaurant above the pub, where their authentic Belgian cuisine has won many converts. This is their beer vinaigrette recipe to go with chicory, a favourite Belgian vegetable – why, I can never quite understand! But it does taste good when mixed with walnuts and a fine Ardennes ham, glistening with a Hoegaarden and honey dressing, in which the flavour of the wheat beer is brought out by the fresh coriander.

2 heads chicory
50 g (2 oz) walnuts, chopped
75 g (3 oz) Jambon d'Ardennes (or Parma ham), sliced thinly
1 orange, all peel and pith removed
*Dressing*
3 tbsps walnut oil
1 tbsp balsamic vinegar

1 tsp grain mustard
3 tbsps Hoegaarden (or Belgian wheat beer)
3 tbsps orange juice, freshly squeezed
1 dstsp clear honey
Salt and white pepper
1 tsp fresh coriander, chopped finely

Separate chicory leaves, removing any bitter core, and place in a large salad bowl. Mix in walnuts and ham, cut into small pieces. Using a very sharp knife, cut the orange into thin rounds, and each of those into segments, and add to the salad.

Make the dressing by whisking the walnut oil with the balsamic vinegar and mustard, then gradually whisk in the Hoegaarden, squeezed orange juice and clear honey. Season to taste with salt and white pepper, then mix in coriander. Toss the salad in the dressing and serve as a starter with hot garlic bread.

*To drink: has to be Hoegaarden itself, served chilled, preferably in its special glass, a thick tumbler with jutting rim. It usually has a slice of lemon on the rim of the glass, but with this dish I guess you should choose orange – and why not? After all, the beer is steeped with dried orange pith, snapped open to release the zest.*

# Chilli Beer and Roast Pepper Salsa (serves 4–6)

Looking along the shelf in a specialist beer shop, you may see a bottle with a chilli in it and think you've stumbled into a deli by mistake and found a flavoured vinegar. Not a bit of it. On the label is a *hombre* on a horse and the legend 'Kill a thirst – hit the heat'! This is genuine chilli beer, produced here for the Mexican market. It is tongue-burning stuff and, for my money, better as a cooking ingredient than a drink. It works brilliantly in this salsa with the beer-steeped chilli as part of the act; serve as a side dish wherever you want a spicy salad – it's good with the roast beer crumbed haddock on page 63.

2 large red peppers
½ firm cucumber (about 225 g
  or 8 oz)
8–10 cherry tomatoes
1 small yellow pepper
Chilli from the beer, chopped
1 tbsp chopped parsley or 1
  dstsp chopped mint

*Dressing*
100 ml (4 fl oz) chilli beer
1 dstsp balsamic vinegar
1 tsp tomato purée
1 fat clove garlic, peeled and
  crushed
Salt and freshly ground black
  pepper

Halve red peppers, scoop out seeds and roast in the oven, cut side down, at 400°F, 200°C, gas mark 6 for 20–30 minutes, until the skins are blackened and blistered. Remove from oven and put in a Polythene bag for 10 minutes to make it easy to remove the skins. Once skinned, cut into strips and blot on kitchen paper.

Peel and dice cucumber and place in a colander; sprinkle with salt and leave to drain for 1 hour, then press to remove more liquid, and drain on kitchen paper. Halve cherry tomatoes and scoop out seeds. Dice yellow pepper, which will add crunch to the salsa. Place vegetables, including chopped chilli, in a plastic storage box.

To make the dressing, blend or liquidize chilli beer, balsamic vinegar, tomato purée and crushed garlic, seasoning with salt and pepper. Pour over vegetables, adding fresh parsley or mint, depending on which you fancy at the time, and mix well. Put the lid on the box and leave to marinate in the fridge until needed – overnight is fine.

## Duck Breast with Bitter Leaf Salad and Fruit Ale Vinaigrette (serves 6)

The Old Coach House is an award-winning coaching inn in Ashby St Ledgers, near Rugby, one of the prettiest villages you could happen on. Coach House chef Mark Cartwright commissioned a one-off raspberry and strawberry beer from the Kitchen Brewery in Huddersfield to create this recipe for me, and also used coarseground Chiltern Ale mustard to create an inspiring vinaigrette for a duck breast salad. You could use Belgian raspberry or strawberry beer or try bottled Pete's Wicked Strawberry Blonde from the US.

2 duck breasts
Clear honey
Salt and freshly ground black
 pepper
*Salad*
1 bag mixed salad leaves or ½
lollo rosso, ½ curly endive, ½
oak leaf lettuce, ½ head
chicory and ½ radicchio
4 tomatoes
¼ cucumber
1 yellow pepper

75 g (3 oz) croûtons
Small punnet strawberries
*Vinaigrette*
2 tbsps Chiltern Ale mustard
 (or one of the other beer
 mustards available)
2 tbsps soft brown sugar
4 tbsps red wine vinegar
150 ml (¼ pint) Chiltern
 Summer Fruit Celebration Ale
150 ml (¼ pint) olive oil

Preheat oven to 425°F, 220°C, gas mark 7. Seal both sides of the duck breasts – starting with the skin side to release fat – in a pan, then brush skin side with honey, season with salt and pepper, place in an ovenproof dish and cook at the top of the oven for 8–10 minutes or until just pink. Remove and leave to cool.

Rinse mixed salad leaves, if necessary, or prepare the other lettuces by tearing leaves into 2.5 cm (1 inch) pieces; de-seed tomatoes and dice with the cucumber; cut pepper into strips. Mix all salad ingredients except strawberries with the croûtons.

Make vinaigrette by blending mustard, sugar and vinegar in a liquidizer; whilst blending, slowly add the ale and olive oil. Pour into a jug. Divide salad among 6 plates, slice duck breasts thinly and arrange on top. Drizzle 4–5 tbsps vinaigrette over each portion and garnish with strawberries.

*To drink: now here I would go for a cherry beer since duck goes with cherry – but not one of the sweet ones. A schooner of Liefmans Kriek, a classic Flemish brown ale with a sour cherry note and wine-like finish, chilled for about 30 minutes, would be a treat.*

# Raspberry Beergrette

The acidity in beer makes it a good ingredient in a salad dressing. This vinaigrette is sweet, sharp and titillates the tastebuds – it can be used on a simple green salad or a main-meal salad. Helen Hayward, who has been a beer cellar cook, devised it to go on a warm chicken liver salad or duck and bacon salad. I like it with smoked chicken breast or smoked lamb, warmed through and thinly sliced then arranged on frisée lettuce (add a little fresh mint with smoked lamb) with a few fresh raspberries for garnish; vegetarians could substitute thinly sliced smoked cheese for the chicken. There are several Belgian raspberry beers – I used Lindemans with its lambic acidity – and a few English versions now as well, though they are available usually as seasonal draught ales.

2 medium egg yolks
1 tbsp Dijon mustard
85 ml (3 fl oz) red wine vinegar

175 ml (6 fl oz) olive oil
300 ml (½ pint) raspberry beer

Place first 3 ingredients in a food processor and set on high for up to 2 minutes to emulsify. Whisk in olive oil slowly, a little at a time, until mixture thickens; then stir in enough raspberry beer to reach the required consistency, about 300 ml (½ pint). Season to taste with salt and pepper.

*To drink: a fairly rich combination of duck livers or smoked meat, so have a clean-tasting English wheat beer, such as Feland Brewery's Sparkling Wit, or a pale pilsner.*

# Summer Roasted Cod Salad with Dark Mild Vinaigrette (serves 6)

A few breweries are starting to adopt the noble practice of throwing a beer banquet. In 1997 Bateman's Brewery of Wainfleet in Lincolnshire put on a stonker at their Vine Hotel in nearby coastal resort Skegness. Head chef Stephen Coggins put together a scintillating seven-course menu based around Bateman's renowned beers, starting with beer and mushroom soup and ending with beer-flavoured truffles. The fish course was roasted cod with a mustard and beer dressing flavoured with Bateman's dark mild, described in CAMRA's *Good Beer Guide* as 'ruby black, topped by a cream head, this is the epitome of a mild'. It won the Silver Award at the 1997 Great British Beer Festival.

500 g (1 lb 2oz) cod fillet, skinned
6 medium eggs, hardboiled
6 rashers middle back bacon, de-rinded
2 slices white bread, crusts removed
150 ml (¼ pint) garlic oil*
Handful mixed lettuce per person (frisée, lollo rosso,
endive, iceberg, rocket)

*Dressing*
300 ml (½ pint) Bateman's mild (or another dark mild)
150 ml (¼ pint) balsamic vinegar
2 tsps wholegrain mustard
Salt and pepper to season
150 ml (¼ pint) garlic oil*

Using sterilized tweezers, remove any remaining bones from cod. Cut into 2 cm (¾ inch) cubes and refrigerate until required. Cut cooled, hardboiled eggs into quarters. Grill bacon rashers until crisp, then slice into strips and allow to cool. Make croûtons by cutting bread slices into neat cubes then crisping in garlic oil; drain on absorbent paper (reserving oil).

Prepare and wash salad leaves and drain well. Make the dressing by bringing the beer to the boil in a saucepan, then simmering

*The best garlic oil is made by steeping 8 peeled, chopped cloves garlic in 300 ml (½ pint) good quality olive oil for 6 days at room temperature, says Steve, though you can buy ready-made.

briskly until half its original volume. Add balsamic vinegar, seasonings, mustard and garlic oil and whisk well; keep warm.

Pre-heat oven to 450°F/230°C/gas mark 8, then brush a roasting tray with some of the reserved garlic oil. Arrange cod cubes on tray and cook near the top of the oven for 6 minutes; while fish is cooking reheat bacon strips in the bottom of the oven.

To serve: divide salad leaves between 6 plates, then arrange egg quarters on top and cover with bacon strips and cod cubes; drizzle over a little dressing, then scatter croûtons over the top and serve immediately.

*To drink: a contrast – either the dark mild slightly chilled or a dry pale pilsner, which is excellent with white fish, served a few degrees colder.*

# Stir-fried Scallop and Bacon Salad with Thai Pickled Ginger and Brown Malt Ale
## (serves 6 as a starter, or 2 as a main dish)

Foodie fads soon fade unless they're good; a warm salad harmonizing hot and cold ingredients is one of the better ones. Here a deep brown, malty ale takes the place of soy sauce or even oyster sauce, but adds a sweetness that goes beautifully with the shellfish. I got the idea for the recipe when Sussex brewers King and Barnes were originating a recipe of their own, recreating an old brown malt ale once made with a pale ale malt roasted over brushwood faggots; it is a bottle-conditioned beer containing a yeast sediment; pour carefully so that the sediment stays in the bottle or it will spoil the flavour. If you can't find this occasional brew, use a dark, sweetish stout.

2 rashers smoked, streaky bacon, cut into small pieces
Hazelnut oil for frying
75 g (3 oz) queenie scallops
2 spring onions, trimmed and chopped
1 level tsp Thai pickled ginger, drained
50 g (2 oz) canned water chestnuts, drained

50 g (2 oz) mangetouts, halved
25 g (1 oz) beansprouts
50 g (2 oz) yellow oyster mushrooms
A little Brown Malt Ale or sweet stout
Mixed young red and green salad leaves including spinach, oak lettuce, a little watercress

Heat oil in a wok and fry bacon until nearly crisp; add scallops and stir-fry for up to 3 minutes until just cooked through. Remove with the bacon, using a slotted spoon, and keep warm.

Get the wok hot again and throw in spring onions with Thai pickled ginger, swiftly followed by the water chestnuts and mangetouts. Cook over a high heat, stir-frying constantly for 2 minutes. Add beansprouts and oyster mushrooms and stir-fry for another minute before pouring in just enough beer to cover the bottom of the wok. Cook down rapidly to a glazing syrup.

Meanwhile, put the salad leaves in a bowl, then add the contents of the wok and mix quickly together before arranging the bacon and scallops on top. Serve as a starter with sesame-coated bread sticks.

*To drink: I love a dryish stout with almost any seafood; Sam Smith's bottled Imperial Stout is a joy, or have a big-bowled wine glass of draught stout with a thick, creamy head.*

# Warm Chicken Liver, Ciabatta and Cherry Beer Salad
## (serves 6)

Hot chicken livers and ripe cherry beer bring out the best in each other in this warm salad, which can either be served as a starter for six or a light supper if you increase the quantities. These Belgian cherry beers provide new taste possibilities: the deep pink dressing, sweet but not cloying, makes a perfect foil for the sautéed livers and mixture of red and green salad leaves. I used Lindemans Kriek (cherry beer), which you have to liberate from a bottle that has both a fat, champagne-style cork and a metal cap to confine this live beer brewed with spontaneously fermenting wild yeasts. Other Belgian cherry beers have a characteristic sour edge, but this one is almost syrupy sweet and a perfect link between the chicken livers and salad leaves.

175 g (6 oz) fresh chicken livers
Unsalted butter
3 slices ciabatta bread
25 g (1 oz) garlic butter (made by mixing softened butter with 1 clove crushed garlic)

Mixed young salad leaves: spinach, watercress, oak lettuce
2 tbsps fresh chives and flat-leaf parsley, chopped finely
A few basil leaves, torn in half
150 ml (¼ pint) cherry beer

Place salad leaves in a bowl and mix in the herbs. Cut ciabatta into cubes and fry in garlic butter until crisp to make croûtons, then remove from pan and drain on kitchen paper.

With a very sharp knife cut the chicken livers into bite-size pieces, and fry on all sides in unsalted butter for 2 minutes, until just cooked; remove from pan and keep warm. Add cherry beer to the pan and reduce over a high heat to a thick syrup; allow to stand for about 30 seconds to cool slightly.

Add warm chicken livers to salad leaves and toss with the warm cherry-beer glaze. Sprinkle over the crisp croûtons and take quickly to table for the diners to serve themselves.

*To drink: a fruity beer but not a fruit beer. Try a bitter that's bitter sweet – sweet for the cherry dressing, bitter for the salad leaves, like Harvey's Sussex Best Bitter or Woodforde's Baldric.*

# PUDDINGS

'Desserts must be the most difficult part of the book, I guess,' said an acquaintance. A fair assumption. When you think of beer you tend to think of bitterness and certainly of savoury tastes. But desserts proved to be a real eye-opener – in the end it was a case of trying to decide which recipes to leave out, not which to put in. In fact, I have a friend who is collecting recipes for an entire book of beer puddings.

Nor was this simply because there are now so many splendid fruit beers, although that helped, giving me the opportunity to lighten and flavour various pastries with raspberry beer, or use cherry or another fruit beer neat in syllabubs and trifles to create an alcoholic dessert since the alcohol was not being cooked out.

No. I think the two great eye-openers were sweet, malty beers and bitter chocolate beers. Malty beers, with their happy knack of caramelizing, are absolute knockouts in puddings such as crème caramel, treacly rice pudding and, above all, a sticky toffee pudding to die for. Those dark chocolate porters and stouts, many with a biting chocolate edge or a hint of espresso coffee, were irresistible in mousses and ice creams, while a more vinous porter proved sweet and winsome in a porter jelly.

High-alcohol fruity beers were again made for puddings, especially when it came to using dried fruit soaked for a couple of days, above all in Christmas pudding. Ginger beer, too, proved its flexibility by proving to be just as much at home in sweet as in savoury recipes and finding a natural partner in rhubarb.

Perhaps the most innovative idea came from *Eat Your Greens* cook Sophie Grigson, who used a French bière de garde to make a yummy French-style beer tart.

With the pudding course drink small glasses of intensely flavoured beer. Both cherry and raspberry beers go well with chocolate puddings, as does a drop of slightly chilled creamy porter, which also sits quite happily beside a strawberry, raspberry or cherry dessert.

In this section I begin with the hot puddings, followed by cold desserts.

# Beer-baked Bramleys with Dates and Walnuts
## (serves 6)

Adding beer to your cooking often lifts a run-of-the-mill dish into the wow category. That's how I felt when I first tasted boring old baked apples transformed at a brewery dinner by the addition of a spicy ale into a dish that made strong men tremble. Giant Bramleys had been cored and stuffed with sultanas soaked in dark, nutty Marston's Union Mild, then simply roasted until the apples had sucked in all the beer and swelled to a soufflé meringue texture. I used King and Barnes's bottle-conditioned Festive Ale at a fairly robust 5.3 per cent, but you could opt for a dark, spicy mild. All the spice is in the beer, you don't need to add any.

| | |
|---|---|
| 6 large Bramley apples | Approx 300 ml (½ pint) |
| 100 g (4 oz) mixed dried fruit | Festive Ale or dark mild |
| 50 g (2 oz) dates, chopped | 6 whole walnuts |
| 50 g (2 oz) walnuts, chopped | 50 g (2 oz) soft brown sugar |

Mix dried fruit and dates in a bowl. Pour over enough ale to come about 5 cm (2 inches) above the fruit. Leave to steep in the fridge for 48 hours until the fruit is swollen with beer. Drain, retaining liquor.

Core apples and cut a line round the diameter of each with a sharp knife. Mix beer-soaked fruit with chopped walnuts and use to stuff apples, adding a little sugar as you go. Place in an ovenproof dish and pour over enough of retained liquor to come about 1 cm (½ inch) up the apples. Scatter any left-over mixed fruit around them.

Bake in the centre of a hot oven (400°F, 200°C, gas mark 6) for 30 minutes. Remove from the oven and place a walnut where the apple stalk was, sprinkling it with brown sugar, and return to the oven for another 30 minutes until the apple is puffed up and marshmallow soft, the ale turned to a toffee syrup.

Serve piping hot with very cold thick yellow pouring cream.

*To drink: Marston's Union Mild, named after their historic union brewing system, would be ideal, or mahogany-hued Tomintoul Stag, brewed in Scotland, for its marked apple-skin tang.*

## Boozy Bread and Butter Pudding (serves 6–8)

Bread and butter pudding is the most popular pub pudding, without a doubt. The best are served with proper custard – but none is as good as mine. Why on earth don't pubs use all that brilliant free beer they have on tap to pep up run-of-the-mill dishes and make them special? I steep the fruit in an incredibly strong barley wine, the brandy of the beer world – options could be Fuller's bottle-conditioned Golden Pride at a stonking 9.2 per cent, also draught around Christmas, or a Christmas ale such as McMullen's, my county brewer in Hertford, luscious Stronghart, a complex, vinous winter beer at 7 per cent available draught seasonally, also bottled.

| | |
|---|---|
| 50 g (2oz) raisins | 6 thin slices buttered light |
| 50 g (2 oz) sultanas | brown bread, crusts removed |
| 50 g (2 oz) stoneless dates, | Soft dark brown sugar |
| chopped | 450 ml (¾ pint) creamy milk |
| 300 ml (½ pint) barley wine – | 2 medium eggs, whisked |
| or a nip-sized bottle | Fresh nutmeg, grated |
| Butter | 1 tsp powdered cinnamon |

Place raisins, sultanas and dates in a bowl and pour over barley wine. Leave for up to 48 hours until the fruit is swollen with the liquor then drain, retaining any unabsorbed beer.

Preheat oven to 375°F, 190°C, gas mark 5. Butter an oblong, glass, ovenproof dish. Cut bread into triangles and layer in the dish, butter side up, sprinkling each layer with the soaked fruit and sugar to taste, finishing with bread. Warm the milk, without boiling, and pour in the eggs slowly, whisking them in. Pour over the bread until almost covered, and leave to stand for 20 minutes. Finally, pour over some of the retained beer and finish with a grating of nutmeg and the powdered cinnamon.

Bake above the centre of the oven for 30–35 minutes until crisp on top, melting underneath and risen to almost soufflé lightness. (You do not need a full ½ pint beer, but barley wine flavoured by the fruit is a luscious cook's perk or can be used to flavour custard.)

*To drink: not barley wine – that is an end-of-meal pleasure. Instead, enjoy a small tumbler of Christmas ale or winter ale in season, such as Stronghart or Woodforde's delectable Norfolk Nog (a Champion Beer of Britain winner), or a hearty, spicy bitter like Ringwood's Old Thumper.*

## Bramble and Bramley Turnovers with Y Fenni Mustard and Ale Cheese (serves 6)

It is not unknown to serve mature Cheddar with apple pie; here I have teamed a beer cheese with blackberries and Bramley apples. Y Fenni is a wonderful Welsh cheese, flavoured with ale and wholeseed mustard – initially sweet but with a hot kick when you bite into a mustard seed. It helps to sweeten these turnovers and give them a creamy tang with a bit of welly as well. Y Fenni is available in delicatessens and supermarkets.

450 g (1 lb) puff pastry
450 g (1 lb) Bramleys, peeled, cored and cut into small chunks
175 g (6 oz) fresh or frozen blackberries
Approx 50 g (2 oz) Demerara sugar
100 g (4 oz) Y Fenni, crumbled
1 medium egg, beaten

Roll out the pastry to about 0.5 cm (¼ inch) thick, then cut into 6 pieces.

Divide apple chunks between them, piling them on one half of the pastry. Sprinkle 1 tsp brown sugar over the apple, then cover with blackberries. Top with crumbled Y Fenni and brush round the pastry edges with beaten egg. Fold the other half of the pastry over to form a turnover, pinching the edges together and crimping them upwards to make a firm seal and decorative rim. Brush with egg, place on a greased baking tray and bake towards the top of a pre-heated oven (425°F, 220°C, gas mark 7) for 30 minutes until puffed and golden brown. Serve with a wickedly thick clotted cream or more virtuous crème fraîche.

*To drink: either Henry Weinhard's Blackberry Wheat Ale from America or one of the Bavarian cloudy wheat beers with their cinnamon and bubblegum flavours – most notably Schneider Weisse.*

*Beer-baked Bramleys with Dates and Walnuts, see p. 207.*

# Crêpes Kriek Susan – or my Variation of Crêpes Suzette! (serves 6)

Beer is used in savoury pancakes as starters, but pancakes with beer are just as successful as a sumptuous dessert. The usual crêpes Suzette are very thin pancakes simmered in orange juice then flamed in brandy. I think this is even more decadent – pancakes made with cherry beer batter, then cooked in the beer. I've used Belle-Vue Kriek from Brussels. Cherries are macerated in the brew, then aged in oak casks to a deep ruby port hue and sweetness, but with that refreshing tart edge of the lambic (wild yeast) beer. You can make almost any quantity of batter you like, just use roughly the same amount of flour and beer. And you'll still need a measure of brandy – beer alone won't cause a conflagration at the dining table!

*Pancakes* (makes 12)
1 cup (235 ml, 8 fl oz) Belle-Vue Kriek
Same cup plain flour
1 dstsp icing sugar
1 tbsp unsalted butter, melted
1 dstsp very cold water
2 large eggs
Lard/butter for frying
*To serve*
Measure of brandy
Fresh cherries
Crème fraîche

Put all the pancake ingredients into a liquidizer and blend to a smooth, cherry-blossom-tinted batter. Rest for 1 hour then pour into a bowl and stir.

Make pancakes in the usual way, using 2 tbsps batter only to create a really lacy pancake. Grease frying pan with a little lard until smoking hot, then add the same amount of butter, which will sizzle and melt, before adding batter. Repeat for each pancake, piling them flat on a plate as you make them, until you have used up all the batter.

Wipe out the pan with kitchen paper to remove any grease, then add the rest of the bottle of Belle-Vue and bring to a gentle simmer. Add the first pancake, warm through, fold over into a triangle (as in crêpes Suzette) and push to one side of the pan. Repeat with the

*Cherry Beer Syllabub, see p. 229.*

other pancakes – have another bottle of Belle-Vue ready in case you need it.

When ready to serve, pour everyone a small wine glass of the beer, then warm a measure of brandy, set light to it and pour it over the pan of crêpes. Take flaming to table and serve with fresh cherries and large dollops of crème fraîche.

*To drink: as above – I bought Belle-Vue easily in my local supermarket, but if you can't find it use another cherry beer, or even a raspberry one.*

## Dunkin' Drunken Apples (serves 6)

This is a sort of toffee apple using Adnams' potent, fruity and caramelly Broadside Ale, which is brewed in Southwold. The beer was chosen by recipe originator Alistair Shaw of the Froize Inn at Chillesford in Suffolk because he serves mainly East Anglian beers. You would get similar results with a strong, malty beer such as Harvey's Old Ale or a malty Scotch ale.

6 cooking apples, peeled, cored
 and quartered
450 g (1 lb) butter

750 g (1½ lb) demerara sugar
300 ml (½ pint) Adnams
 Broadside

Put butter in a thick-bottomed frying pan and heat till foaming. Add the sugar by sprinkling it all over, then stir until the mixture starts to caramelize. Add the Broadside and reduce to a thick liquor. Add the apple quarters and cook one side until browned, then turn over and repeat. Remove the apples and keep warm.

Lay out the apple quarters on a large plate and serve the sauce as a dip. (Alistair says that the secret of this dessert is to not over-cook the apples.)

*To drink: a malty, burnt-caramel type of beer such as tongue-curling Traquair House Ale, which has apple notes to boot, or you can choose one of the 'toffee apple' barley wines.*

# Fruit Ale Bread and Butter Pudding with Mash Tun Marmalade and Sauce Anglaise (serves 6)

In my recipe for bread and butter pudding (page 208) the beer is in the barley wine. Mark Cartwright, the chef at the Old Coach House, Ashby St Ledgers in Northamptonshire, uses a different approach. His recipe is doubly beery, flavoured with Summer Fruit Celebration Ale (no longer available, so try Henry Weinhard's Blackberry Wheat from America, bottled in supermarkets) and Chiltern Brewery's dark Mash Tun Marmalade made with Seville oranges and roast malt from the brewery (or use a bitter, coarse-cut marmalade). Mark serves it with Sauce Anglaise (that's posh custard).

*Pudding*

6 thin slices wholemeal bread, buttered
Chiltern Mash Tun Marmalade (or Seville marmalade)
450 ml (¾ pint) fruit beer
150 ml (¼ pint) full-fat milk
4 medium eggs
150 g (5 oz) sugar
50 g (2 oz) dried mixed fruit, chopped
Ground nutmeg

Spread buttered, de-crusted bread with marmalade and cut into triangles. Whisk together beer, milk, eggs and sugar. Layer the marmalade bread with the fruit in a square or rectangular oven-proof dish. Pour over the beer, egg and milk mixture and allow to soak for 20 minutes. Sprinkle with nutmeg and bake towards the top of a pre-heated moderate oven (400F°, 200°C, gas mark 6) for 40 minutes until nicely risen, crisp and golden.

*Sauce Anglaise*

450 ml (¾ pint) milk
75 g (3 oz) sugar
1 tsp grated nutmeg
4 egg yolks
½ vanilla pod

Blend egg yolks with sugar and nutmeg in a bowl. Heat milk with vanilla pod. Remove from heat and whisk into the egg-yolk mixture.

Return to pan and stir constantly over a low heat until the mixture thickens. Remove vanilla pod and serve with the bread and butter pudding.

To make the pudding look more elegant, cut out rounds with a fluted 7.5 cm (3 inch) metal cutter and serve with custard poured round it.

*To drink: one of the stronger, spicy bitters like King and Barnes's Festive Ale, with its beaten copper hue, or Monkey Wrench from Daleside Brewery, which has a wine feel and dried-fruit flavours (both available bottled).*

# Ginger-Beer Pancakes Filled with Spiced Rhubarb Fool
## (serves 6)

Ginger and rhubarb are traditional bedfellows, but in this recipe the ginger carries through to the pancakes in the shape of a ginger wheat beer called Gingersnap, brewed by the Salopian Brewing Co., which gives the pancakes a crisp, lacy texture as well as the flavour of ginger ale. There are a few ginger beers available now, bottled and draught, which are usually seasonal. Although it's only available sporadically, Gingersnap is ideal, with its sharp, tart wheat-beer flavour and true root ginger – also, it's a bottle-conditioned beer containing live yeast, so use the yeast sediment in your beer batter.

*Pancakes*
1 cup plain flour
1 cup ginger beer*
2 medium eggs
1 tbsp unsalted butter, melted
Vegetable fat and butter for
 frying
*Filling*
450 g (1 lb) fresh rhubarb,
 washed and chopped

3 cardamom pods
½ tsp mixed spice
Soft light brown sugar to taste
More ginger beer
150 ml (5 fl oz) double cream
*To garnish*
Icing sugar
Powdered ginger
Stem ginger, sliced thinly

To make pancakes, place first 3 ingredients in a blender and liquidize, adding either a little extra flour or a drop of very cold water if mixture seems to thin or too thick. Pour into a bowl and rest in the fridge until needed.

Meanwhile, place the rhubarb in a pan with cardamoms, mixed spice, sugar to taste (start with 1 heaped tbsp) and almost cover with ginger beer. Simmer with the lid on until tender, then taste and sweeten further if necessary. Continue to cook with the lid off until rhubarb becomes a thick purée; chill in the fridge.

* If ginger beer is not available, use an English wheat beer plus 1 tsp powdered ginger in the pancakes and ½ tsp in the filling.

Add melted butter to the batter and make thin pancakes, using about 2 tbsps batter per pancake; keep warm.

Whip cream until it is stiff, remove cardamom pods from rhubarb purée, then fold purée into the cream. Use to fill the hot pancakes, folding them over to form a triangle, and serve on a plate which has the rim dusted with icing sugar mixed with powdered ginger, then arrange a little stem ginger on each pancake.

*To drink: the chocolatey edge of a thick, sweet stout is superb with the ginger and rhubarb; bottled, choose a slightly sour Flemish brown beer.*

## Pears in Porter (serves 6)

Pears in red wine is a classic dish, though goodness knows why since it always seems to me to be a rather insipid version of stewed fruit. But I had a picture in my mind's eye of how the pears might look, all dark and glossy, with the stem at the top, a sharply sweet coating in contrast to the more delicate flavour of the pears; a sort of pear toffee apple. Some porters have a port-like, fruity or nutty finish, but for this dessert choose the other sort, a jet black drink with a roast-malt style, such as Young's London-brewed porter, King and Barnes's Old Porter full of body and chocolate malt, Butterknowle Brewery near Newcastle's 'bible black' Lynesack Porter – but you'll find many more in the bar and on off-licence shelves.

| | |
|---|---|
| 6 firm, plump pears | 1 tbsp dark soft brown sugar |
| 300 ml (½ pint) dark, bitter- | 1 knob unsalted butter |
| sweet porter | *To serve* |
| 1 tsp powdered cinnamon | Clotted cream |
| 1 dstsp dark, clear honey | Grated bitter chocolate |

Peel pears, but leave stalks attached. Sit them side by side in a large pan, stalks uppermost. Pour in enough porter to come about one-third of the way up the pears and bring slowly to simmering point. Add cinnamon and honey; cover and cook gently for around 30–40 minutes until the pears are soft, turning them occasionally in the liquor towards the end of cooking time to give a dark patina all over.

When cooked, remove pears with a slotted spoon and keep warm. Pour porter liquor into a frying pan and bring to a brisk simmer to reduce, stirring frequently. Add sugar. Continue cooking until the mixture thickens and caramelizes slightly. Stir in butter to give the sauce a glossy finish. Pour over pears, making sure they are coated.

Serve the burnished pears hot with a large dollop of really cold clotted cream decorated with a little grated dark chocolate.

*To drink: another dark brew but with a peardrop and cinnamon sweetness – bottled strong Aventinus, at a pause-giving 8 per cent. Serve in sipping glasses.*

# Rich Almond and Plum Slice in Raspberry Beer Pastry (serves 6)

When I made raspberry beer tartlets, my husband commented that the pastry would be wonderful with almonds. His tastebuds did not betray him. Here it is in a summer flan with fresh plums, a few glacé cherries and loads of ground almonds cooked to a light consistency. Even with the almonds and plums on board, it is the raspberry beer you smell during baking and the flavour is still quite distinct when you bite into the crisp base. The combination of sweet, juicy plums with their almond covering and the raspberry beer is irresistible.

225 g (8 oz) raspberry beer pastry (page 241)
75 g (3 oz) caster sugar
3 large eggs
½ tsp almond essence

100 g (4 oz) ground almonds
6 small, sweet, fresh plums
25 g (1 oz) almond slivers
5–6 natural-coloured glacé cherries

Roll out the pastry thinly and use to line a 30 cm (12 inch) greased flan dish; prick the base with a fork. Pre-heat the oven to 400°F, 200°C, gas mark 6.

Tip sugar into a large bowl and break in eggs, then whisk vigorously for a few minutes until the mixture is thick and foaming. Stir in almond essence, then slowly fold in the ground almonds.

Wash and dry plums, then halve them lengthways with a sharp knife, removing stones; arrange plums cut side down on pastry base.

Pour egg and almond mixture over the plums and scatter almond slivers over the top, then drop on the glacé cherries, which will sink in. Bake in the centre of oven for 15 minutes, then turn down the heat to 350°F, 180°C, gas mark 4 and cook for a further 30 minutes until the filling is set and risen, the top golden brown (check after the first 30 minutes and, if it is browning too quickly, cover with foil while the filling sets). Serve hot or cold with pouring cream.

*To drink: plum beer would be perfect and does exist, but is not easy to find; otherwise find a deep red beer with some malty sweetness, such as Ushers' bottled Ruby Ale.*

# Thomas Hardy's Sticky Toffee Pudding (serves 6)

In *The Trumpet Major* Hardy wrote of Dorchester strong beer: 'It was of the most beautiful colour that the eye of an artist in beer could desire; full in body, yet brisk as a volcano; piquant yet without a tang; luminous as an Autumn sunset . . .', an evocative description which now applies to the beer named after him, Thomas Hardy's Ale. A giant among beers – and, at 12 per cent, one of the strongest in the world – this dark, vinous brew is bottled with natural yeast and can be laid down for a number of years like a fine wine. I once tasted a thirty-year-old bottle and it was still perfectly drinkable; in all honesty, it should only be drunk, not used for cooking. Thick as molasses and tasting of treacle and Marmite, this is a feet on the fender at the end of a meal vintage beer. I decided to use it in just one glorious pudding, which takes only a little, so there is just enough left in one bottle to serve small glasses as a 'dessert beer'.

100 g (4 oz) unsalted butter
50 g (2 oz) soft dark brown
  sugar
2 eggs, beaten
75 g (3 oz) mixed dates and
  walnuts, chopped
175 g (6 oz) self-raising flour
150 ml (¼ pint) equal amounts

milk and Thomas Hardy's Ale
  mixed
*Sticky sauce*
50 g (2 oz) unsalted butter
50 g (2 oz) soft dark brown
  sugar
85 ml (3 fl oz) Thomas
  Hardy's Ale

Butter a 900 ml (1½ pint) pudding basin.

In a large bowl, cream together butter and sugar until light and fluffy, then add the beaten eggs a little at a time, beating them in well. Stir in the chopped dates and walnuts, then fold in the flour, using a metal spoon. Finally stir in the milk and ale and mix to create a dropping consistency, adding a little more ale if necessary.

Pour into the prepared bowl, cover with foil and secure with a rubber band. Steam in a large covered pan for 90 minutes (the water should come about 5cm (2 inches) up the bowl; top up with boiling water as needed).

Prepare sticky sauce by melting butter and sugar together in a thick-bottomed pan until the mixture thickens and caramelizes, then stir in enough Thomas Hardy's Ale to make a pouring syrup (as little as possible!).

Turn the pudding out on to a serving dish and pour over the syrup. Decadence on a plate.

*To drink: Thomas Hardy is a collector's ale and is generally only to be found in specialist beer shops. It is also expensive, but fortunately you only use a small amount in the pudding; 2 bottles ensure a convivial evening. If you can't find it, a heavyweight barley wine is quite acceptable.*

# Three Pints of Christmas Pudding
## with Brandy and Barley Wine
### (Makes enough for a 2-pinter and a 1-pinter)

There is no end to the enterprise of Bob and Theresa Miller at the White Swan in Sileby, Leicestershire. Bob used to be a butcher and still makes brilliant bangers, including one flavoured with real ale, which he sells over the bar. Theresa is a talented chef (I was once judging when she reached the finals of the Guinness Pure Genius pub food awards with a delicious dish using trout caught in nearby Rutland water), and her menu is a magnet for diners. She also sells her produce over the bar, from home-made salmon and courgette quiches to plum chutney and crab apple jelly, while a local store sells her puddings, such as date and butterscotch or damson pie. One Christmas I received a mysterious package through the post and opened it to find the most delicious Christmas pudding I have ever tasted. Here is the recipe.

175 g (6 oz) currants
175 g (6 oz) sultanas
225 g (8 oz) raisins
6 tbsps barley wine
275 g (10 oz) fresh white or mixed brown and white breadcrumbs
100 g (4 oz) glacé cherries, chopped
175 g (6 oz) shredded suet (or vegetarian suet)*

100 g (4 oz) chopped mixed peel
1 275 g (10 oz) cooking apple, peeled and grated
Grated rind and juice of 1 orange
1 tsp mixed spice
½ tsp ground cinnamon
½ tsp ground nutmeg
3 medium eggs, beaten
225 g (8 oz) soft brown sugar
3 tbsps brandy

Soak currants, sultanas and raisins overnight in the barley wine, then thoroughly combine with all the ingredients in a large mixing bowl – this is a stiff mixture to stir so get the kids to help. Turn

*For vegetarians Theresa sometimes omits the suet altogether because she feels vegetarian suet is a contradiction in terms. Instead she doubles the amount of barley wine, which, she says, makes a moister pudding.

into well-greased 1.2-litre (2 pint) and 600 ml (1 pint) pudding basins and cover with greaseproof paper, then double-wrap with foil. Tie securely with string.

Place each pudding in a saucepan and pour in boiling water to come halfway up the sides. Briskly simmer the bigger pudding for 8 hours and the smaller one for 5 hours, topping up the pans with water as necessary.

Remove the puddings from the pans and leave overnight to cool completely. Remove the coverings and cover again with fresh greaseproof paper and foil or a pudding cloth. Store in a cool, dry place away from direct sunlight until you want to cook them.

To serve: reboil the big pudding for 4 hours or the smaller one for up to 3 hours and turn out onto a warm dish. Serve with rum sauce or brandy butter.

You need a powerful barley wine for this pudding or wait until early December and choose one of the stronger Christmas or winter ales. For me, McMullen's Stronghart is irresistible; not only is it a Christmas Ale so strong (7 per cent) that it has won a barley wine competition, but at a tasting I once referred to it as 'liquid Christmas pudding' and the name stuck. Legendary bottle-conditioned Gale's Prize Old Ale is also highly recommended, and as an accompanying drink in dessert wine glasses. You can save the smaller pudding and cook it when you need cheering up.

*To drink: definitely the beer you have used to make the pudding, served in chunky little glasses you can warm with your hands.*

## Traquair Rice (serves 6)

'A potent liquor as brewed by the Laird in the ancient brew house of the oldest inhabited house in Scotland,' it says on the bottle. And yes, it's a malt – but not a whisky, though your tastebuds will draw comparisons. Traquair House Ale at a socking 7.2 per cent strength is an unctuous, malty beer brewed in a romantic Borders stately home by the descendants of the Stuart who fell with his king at Flodden in 1513. Today Catherine Maxwell-Stuart is the brewing 'laird', producing heart-warming brews full of treacle and burnt sugar, but with a distinct yeast extract follow-through. There are only two or three places where you can drink her beers on draught, but I managed to pick up a bottle in my local supermarket and it is becoming more available, as is its sister brew Jacobite Ale. Scottish beers tend to have a denser, maltier character than sassenach ales – perhaps that's why they call them 'wee heavies' and why they turn an ordinary rice pudding into golden gooeyness under a caramel crust.

| | |
|---|---|
| 40 g (1½ oz) short grain pudding rice | 250 ml (8 fl oz) Traquair House Ale or a dark, malty beer |
| 1 oz soft dark brown sugar | |
| 350 ml (12 fl oz) creamy milk | 25 g (1 oz) unsalted butter |
| | Nutmeg, grated freshly |

You need a cool oven (300°F, 150°C, gas mark 2), and a buttered ovenware dish.

Rinse the rice and scatter it over the bottom of the dish. Measure the milk into a measuring jug and top up to 600 ml (1 pint) with the beer. Sprinkle the sugar over the rice, then pour over the milk, dot the surface with butter and finish with a grating of fresh nutmeg to taste.

Place on a low oven shelf and cook for 45 minutes. Remove from the oven and stir, then cook for another hour and stir again. Return to the oven for around 30 minutes and serve when the rice has absorbed virtually all the beer and milk to reach a thick, sticky texture with a toast-brown skin. (You can add flavourings like cardamoms or sultanas, but I find the beer contributes such a complexity of spices that it's best left straight.) I serve it unrepentantly with chilled, clotted cream to offset the hot rice.

*To drink: definitely the Traquair in whisky shot glasses, though a dessert flute of lambic banana beer, chilled, makes a shock contrast!*

## Weissbier Fritters with Spiced Pear Compôte and Crème Fraîche (serves 6)

Weissbier is literally 'white beer' from Bavaria, a brilliant effervescent brew produced with top-fermenting yeast to deliver a complex, spicy beer frothing to a refreshing tartness. Its distinctive characteristic is a 'boiled sweet' fruitiness, often with a marked banana, apple or pear tang. Schneider Weisse, with its 150-year pedigree, is the classic example of the style and has gained a huge following since it arrived in the UK from Bavaria a few years ago. It is widely available bottled in pubs and off-licences; leading supermarkets also have their own brands of weiss. Its airy yeastiness makes it the perfect ingredient for a light fritter.

*Fritters*
1 cup plain flour
1 dstsp cornflour
Pinch salt
1 cup Weissbier
2 tbsps very cold water
Oil for deep frying
Icing sugar and cinnamon for
 finishing

*Spiced pear compôte*
4 red-skinned dessert pears
3 cloves
Sugar to sweeten if wished
Large tub crème fraîche
Fresh mint

Combine plain flour, cornflour and salt, then whisk in the Weissbier a little at a time to produce a batter the texture of thin cream. Stir in cold water, then rest for at least 30 minutes in the fridge until ready to cook.

Heat oil in a deep pan until medium hot, then give batter a good stir and drop 3–4 tbsps batter separately into the hot oil – they will sink, then rise to the surface. Allow to cook for 2–3 minutes, flipping over once with a slotted spoon, until puffed, crisp and golden. Drain on kitchen paper and keep warm while you make the rest of the fritters – use dstsps as well, and pour some from the side of the spoon and some from the tip, so you get a mix of shapes and sizes.

Make the pear compôte by peeling, quartering and slicing up the pears, then simmering them in a little water with the cloves until soft; remove cloves, taste and add sugar if wished. Mash well and force through a sieve, or liquidize, then chill until ready to serve. Tip crème fraîche into a bowl and whisk well to smooth and thicken.

Serve the fritters piping hot dusted with icing sugar and cinnamon, with half-moons of pear compôte and crème fraîche either side as dips, and garnished with sprigs of fresh mint.

*To drink: a golden beer with a hint of spice such as Hall and Woodhouse's Tanglefoot at 5 per cent strength, or lighter Deakin's Golden Drop from Mansfield brewery.*

## Brown Bread Ice Cream with Traquair Ale (serves 6)

The gloopy, almost Marmite thickness of this black and potent brew makes it as effective in ice cream as it is in rice pudding (see page 224). It was devised by sparkling cook Heather Humphreys, now of the Rising Sun at Woodland near Ashburton in Devon, to serve at beer banquets for members of her local branch of the Campaign for Real Ale when she ran a pub in Berkshire. Traquair House Ale, brewed in Scotland's oldest stately home, is now available in some supermarkets and off-licences. Otherwise choose a small bottle of strong, dark barley wine or a treacly Russian-style stout.

150 g (5 oz) wholemeal breadcrumbs
250 ml (8 fl oz) double cream
200 ml (7 fl oz) single cream
100 g (4 oz) icing sugar (or

light brown sugar for a
darker result)
125 ml (4 fl oz) Traquair
House Ale
2 medium eggs

Toast breadcrumbs lightly by spreading them in a single layer on a baking sheet and placing them under a medium to hot grill for a few minutes, turning them a few times until just crisp and brown.

Whisk together double and single cream, sugar and the Traquair House. Separate the eggs and add the yolks to the cream mixture, beating well. Gently fold in toasted crumbs, then whisk egg whites until stiff and fold in gently.

Pour into a loaf tin lined with clingfilm and freeze – there is no need to stir during freezing.

*To drink: do drink the Traquair, at room temperature and in small goblets, toasting Bonnie Prince Charlie as you do; or barley wine or thick Russian stout – but in sipping, not swigging, glasses.*

## Cherry Beer Syllabub (serves 6)

'Sheer sex in a glass,' a guest once said on tasting my cherry beer syllabub, a decadent coupling of Belgian fruit beer and thick cream. Alcohol, of course, evaporates during cooking, but this is a cold dessert, using the beer neat to give a heady end to the meal. It is a lambic beer – that is, a spontaneously fermenting wheat beer impregnated with wild yeasts – and the cherries steeped in the cask give it the name kriek, meaning cherry. Use either Kriek of the famous farmhouse brewery Lindemans – a bright cherry red with an intense fruit flavour and almost syrupy sweetness – or bitter-sweet Liefmans; both are readily available here. In addition to its aphrodisiac qualities, this syllabub is dead easy to make!

300 ml (½ pint) double cream
300 ml (½ pint) cherry beer
1 level tsp almond essence

225 g (8 oz) fresh ripe cherries
Toasted flaked almonds for
   decoration

Add almond essence to the cream and whip until stiff – you can sweeten the cream with icing sugar; I find the beer makes it sweet enough, but I like it slightly tart. Slowly fold in the cherry beer a little at a time until the cream turns blush pink and just holds the beer (the proportions are roughly the same amount of cream and beer, but do not add quite all the beer).

De-stone the cherries, saving 6 pairs linked by stalks for decoration. Drop spoonsful of cream into 6 wine flutes, leaving a few small 'air pockets'. Place a layer of cherries halfway up. Trickle in a little of the remaining beer to work its way through the gaps, giving a marbled effect. Decorate with flaked almonds and loop a pair of cherries over the rim.

*To drink: the cherry beer, obviously, slightly chilled in port glasses – or for contrast a dense, chocolatey porter.*

# Chocolate Beer Truffles (doesn't make enough!)

All good things must come to an end, even the annual Beer Banquet staged by the British Guild of Beer Writers. When you've munched your way through a beer starter, beer main course, beer vegetables, beer dessert, ripe beer cheese with ripe English apples you feel so totally stuffed you couldn't manage another mouthful. And then our caterers, Focus on Food, who interpret my beer recipes for this feast, bring on the coffee, barley wine . . . and these. And suddenly your jaded appetite perks up.

| | |
|---|---|
| 100 g (4 oz) dark Belgian chocolate (the other thing the Belgians do so well!) | 4 tbsps dark cocoa powder |
| | 16 glacé cherries, halved |
| | 1 cup dark spicy ale* |
| 225 g (8 oz) Genoese sponge, crumbled | Strawberry jam |
| | Dark chocolate vermicelli |
| 2 tbsps sultanas | |

Combine first 5 ingredients, adding enough dark, spicy ale to bind the mixture together without making it mushy; if it is too wet, add more Genoese sponge. Mould or form mixture into balls and freeze for a short time. Take out and coat with strawberry (or apricot) jam, then roll in dark chocolate vermicelli, and refrigerate until ready to serve.

*To drink: a dark porter with espresso coffee notes, port-hued strong ale Hobgoblin from Wychwood Brewery at 6.5 per cent (widely available bottled), or whatever was used to make the truffles! For a contrast, chill a raspberry beer which is sensuous with chocolate.*

*At this point in the meal Terry Smith of Focus on Food uses one of the beers we have drunk during the evening – could be a chocolatey porter, a Christmas ale, a dark spicy Belgian beer or one of the German doppelbocks (double strength).

# Double Chocolate Beer and Hazelnut Parfait (serves 6)

Come Easter, Young's Brewery in south London makes a more than usually self-indulgent ale – Young's Double Chocolate Stout, originally for Easter, but now widely available bottled all year. Many dark stouts and porters have a strong hint of bitter chocolate, but this one accentuates the style by adding real chocolate. It was used by the brewery's first executive chef, Paul Jefferys, to create a double chocolate parfait that is even better than death by chocolate.

| | |
|---|---|
| 40 g (1½ oz) caster sugar | 8 tbsps Double Chocolate Stout |
| 4 egg yolks | 100 g (4 oz) milk chocolate |
| 450 ml (¾ pint) double cream | 50 g (2 oz) chopped hazelnuts |

In a heavy pan, boil the stout to reduce by half, being careful not to boil over. Add sugar and stir constantly with a wooden spoon until dissolved. Bring to the boil again and simmer briskly until you get a light syrup – about 2–4 minutes, then set aside to cool slightly.

In a mixing bowl, whisk egg yolks, then pour on the beer syrup, whisking continuously. Melt chocolate in a small glass bowl over hot water, whisk into the beer syrup and egg mix, then leave to cool.

When cold, fold in the double cream gradually, then churn in an ice-cream machine – or pour into a plastic container and freeze, removing occasionally to stir as it sets – mixing in the chopped hazelnuts as it freezes.

Serve 2 scoops per portion with thick clotted cream.

*To drink: either the Young's or a dark porter with bitter chocolate tones will do well because it will be a contrast to the sweeter chocolate taste of the dessert.*

## Elderbeer Trifle (serves 6)

Elderberry Beer is the sister beer to St Peter's Ale, which is featured in the lamb and artichoke pie on page 130. They are both brewed at St Peter's Hall near Bungay in Suffolk, and distributed in the brewery's distinctive flat bottles, which are copies of the flask-shaped vessel made around 1770 for Thomas Gerrard, who lived across the Delaware River from Philadelphia. The beer shares the ale's unmistakable ripe, fecund notes, but is flavoured subtly with elderberries to produce a lighter more astringent taste than in continental berry beers or English fruit wines; the fruit is more elusive than in traditional heavier Belgian brews. The recipe was created by Alistair Shaw, chef/proprietor of the Froize Inn, Chillesford in Suffolk, who hunts down East Anglian beers to serve in his pub.

| *Sponge mix* | *Filling* |
|---|---|
| 225 g (8 oz) margarine or butter | 3 tubs mascarpone |
| 225 g (8 oz) caster sugar | 1 bottle St Peter's Fruit Beer* |
| 225 g (8 oz) self-raising flour, sifted | 275 g (10 oz) sifted icing sugar |
| 4 medium eggs | Whipped double cream to serve |

To make sponge, pre-heat oven to 350°F, 180°C, gas mark 4. In a bowl cream together the margarine and caster sugar until light then beat in the eggs, 2 at a time. Fold in the flour until the mixture is light and fluffy. Spoon it into a lightly greased baking tin and put in the pre-heated oven for about 10 minutes; remove and allow to cool.

To make the filling, mix together the mascarpone, icing sugar and three-quarters of the bottle of fruit beer. Chill for around 15 minutes. Slice the sponge into strips and dip into the remainder of the beer, then use to line the bottom and sides of a medium-sized glass bowl. Spoon the chilled mascarpone and beer mix into the bowl, then cover with remaining sponge and sprinkle the top with any

*St Peter's Fruit Beer (elderberry) is available bottled, but you could use one of the Belgian fruit beers – apricot or strawberry are alternatives. Or even recently available Henry Weinhard's Blackberry Wheat from Portland, Oregon.

remaining beer. Chill for at least 2 hours. To serve: put a portion on each dessert plate and accompany with freshly whipped cream.

*To drink: the elderberry beer is not a sweet beer so is all right as a contrast to this sweet dessert. Or go for something darker and weightier, bubblegum and spice dark Aventinus brewed by Schneider in Bavaria, whose bottle-conditioned lusciousness now has a cult following here.*

## Hot Lemon and Beer Mousse with Toasted Marshmallows and Coffee Ice Cream (serves 6)

The intense flavour of this powerful lemon sherbet mousse originates from Hoegaarden brewery in Belgium. There the chefs who cook for the brewery hall have devised many ways of using their beers – in this case their awesome bottled Hoegaarden Grand Cru; as with wines, Grand Crus are the beers with the greatest character and complexity, at an almost vinous strength. At the brewery they serve the mousse hot to accompany crisp, butter-fried sweet bread balls, but I think it should be the main event. It can be adapted to all sorts of desserts: poured into a pastry case and topped with whisked, sweetened egg whites then baked as a lemon meringue pie; as a thick, pouring mousse over a featherlight vanilla sponge; or poured into small ramekins and chilled to set as a cold mousse, then topped with a blob of double cream and little slices of candied lemon. And married with rich coffee ice cream (Belgian for preference) and melting marshmallows it is irresistible.

150 ml (¼ pint) Hoegaarden Grand Cru
1 medium egg
1 egg yolk
Juice ½ lemon
3 tbsps caster sugar
Belgian coffee ice cream
12 small white marshmallows

Mix the Hoegaarden Grand Cru with egg, egg yolk, lemon juice and sugar and whisk together in a glass dish over a pan of simmering water until the mixture thickens and forms peaks.

Leave the dish over the pan to keep warm while you heat the grill to very hot and arrange the marshmallows on a heat-proof sheet.

Put a scoop of coffee ice cream on each of 6 dessert plates, then thrust the marshmallows under the grill for a few seconds while the tops caramelize. Arrange 2 on each plate and spoon the hot lemon mousse around the ice cream.

*To drink: something clean and effervescent with a hint of citrus – the same brewery's Hoegaarden Weisse in a champagne flute is ideal; or contrast with a thick, bitter-sweet chocolate porter.*

# Macerated Summer Berries with Honey and Ale
## (serves 6)

The Star Inn at Weaverthorpe in the Yorkshire Wolds is the right place for my friend Susan Richardson because she is a real star of the kitchen, her imagination putting the most delicious combinations on your plate. It is just like her to think of mixing summer fruits with dark ale and honey. Beers you might choose are Theakston Old Peculier, a multi-layered, vinous dark ale famous worldwide, or Marston's Merrie Monk – their oak-fermented Pedigree with caramel added. I think the result harks back to the Elizabethans.

300 ml (½ pint) strong dark
  ale
1 tbsp dark clear honey
4 strips lemon rind

550 g (1¼ lb) summer berries
  (including blackberries,
  red and blackcurrants,
  raspberries)

Pour the beer into a heavy pan, add honey and lemon rind, then heat slowly until honey melts and a syrup forms. Add the berries and poach for a few minutes, then remove from heat and leave to cool and stand for 24 hours or longer. Remove lemon rind, chill, and serve with crème fraîche or Greek yoghurt flavoured with honey. 'Yummy,' says Susan.

I have also used Susan's recipe to create a sort of summer/autumn pudding by lining individual ramekins with thinly sliced malted fruit loaf then filling them with the mixture and chilling for at least 24 hours.

*To drink: this is a strong, fruity dessert best set off by something lighter and summery, such as spritzy Belgian raspberry beer or, from Scotland, Fraoch Heather Ale.*

# Malted Caramel Cream with Toffee Apple (serves 6)

Dark, roasted malt is a brewing ingredient which makes beer ideally suited for many caramelized dishes. None more so than crème caramel itself, where a strong, black/brown malty beer full of the flavours of toffee brittle, treacle and burnt sugar makes a perfect topping. You find the flavours you are seeking in a host of strong beers – dark old ales or Christmas ales, some of the heavier stouts and barley wine. I got excellent results with Greene King's Strong Suffolk vintage ale, high in roast caramel, and with an almost Elizabethan sweet spiciness to the flavour. Alternatives might be Hop Back Entire Stout (a vegan beer), Cottage Brewery in Somerset's Norman Conquest and Baz's Bonce Blower or BBB, the 11 per center from Parish Brewery in Leicestershire. As you can see, some of them are very strong indeed and, served in small tumblers, make an ideal accompaniment.

150 g (5 oz) soft dark brown sugar
150 ml (¼ pint) dark, sweet malt beer
4 eggs
600 ml (1 pint) creamy milk
1 vanilla pod or 2 drops essence
1 eating apple, sliced but not peeled

Warm 100 g (4 oz) brown sugar gently in a thick-bottomed pan until it starts to melt. Stir in the beer and cook, stirring with a wooden spoon for a few minutes until it caramelizes and thickens. Use some of the caramel to cover the bases of 6 warmed ramekins, and reserve the rest. Dip apple slices in remaining hot caramel and cool to crisp.

Stand ramekins in a baking dish one-third filled with water. Whisk together eggs and remaining sugar, then warm the milk in a pan with vanilla pod or essence and mix into the eggs. Strain into ramekins and bake for 45 minutes in a warm oven (325°F, 160°C, gas mark 3) until just set.

Remove from oven, cool, and chill in the fridge. When ready to serve, turn out on to serving dishes so that the beery syrup forms a pool round them. Decorate each plate with 2 caramelized apple slices.

*To drink: as above!*

## Old Nutpecker Ice Cream (serves 6–8)

You've heard of rum and raisin ice cream. Well, this is ice cream flavoured with strong, vinous ale that adds loads of flavour and colour. The recipe comes from brewer-turned-cook Barry Horton of the Elsted Inn at Elsted Marsh near Midhurst in West Sussex – an old railway pub 'Beechinged' in the Fifties. At what was the original brewery of Ballard's peerless ales they serve Ballard's full range and in this recipe use their strong vintage ale, a different one in the series brewed every year – when Barry devised this recipe it was Old Pecker, with its undercurrents of citrus and marmalade. You can equally use their current 'pecker' or a head-knocking, fruity barley wine.

175 g (6 oz) raisins
275 ml (1 bottle or ½ pint)
   Old Pecker or barley wine
4 dstsps caster sugar

75 g (3 oz) walnuts, chopped
   roughly
600 ml (1 pint) double cream –
   at the Elsted they use 'best
   fresh natural Jersey'

Soak the raisins in all the ale overnight. Mix all the ingredients together and freeze in an ice-cream machine.* 'Wonderful!' says Barry's partner, Tweazle, who used to be a restaurant guide inspector.

*To drink: the barley wine would certainly complement the ice cream, and is appropriate for the end of a meal; but if you want the dessert to be the dominant flavour, choose a creamy dark mild with lots of head and a hint of vanilla.*

---

* If you do not have an ice-cream machine, make as above, but remove from the freezer compartment and stir briskly a few times during freezing to prevent crystals forming.

## Poached Peaches with Tuille Biscuits and Framboise
### (serves 6)

In the traditional peach melba, raspberry syrup is used. Here peaches are lusciously partnered with raspberry beer to create a more complex dessert of cold peaches set off by the less sweet tones of Belgian fruit beer Liefmans Framboise and the crunch of home-made tuille biscuits. The recipe comes from the eclectic White Horse in Parson's Green, south-west London, where Mark Dorber is host of much more than a pub. Always ready to experiment, the kitchen came up with this sweet notion for a beer dessert.

| | |
|---|---|
| 10–12 peaches | 3 egg yolks |
| 370 ml (1 bottle) Liefmans | *Tuilles* |
| Framboise | 2 size 2 eggs |
| 1 stick cinnamon | 100 g (4 oz) white sugar |
| 2 punnets strawberries, | 75 g (3 oz) plain flour, sieved |
| washed and hulled | 275 g (10 oz) unsalted butter |

To make tuilles place eggs, sugar and sifted flour in a food processor and blend thoroughly; melt butter gently in a pan, or microwave, and add to the mixture whilst blending.

Line a baking tray with baking paper and place tbsps of mixture on it, using the back of the spoon with a circular motion to make biscuits about 5 cm (2 inches) across. Bake towards the top of a pre-heated oven (350°F, 180°C, gas mark 4) for 3–5 minutes or until golden brown. Remove from tray, cool, then peel off.

In a saucepan boil sufficient water to cover the peaches. Score each peach with a knife, cut a 1 mm-deep ($^{1}/16$ inch) cross on each end and plunge in boiling water for 10–15 seconds; remove and refresh under cold running water. The peach skins should now slide off – if not, repeat boiling process for up to 10 seconds. Using a sharp knife and starting from the stem, cut all the way round the peach to the stone; separate the halves, remove stone and slice each half into 6 slices.

In a separate pan place the beer, cinnamon stick broken roughly in 3–4 pieces, sliced peaches and half the strawberries. Place on heat and bring gently to simmer for around 1 minute until the peaches are soft but not mushy. Remove peach slices with a slotted spoon and refrigerate. Increase heat and simmer beer for another minute, then strain liquor.

Place 150 ml (¼ pint) of liquor in a stainless-steel bowl with the egg yolks; place in a double boiler and whisk constantly until the mixture forms frothy peaks. Arrange layers of peach slices then the tuilles alternately in deep dessert dishes and top with the whisked Framboise sauce; garnish with remaining strawberries and trickle rest of poaching liquor around.

*To drink: the Framboise is fine; or a drop of spiced Morocco Ale made to an Elizabethan recipe by the Daleside Brewery near Harrogate (available bottled) might be appropriate.*

## Porter Jelly with Figs (serves 6)

Funnily enough, I first had *port* jelly at a brewery function and it was a rich, ruby delight. So I thought, why not make it with porter and see what happens? It was stunningly good, a jelly for grown-ups, not quite black, but certainly an uncompromising purple. Thinly sliced fresh figs look lovely alongside; or soak dried figs overnight in a little porter, cut them thinly and set them in the jelly. For this recipe you should choose a porter with some sweetness and muted fruit (rather than one of the bitter chocolate or roast styles), such as Larkin's luscious draught porter, using hops grown on their own farm in Kent or Shepherd Neame's Original Porter, which is available bottled.

| | |
|---|---|
| 1 450 ml (¾ pint) bottle porter | 3 dried or fresh figs |
| Water | 50 g (2oz) soft dark brown sugar |
| 1 sachet gelatine or vegetarian | Grating fresh nutmeg |
|   equivalent | Thick yellow pouring cream |

If using dried figs, cover with porter and soak overnight. Next morning, drain, then pour beer into a measuring jug and make up to 600 ml (1 pint) with cold water. Sprinkle on the gelatine (or vegetarian gel) and stir well until it is fully amalgamated. Stir in sugar and a good grating of nutmeg and bring slowly to simmering point.

Pour into a wet 600 ml (1 pint) mould; if using dried figs cut into thin rounds, add to the jelly and stir, then leave somewhere cool to set – beer jelly sets amazingly quickly.

To serve, turn out on to a platter and pour cream around it; if using fresh figs, slice them and place in a circle round the cream. Alternatively, you could make the jelly in 6 small moulds, turn each on to an individual serving dish and surround with cream, arranging slices of fresh fig alongside. If you want jelly and ice cream you could serve with beer ice cream (see page 247).

*To drink: this turns out very rich, fruity and spicy, so I would choose a Christmas-type beer in winter or one of the stronger, spicier brews such as King and Barnes's Festive Ale, always buyable bottled. Hoegaarden's Forbidden Fruit could be good, too.*

## Raspberry Beer Pastry Tartlets

Using one of the effervescent raspberry beers in pastry has two virtues – flavour and a light crisp texture. The taste is so powerful that a little goes a long way – just the tiny amount used to make these open tarts fills the kitchen with a smell of raspberries during cooking and is immediately there when you bite into the crisp pastry. This quantity is enough to make 24 open tarts, or you can freeze half the pastry and use it on another occasion to make a Bakewell tart, in which the raspberry flavour goes right through to the pastry; it is a natural with almonds. In the pastry the beer emerges sweetly, but carried through to the filling it lends the contrasting tartness characteristic of lambic beers – and gives the dish a bit of an alcohol kick since the beer is neat.

*Pastry*
225 g (8 oz) plain flour
1 dstsp icing sugar
100 g (4 oz) unsalted butter
1 small egg, beaten
50 ml (2 fl oz) Lindemans
  raspberry beer

*Filling*
150 ml (¼ pint) double cream
Icing sugar to taste
1 tsp ground almonds
225 g (8 oz) fresh raspberries
50 ml (2 fl oz) raspberry beer
  (approx.)
Toasted almond flakes

To make the pastry, sift flour and icing sugar into a mixing bowl, cut the butter into small pieces and rub in as lightly as possible until it resembles fine crumbs. Make a well in the middle and pour in the egg, then mix in with your fingers. Add enough raspberry beer to make a soft dough, just as you would if you were using water. Wrap in clingfilm and rest in the fridge for 2 hours. Remove at least 1 hour before use to bring back slowly to room temperature.

Pre-heat oven to 425°F, 220°C, gas mark 7, and grease tartlet tins. Roll out pastry thinly, cut out tarts and line the tins, pricking the bases, then bake blind towards the top of the oven until crisp and golden (around 10–15 minutes). Remove from baking tin and put on a cooling rack.

Make the filling by adding icing sugar and ground almonds to the double cream, then whipping until stiff; fold in enough beer to pinken and flavour the cream, but leave it firm enough to spoon. Gently mix in half the raspberries and fill the cooled tartlets with the mixture. Scatter toasted almond flakes on top and place a large raspberry in the centre of each.

*To drink: Lindeman's luscious Framboise, all fizzy and chilled, is as good as a dessert wine any day. But a chocolatey porter or stout with a well-roasted edge makes a perfect contrast in sherry schooners – colourwise, too.*

# Really Wild Raspberry Beer Choux (serves 6)

Two wilds here – Framboise, the spontaneously fermenting Belgian raspberry wheat beer fermented with wild yeasts as well as, if you can find and gather them, wild raspberries. Beer is mixed with water to make a light airy choux, which is then filled with whipped cream flavoured with the sparkling beer. This differs from the usual method of making choux pastry; I used slightly less butter and melted it separately from the beer to produce a lighter puff. I used Lindemans' Framboise, which is sweet enough not to need any sugar, but has just that slight edge to prevent the dessert from being cloying.

300 ml (½ pint) bottle
 raspberry beer
40 g (1½ oz) unsalted butter,
 melted
150 g (5 oz) plain flour

3 medium eggs, whisked
150 ml (¼ pint) double cream
100 g (4 oz) fresh raspberries
Icing sugar
Few springs mint

Heat the oven to 400°F, 200°C, gas mark 6. Sift flour into a bowl. Pour two-thirds of the raspberry beer into a ½ pint mug and make up the rest with water. Bring to boiling point in a thick-bottomed pan.

Remove from heat and tip the flour into the boiling liquid all in one, swiftly followed by the melted butter. Beat briefly with a wooden spoon to form a ball in the centre of the pan; beat in the whisked eggs little by little until the mixture is glossy and of piping consistency. Pipe small balls about the size of a walnut on to a baking tray lined with buttered foil or baking parchment and bake towards the top of a hot oven for 25 minutes until risen and golden (do not open oven door).

Remove choux and make small slits to let out the steam, then turn off oven and return them for 10 minutes to dry out, leaving the door open.

Whisk double cream until stiff then fold in the remaining beer – just enough to flavour the cream and turn it pale pink. Mix in most of the raspberries and use to fill the choux.

Pile on a decorative glass serving dish and dredge with icing sugar, decorating with the remaining raspberries.

*To drink: serve the Framboise in champagne flutes alongside the dessert or, if you can get it, sour Flemish Rodenbach in a bottle which is sold thickly wrapped in tissue; add a little blackcurrant cordial as the Belgians do, kir style.*

# Sophie Grigson's Tarte à la Bière (serves 10–12)

I first met Sophie Grigson when we were judging the finals of the Guinness Pure Genius pub food awards – we both went overboard for a Hokkien pork dish cooked by a pub landlady from Brunei. Sophie has given me this recipe for a sweet beer tart and says, 'This most unlikely but remarkably good tart comes from the Nord–Pas de Calais. The method is unorthodox, the balance of pastry to filling seems all wrong, but it works. The finished tart derives a clear taste of beer from the thin layer of filling, but it is perfectly balanced by the underlying syrupy sugar and thick almondy pastry. It's a great party piece, but it tastes just as good a day or even two after it is made, so you don't have to have a crowd to feed to justify making it. I used Sainsbury's Bière de Garde, as recommended by Michael Jackson.*

*Pastry*
450 g (1 lb) plain flour
¼ tsp salt
100 g (4 oz) caster sugar
150 g (5 oz) ground almonds
300 g (11 oz) butter
4 medium eggs
½ tsp vanilla essence

*Filling*
150 g (5 oz) granulated sugar
3 medium eggs
150 ml (¼ pint) bière de garde
25 g (1 oz) butter, melted and
  cooled to tepid

For the pastry, sift the flour with the salt. Mix with caster sugar and almonds, then rub in the butter. Add eggs and vanilla essence and mix to a soft dough. Knead briefly to smooth out, then wrap in clingfilm and chill for 30 minutes. Bring back to room temperature and roll out to a thickness of about 1 cm (½ inch), then use to line a 28–30 cm (11–12 inch) tart tin.

Prick the base all over with a fork and sprinkle evenly with the granulated sugar. Cover loosely with foil and bake for 15 minutes at 350°F, 180°C, gas mark 4. Remove foil and bake for a further 15 minutes.

* Other bières de garde readily available are Jenlain and La Choulette.

When the pastry is almost done, make the filling. Beat eggs lightly, then gradually beat in beer and melted butter. Pour over the sugar in the baked pastry case and return to the oven for 15–20 minutes until just set. Leave to cool completely.

*To drink: just as raspberry beer works well in pastry with almonds, so here it is a perfect foil to the almond sweetness of this tart, served in a dessert wine flute. Alternatively, choose a bitter chocolate porter or stout such as London brewer Young's Double Chocolate Stout.*

# Two-tone Beer Ice Cream in an Ale and Almond Tuille Basket with Hot Toffee Sauce (serves 6)

Two different beers produce a duo of ice creams, dark and light, in this stunningly pretty dish. It was originated by Stephen Coggins, head chef of the Vine Hotel in Skegness – a man who displays great creativity on the cooking with beer front. His hotel cum pub is owned by brewers George Bateman and Son (though it's the brewing daughter Jacqui Bateman who swaps beer recipes with me), so Stephen used Bateman's famous Salem Porter with its malt character and hint of licorice to create the dark ice cream, and their summer elderflower beer to flavour the pale one. 'Either mix together at the last minute or serve side by side in a crisp almond biscuit basket,' he says.

| *Dark beer ice cream* | *Light beer ice cream* |
|---|---|
| 600 ml (1 pint) dark, sweetish porter | 600 ml (1 pint) Elderflower beer (or a golden, flowery beer) |
| 4 medium egg yolks | |
| 450 ml (¾ pint) double cream | 4 medium egg yolks |
| 85 g (3 oz) runny honey | 450 ml (¾ pint) double cream |
| 1 tsp coffee granules | 85 g (3 oz) runny honey |

In 2 separate saucepans rapidly boil the beers until each is reduced to a thick glaze or about ⅛ pint (75 ml). In 2 separate bowls put remaining ingredients apart from the double cream. Pour each beer syrup into appropriate bowl, then mix well and place each bowl over a pan of simmering water and whisk (an electric whisk is ideal at this stage) until both mixtures double in volume, becoming light and fluffy, then chill both beer custards.

Whip both quantities of double cream separately until they form peaks, then gently fold into the chilled custard mixtures. Pour into separate containers and freeze, whisking every 2 hours until set (or use ice-cream machine). At the point when each is nearly set they can be gently stirred into each other to give a marbled effect – or be left separate.

*Beer and Almond Tuille Baskets*
*(makes 6)*
120 ml (¼ pint) light ale
275 g (10 oz) caster sugar

100 g (4 oz) melted butter
175 g (6 oz) ground almonds
150 g (5 oz) plain flour, sieved

Mix all ingredients well in a mixing bowl. Lightly oil a baking sheet or use silicone paper and place 6 heaped dstsps of mixture separately on to the sheet, spacing well apart; flatten each with a fork and bake at 350°F, 180°C, gas mark 4, for 5 minutes.

Remove tuilles from baking sheet and, whilst still warm, place each in a small fluted mould, then gently press a smaller mould inside to form a tulip-shaped container (or use a small dessert bowl with glass tumbler inside.) Carefully remove moulds and place the tuilles on a wire rack until cold and firm.

*Toffee Butterscotch Sauce*
150 ml (¼ pint) water
425 g (15 oz) caster sugar
100 g (4 oz) butter, diced

225 g (8 oz) golden syrup
600 ml (1 pint) whipping
 cream
½ tsp vanilla essence

Place water and sugar in a thick-bottomed pan and bring slowly to the boil; cook until caramelized, thick and dark golden. Add diced butter (beware of splashback!), stir well, then add the cream and vanilla essence; bring back to the boil and leave on a slow boil for 10 minutes, strain and keep warm. (Steve makes twice this amount because it keeps well; if you make a large quantity and don't want to use it at once, strain it into a clean tub, cover with clingfilm, allow to cool, label, date and store in the fridge for up to 2 months. Re-heat gently to use.)

To serve: put a scoop of each ice cream into a tuille basket, place basket on the centre of a plate and trickle heated sauce around.

*To drink: two different beers, obviously, but don't mix them! Serve Bateman's famous and award-winning Salem Porter in a thick little tumbler, the elderflower beer in a flute, if available. Alternatively, try St Peter's bottled fruit beer, golden hued and lightly flavoured with elderberries.*

# BAKING

The baking process is where brewing and cooking really come together in the kitchen. Brewing beer and baking bread not only have ingredients in common — yeast, grain, water and sugar – but methods as well. Historically, it was natural for households to both brew beer and bake bread, and both fed each other, brewer's yeast being used for centuries to make bread rise.

Whenever I go into a brewery my nose picks up the aroma of baking bread; conversely, in a bakery I can distinguish brewing smells. You talk about dough fermenting just as you talk about beer fermenting. I like the definition given by the hero in Dick Francis's racing thriller, *Banker*: 'Bread that is made with yeast definitely does contain alcohol. If you mix yeast with water and sugar you get alcohol and carbon dioxide, which is the gas which makes the dough rise. The air in a bakery smells of wine – simple chemistry.'

Well, not quite that simple, Dick. During its early use, yeast was invested with mysterious and sometimes vaguely sinister properties because its vigorous action in brewing beer and making bread seemed, quite simply, magical. It can be 'tamed' to the extent that breweries cultivate their own yeast strains which help give their beer its unique character, but this living organism is also in the air in the form of wild yeasts and, as I've described on page xvii, a small group of Belgian lambic and Gueuze beers are deliberately exposed to the wild yeasts floating in through open windows. Magic.

Put simply, yeast is a single-cell plant that multiplies rapidly as it turns sugar into alcohol and carbon dioxide – performing roughly the same function in both brewing and baking. In brewing, the natural carbon dioxide gives the beer its sparkle; in yeast cookery the air bubbles make the bread rise and give it its light texture, while the heat of the oven kills off the alcohol.

Today, brewer's yeast might still be used in making some types of bread, such as sourdough – it was only in the last century that brewer's yeast and baker's yeast became separated. Until then ale yeast, or barm (is that why in some areas tea cakes are still called barm cakes?) had been used to make bread – a major discovery, since pre-yeast unleavened bread was flat, solid and heavy. But brewer's yeast was not ideal – early bread recipes advised soaking it in plenty of water to get rid of the hop taste, which made bread bitter. So eventually 'compressed' or baker's yeast was developed.

Yeast works well with the starchy ingredients used in brewing and distilling as well as baking – potatoes, all kinds of grain from rye to oats, wheat and barley. While wheat is more generally used in bread-making and barley in beer, only certain strains of barley can be used to produce malt for brewing; in England, Maris Otter is a famous variety. And yeast not only turns sugar into alcohol; it adds aroma and flavour such as spiciness or fruitiness, one reason why beer is so good in cooking.

In baking, always use a live cask- or bottled-conditioned ale as it responds so well with flour. Bread will have a better taste and rise that much more if you use beer, with its yeast sediment to boost the bread yeast, instead of water; it helps the texture of cakes, scones and pastry, too. And you can experiment with different types of beer, perhaps a porter or dark wheat beer, as long as they are live ales, gently warmed and mixed with baker's yeast as the starter for bread dough.

In this chapter you'll find that the different flavours and textures of beer enhance everything from a sensuous chocolatey porter sponge to a traditional Geordie Stottie bread and the ultimate Christmas cake flavoured with barley wine.

# Beer and Seed Bread

When I make bread with real ale, I feel as if I'm getting a double dose of yeast – some from the beer, some from the fresh or dried yeast used neat. This recipe by Annie Clift at the Talbot at Knightwick in Worcestershire goes with her recipe on page 69 for scallops in beer batter. She has always used a draught, cask-conditioned medium-hopped beer from their bar to make their bread, but from 1997 was able to use one from their own brewery made with hops grown on the farm, and by now should be using their own home-grown barley malt as well. Her brother Philip, the brewer, named his three beers This, That and T'Other because regulars tend to come into the bar and say, 'I'll have a pint of this', or 'A half of that'; which only left T'Other! Before that she sometimes used well-hopped Hobsons brewed not far away at Cleobury Mortimer or draught Bass, and says you can mix bitter and stout.

50 g (2 oz) fresh yeast
50 g (2 oz) granulated sugar
1.5 kg (3 lb) wholemeal brown
bread flour
1 kg (2 lb) unbleached white
bread flour
50 g (2 oz) salt

100 g (4 oz) mixed seeds (i.e.
pumpkin, poppy, sunflower,
caraway, sesame)
100 g (4 oz) black treacle
50 g (2 oz) melted lard or
sunflower oil
1.5 litres (2½ pints) draught
medium bitter

Put the yeast and sugar together to cream in a 1.5 litre (3 pint) measuring jug. In a large bowl mix the flours, seeds and salt. Make a well and pour in black treacle and melted lard or sunflower oil.

Make the yeast mixture up to around 1.5 litres (2½ pints) or 1.6 litres (2¾ pints) with the beer (amount used will vary with different flours, which absorb different amounts of liquid). Pour the beer mixture into the well in the flour to make a dough, then turn on to a floured surface and knead for at least 5 minutes (10 is better). Return to the bowl, cover with a damp cloth, and leave to rise for approx 1 hour or until double the size.

Knead again and form it into the required number of loaves –

Annie makes 6, though you can freeze half the dough for future use. Leave to rise till double the size, then bake. Annie says, 'Yeast likes to be cooked in a falling oven, i.e. an oven which is losing its temperature. An oil-fired Aga is excellent.' Otherwise, put the dough into an oven pre-heated to 475°F, 240°C, gas mark 9, then turn down immediately to 425°F, 220°C, gas mark 7 for 20 minutes, then turn the bread and give it another 20–30 minutes at 400°F, 200°C, gas mark 6. It is cooked when the bread sounds hollow if you tap the bottom lightly.

## Drowning by Porter Cake

As chocolate cakes get more and more chocaholic, the flavour seems to get more and more artificial. This cake harks back to the traditional rich chocolate cake, in which the texture of the sponge is as important as the flavour. The dark plain chocolate is enhanced by the dark chocolate malt in the porter – and black coffee in the cream filling echoes that hint of espresso you also find in the porter, here mingled with melted plain chocolate in the mixture. Buy the best plain chocolate you can – you could even go full circle by using Belgian dark chocolate and drinking a small glass of Belgian cherry beer with the cake!

*Cake*
100 g (4 oz) unsalted butter, softened
150 g (5 oz) soft brown sugar
2 size 2 eggs, beaten
175 g (6 oz) self-raising flour
½ level tsp cream of tartar
Pinch salt
1 tbsp cocoa powder
50 g (2 oz) good plain chocolate
150 ml (¼ pint) porter

*Filling*
150 ml (¼ pint) double cream
25 g (1 oz) icing sugar
Up to 2 tbsps strong real coffee (not instant)
*Icing*
100 g (4 oz) dark plain chocolate
3 tbsps porter
1 dstsp dark sugar
25 g (1 oz) unsalted butter
About 10 sweet coffee beans or pecan nuts

Pre-heat oven to 350°F, 180°C, gas mark 4. In a large bowl cream together the butter (softened but not melted) and sugar with a wooden spoon, beating until light and fluffy. Gradually beat in the eggs, adding just a little flour if the mixture starts to curdle. Mix together the flour, cream of tartar, salt and cocoa powder.

Meanwhile melt the chocolate in a glass bowl over hot water. Sift about a quarter of the flour into the beaten butter and eggs, and fold in with a metal spoon. Stir in a little of the porter, then sift in the same amount of flour again, and fold in. Stir in the melted chocolate and a little more porter, then sift in half the remaining flour and fold in, stirring in a little more porter. Sift in the rest of the flour and fold in, then gently stir in the rest of the porter.

Line the bottom of an 18 cm (7-inch) cake tin with lightly greased greaseproof paper and grease the sides. Spoon in the cake mixture evenly and bake slightly above the centre of the oven for 80 minutes, not opening the door for at least the first hour. The cake is cooked when it is risen, slightly springy to the fingertips – when you insert a thin skewer it should come out clean.

Leave to stand for about 5 minutes, then remove from cake tin and leave to cool on a wire rack. Make the filling by whipping the double cream with the icing sugar and cold black coffee to taste, then halve the cake and spread evenly on the bottom half and replace the top half.

Make the icing by heating the chocolate with the porter and sugar in a glass dish over simmering water until melted, then stir in the butter and leave until cool and thickened but spreadable. Spread over the cake and round the sides, filling any cracks in the top, then decorate with sweet coffee beans or pecan nuts and chill until the icing sets.

# Geordie Stotty Cake with Best Bitter

Beer gets back to its roots in a yeast dough; in the very early days of bread and beer making the same yeast was used for both, before it was realized that brewer's yeast and baker's yeast had different roles. At the Cooperage pub and restaurant on the Tyne quayside in central Newcastle head chef Colin Cunningham uses best bitter in this local bread called Geordie Stotty Cake. It's important to choose a live ale with the yeast still working, preferably a draught cask ale, though bottle-conditioned is acceptable. Colin adapted this from a very old traditional recipe of his mother-in-law. He thinks the name stotty came from the bits of dough left over from making loaves, roughly shaped into rounds and put in the bottom of the oven. They are still very popular and widely on sale in the north-east. 'A ham and pease pudding sandwich made with stotty cake – nothing like it,' says Colin.

| | |
|---|---|
| 1.5 kg (3 lb) unbleached plain flour | 1 tsp salt |
| 50 g (2 oz) fresh yeast (or equivalent dried) | 1 tsp sugar |
| | White pepper |
| | 550 ml (15 fl oz) best bitter |

Warm a large bowl and put in flour and salt. Gently warm a little of the beer to lukewarm, then add the yeast and stir with a fork until dissolved. Cover the bowl and leave in a warm place for 15 minutes until frothy, then stir in the sugar and a dash of white pepper.

Heat two-thirds of the beer to simmering point then pour into a jug and mix in the remaining cold beer. Make a well in the flour and pour in the yeast mixture. Add enough of the warm beer to make a stiff dough (the amount varies with different flours, you may need to add a little lukewarm water as well); turn on to a floured surface and knead for at least 10 minutes until no longer sticky (or use dough hooks). Punch dough with your fists, cover with clingfilm, and leave to rise in a warm place for 30–40 minutes until almost doubled in size. Preheat oven to very hot (475°F, 240°C, gas mark 9). Cut dough into 3 or 4 portions and roll into 2.5 cm (1 inch) thick rounds, place on floured baking sheet and bake on the very bottom of the oven for 30 minutes until browned on both sides.

## Leicester and Lightning Scones (makes 18)

Red Leicester is a powerful, rounded cheese that needs a powerful, rounded beer, but not a heavy one or the scones will be lumps of lead. I chose one of my favourite beers with a name that describes its flavour – Hopback Summer Lightning, a straw-coloured ale that makes you think of hay and open fields, with a hoppy character and elusive citrus fruit. Winner of its class at CAMRA's 1997 Great British Beer Festival as a draught beer, it is now available bottled-conditioned so the yeast is still working. This helps give these scones their 'Lightning' texture. The ale takes the place of milk, giving the scones a melting texture and hint of hops.

225 g (8 oz) self-raising flour
Pinch salt
50 g (2 oz) unsalted butter
100 g (4 oz) mature Red
  Leicester, grated

1 level tsp mustard powder
150 ml (5 fl oz) Summer
  Lightning, or a golden bitter
  balancing fruit and hops

Sieve flour into a bowl, add salt and rub in the butter as lightly as possible. Stir in three-quarters of the cheese and then the beer, mixing lightly with your fingers to make a soft dough. Do not roll it out as you will crush the natural carbonation in the living ale, which makes the scones light. Instead, flour a flat surface and your hands and gently flatten the dough until it is around an inch thick.

Cut out with a plain 7 cm (3 inch) cutter, brush the tops with beer, and sprinkle on the remaining grated cheese. Arrange on a greased baking tray, then cook near the top of a hot oven, 425°F, 220°C, gas mark 7, for 15 minutes.

Cool and serve split in two and buttered.

*To drink: believe it or not, there is now a Belgian beer flavoured with tea which I find quite pleasant, chilled on a summer's afternoon. But probably the brew for this is served in a cup, not a glass.*

# Oatmeal Bread with Samuel Smith's Oatmeal Stout

There is a fascinating parallel between brewing and bread-making in this recipe. When producing oatmeal stout brewers use only a small proportion of pinhead oatmeal to malted barley – it tends to clog up pipes and just a little is needed to add the flavour and creamy smoothness characteristic of the beer. So it is in this staff-of-life loaf made by Heather Humphreys of the Rising Sun near Ashburton in Devon to go with her beer soup; she uses one-tenth oatmeal to malted brown flour. Then there's the yeast, the malt extract and stout as well, making a loaf that you might say is brewed rather than baked. Samuel Smith's bottled Oatmeal Stout is easily obtained and has a delightful hint of frothy coffee.

1 kg (2 lb) malted brown
  bread flour
100 g (4 oz) medium oatmeal
1 tsp salt
25 g (1 oz) lard or margarine
25 g (1 oz) fresh yeast (or 1

sachet fast-action dried yeast)
1 tbsp black treacle
1 tbsp malt extract
Approx 600 ml (1 pint)
  Samuel Smith's Oatmeal Stout
  (plus extra water as needed)

Mix the salt into the flour and oatmeal; rub in the lard or margarine. Next rub in the fresh yeast or stir in dried yeast. Warm black treacle and malt extract gently with the stout to blood heat. Mix to a soft dough with the flour, adding lukewarm water as necessary (some flours need more liquid than others, but make it soft rather than wet), and knead well until smooth. Place in a polythene bag and refrigerate overnight.

The next day knead again for 5 minutes and again refrigerate overnight; knead again and shape into rolls or loaves – if using loaf tins use 2 450 g (1lb) greased loaf tins or 1 loaf tin and use the rest of the dough to make rolls. Leave in a warm place to prove for 30–40 minutes. Bake in a pre-heated hot oven, 425°F, 220°C, gas mark 7; 15 minutes for rolls, 30–40 minutes for loaves until they leave the baking tray or loaf tin easily and sound hollow when tapped on the base.

# Old Tom's Barley Cake

Old Tom is some of the most heavenly barley wine you will ever drink, dating back to 1899, almost black, but up against the light it has ruby glints that go with its port-like palate. Apparently, Old Tom was the brewery cat at brewer's Frederic Robinson in Stockport and this is the brewery's old recipe for a quickly made ale cake, which, unusually, involves boiling the beer with the butter beforehand. As you do, overpowering alcoholic fumes fill the kitchen and make you feel quite light-headed – it's like sitting by a pub fire on a winter's afternoon. And the rich, fruity cake is best eaten in a similar situation, served warm in thick slices spread with butter, perhaps accompanied by a really mellow Cheddar and a wine glass of Old Tom.

100 g (4 oz) unsalted butter
100 g (4 oz) dark soft brown
  sugar
180 g (6 oz ) mixed dried fruit

180 ml (¼ pint) Old Tom or
  vinous barley wine
350 g (12 oz) plain flour
1 level tsp bicarbonate of soda
1 level tsp mixed spice

Place butter, sugar, fruit and ale in a saucepan; melt all together and then boil for 2–3 minutes.

Sieve flour, bicarbonate of soda and spice into a bowl, add fruit and ale mixture and stir thoroughly. Put into a greased 1 kg (2 lb) loaf tin and bake for 1 hour in the centre of a moderate oven, 350°F, 180°C, gas mark 4. Remove from oven, loosen with a knife, then leave to cool for 30 minutes.

Serve warm or cold, sliced and spread with butter.

## Owd Rodger's Christmas Cake

This is the ultimate Christmas cake and it is dedicated to world famous beer writer, my friend Roger Protz, winner of more beer-writing awards than he can probably recall. With his Campaign for Real Ale hat on, he was the man who persuaded me to take on the first *CAMRA Good Pub Food Guide*, thereby starting me on this whole trail a decade ago. Owd Rodger is the extraordinary barley wine brewed with love by Marston's Brewery in Burton upon Trent. Get yourself an invite and see it fermenting in the Union squares (open square vessels) – while their other cask beers show a moderate yeast head, Owd Rodger goes totally berserk, towering above the troughs and even escaping down the sides. They have a joke in the brewery that Owd Rodger goes walkabout round the brewery yard before climbing back into the vessels. This is also a wonderful addition to a raised game pie set in barley-wine jelly, but that would not be a dish to name after Mr Protz, he being a vegetarian.

225 g (8 oz) currants
400 g (14 oz) sultanas
275 g (10oz) raisins
150 ml (¼ pint) barley wine
225 g (8 oz) unsalted butter
225 g (8 oz) dark soft brown sugar
5 size 2 eggs
225 g (8 oz) plain flour, sifted
Pinch salt
½ tsp mixed spice
½ tsp cinnamon

Grating nutmeg
175 g (6 oz) glacé cherries, halved
100 g (4 oz) mixed peel
50 g (2 oz) ground almonds
100 g (4 oz) walnuts, chopped
1 tbsp molasses or treacle
Rind of 1 large lemon, grated finely

*To decorate*
Whole blanched almonds
Walnut halves

48 hours before making the cake, put currants, sultanas and raisins in a Polythene box and pour over the barley wine, mixing thoroughly; put the lid on and leave in a cool place.

Preheat oven to 275°F, 140°C, gas mark 1. Line the base of a 23 cm (9 inch) cake tin, preferably loose-bottomed, with greaseproof paper.

Grease the sides and tie a double thickness of greaseproof or brown paper round the outside of the tin so it protrudes above the rim.

Put butter and sugar in a large bowl and cream together, beating robustly, until light and fluffy. Whisk the eggs one at a time and beat into the mixture a little at a time – it may curdle slightly, but don't worry. This takes quite a while.

The next step is to mix the flour with the salt, mixed spice, cinnamon and nutmeg, then fold into the egg mixture as lightly as possible. By now the dried fruit should have swelled up in the barley wine, so stir it in gently, plus any unabsorbed beer, followed by the cherries, mixed peel, ground almonds, chopped walnuts and molasses or treacle. Lastly add the lemon rind.

Spoon the mixture into the tin, smoothing the top evenly, and place the almonds and walnut halves on top, pressing in slightly. Bake on the lowest shelf of the oven for 4–5 hours, depending on your oven. After about 3 hours open the oven door carefully without causing drafts and place a pre-cut round of greaseproof paper on top of the cake to stop it burning.

The cake is ready when the top feels fairly firm when pressed and a skewer, inserted in the centre, comes out clean – if not put it back for 15 minutes and try again. Remove from the oven and cool in the cake tin, then wrap it in greaseproof paper and store in an airtight tin or polythene box until Christmas.

This matures rather like live beer in the cask; I kept mine for two months and it just got better and better.

# Scotch (Ale) Pancakes (makes about 12)

Here's a way to bring ale to the tea table – and an example of beer's superiority to milk in making airy batters with a hint of hops, as you'll see when they rise on the hotplate. It seemed appropriate to choose a Scottish beer, but you don't want a heavy, malty one for these griddle cakes. I settled on Caledonian Golden Promise, brewed in a Victorian brewhouse in Edinburgh in direct-fired open coppers using only organic hops and barley. It has a hop aroma but a summery taste of clover creeps in with a 'slice of lemon' on the edge (bottled in supermarkets). Choose a straw-coloured medium-strength beer which balances hops and flowers – nothing too weighty.

| | |
|---|---|
| 100 g (4 oz) self-raising flour | 1 medium egg, beaten |
| 25 g (1 oz) light soft brown sugar | 150 ml (5 fl oz) golden-hued lightly hopped ale |
| 1 tsp mixed spice | Fat and butter for frying |

Mix dry ingredients togther, then add egg and stir in the beer a little at a time, with as light a hand as possible, to produce a batter the texture of thick cream. If you've got a liquidizer, give it a zizz, then rest it in the fridge for 30 minutes.

Get the griddle (or a heavy-based frying pan) hot then turn down to medium and grease with a little fat; as soon as it melts put on a small knob of butter for flavour, then drop dstsps of the mixture on to the griddle and cook for up to a minute, until bubbles rise. Flip over and cook for another minute.

You're supposed to serve them cold like scones, but I prefer them hot and indigestible with butter and Scottish clover honey.

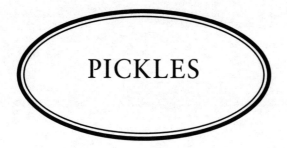

PICKLES

# Cameron's Tomato Relish

Beer gives chutney a bit of bite and works as a preservative. This sweet and spicy tomato relish is tasty enough to serve on toast as a snack or use to accompany cold meats. The beer used by Susan Richardson of the Star Inn, Weaverthorpe, North Yorkshire, was Cameron's Bitter, brewed in Hartlepool, because she wanted a fruity bitter with a touch of dry hoppiness; you can equally use a full-flavoured, medium-strength bitter that has some sweetness, such as Adnams' Broadside.

4 large tomatoes, skinned and de-seeded
3 cloves garlic
1 large onion
1 dstsp each fresh basil and coriander, torn
3 tbsps olive oil
150 ml (¼ pint) fruity bitter
1 tsp sugar
salt and black pepper

Finely chop tomatoes, garlic and onion, then mix with the fresh herbs. Combine olive oil, beer, sugar and seasoning, then pour over the tomato mix, stir well, cover with clingfilm and leave in the fridge for at least 48 hours. It will keep in the fridge, covered, for several days.

## Lucy's Dark Lager Mustard

Lucy Saunders is well known in the USA as a beer and food writer, and we became friends during her forays to Britain and Europe to find out about our pub food and Belgian beer cuisine – she spent time in the kitchens of the famous In't Spinnekopfe restaurant in Brussels. On one of her trips she spent a night at my home, where she first tried a German smoked beer and decided it would be great with barbecued pork ribs. I find her tangy recipe for mustard from her US recipe book, *Cooking with Beer*, is wonderful with cold gammon, in salad dressings and even spread on pork escalopes when grilling.

40 g (1½ oz) soft brown sugar
225 ml (8 fl oz) dark lager
2 tbsps brown mustard seeds
2 tbsps yellow mustard
 powder
100 ml (4 fl oz) cider vinegar

2 shallots, chopped
1 tsp salt
Pinch white pepper
2 medium egg yolks
2 tbsps melted butter

Blend all the ingredients in a liquidizer or processor, then place in the top of a double boiler or steamer over simmering (not boiling) water. Cook until thickened and steaming (about 10 minutes), whisking often to prevent curdling. Leave to cool to room temperature before chilling. Serve as a condiment with all kinds of meats and deli sandwiches. (Keeps up to 2 weeks in a tightly sealed container in the refrigerator.)

# Spiced Elderberry Chutney with Apples and Guinness
## (Makes 1.5 litres or 2½ pints)

Food for free is always tastiest. Though the elderberry season is short, it is abundant, and you can easily go out to the hedgerows and pick enough to make twice this amount to see you through the winter. The recipe was created for me some years ago by an enterprising pickle and preserve inventor called Julie Hooper when I wrote an article about a cottage industry she had launched called Hoops Exquisite Catering. She was then making all sorts of goodies, from kumquat marmalade to peach, mint and pecan preserve. Her recipe is delicious: black, bitter-sweet elderberries are fortified by a 'a pint of plain' – one of the world's most famous porters – added neat right at the end. Be careful to pick clean elderberries away from roads – and leave as many on the tree as you pick, to follow the countryside code.

450 g (1 lb) elderberries
1.5 kg (3 lb) cooking or wind-
  fall apples, peeled and cored
225 g (8 oz) raisins
50 g (2 oz) fresh ginger, grated
2 dried red chillis, chopped
1 stick cinnamon

Pinch ground cloves
900 ml (1½ pints) cider
  vinegar
750 g (1½ lb) demerara sugar
1 mulled wine sachet
150 ml (¼ pint) Guinness

Wash berries, then remove from the stems using the prongs of a fork. Slice apples and put them into a large non-aluminium pan with the elderberries; add all the rest of the ingredients (apart from the Guinness) and simmer gently for 75 minutes until the chutney turns thick. Remove from the heat and stir in the Guinness, then ladle into warm, sterilized jars. Cover and seal at once. Store 4–6 weeks before use.

# BEER COCKTAILS

To be frank, I am totally agin mixing beer with anything. But there are people who make beer cocktails, and even those who drink them.

They are not new, either. One of the earliest known was a twelfth-century recipe for a caudel, in which ale was heated with sugar or honey and saffron to provide a warming drink for travellers cold from coach riding. A posset was a sixteenth-century hot drink made with eggs, milk and ale (see page 272). Brown Betty mixes ale with cognac, cloves and spices before chilling, while a beer nog heats stout with dark rum, eggs and honey. A drink called a Yard of Flannel was a yard of ale with a difference – mild flavoured with cognac, sugar and spices, and mixed with separated beaten egg yolks and folded-in egg whites. Then there was another medieval drink called Figgy Sue, in which dried figs were simmered in beer and water then sweetened and flavoured with ginger. Not terribly inspiring.

One drink I do love, though, is Black Velvet – equal amounts of Guinness and chilled champagne. It works. Other stout drinks include a Black Russian of Guinness with vodka, a Blacksmith of Guinness with barley wine, a Red Witch of Guinness with Pernod, cider and blackcurrant, which sounds truly disgusting, and the more traditional Black and Tan of Guinness with bitter.

Here are a few you might like to try.

## Beer Fruit Cup

You don't have to stick to wine in punch. Here is a summer fruit cup mixing fruit beers with soft fruit, pepped up by a little Bacardi.

Ingredients – elastic!

Chill 3–4 bottles fruit beer – you can get cherry, banana, peach, raspberry and strawberry from Belgium and, from the USA, Pete's Wicked Strawberry Blonde or Henry Weinhard's Blackberry Wheat Ale are available here – and some soda water. Make lots of ice cubes. In a large bowl slice up some mixed fruit – apples, bananas, strawberries, halved cherries, melon cubes, and anything else you fancy. Pour over 3 large measures of Bacardi, add the beer, give a good stir, top up with soda water, drop in several ice cubes and supply a small ladle for people to serve themselves.

## Double Chocolate Glory (serves 4–6)

This is a knickerbocker glory for grown-ups – a thick, dark mix of Young's chocolatey stout with chocolate ice cream and, yes, more chocolate topped with a dollop of cream. Almost a pudding – and definitely not for waist-watchers!

| | |
|---|---|
| 1 bottle Young's Double Chocolate Stout (chilled) | 2 level tsps coffee powder |
| 3 dstsps soft dark brown sugar | 2 scoops rich chocolate ice cream |
| 50 g (2 oz) plain Belgian chocolate | Double cream, sweetened and whipped |

Pour stout into a liquidizer. Add sugar, most of chocolate, coffee powder and ice cream. Liquidize to give a thick, frothy drink. Grate rest of chocolate. Pour the drink into tall goblets, topping each with a dollop of cream, and finish by sprinkling grated chocolate on the cream.

# Hoegaarden Royale

When Soho Brewing Company opened in Covent Garden in summer 1998 – a brew restaurant producing beer in a small micro brewery with modern-style cuisine in an open-plan kitchen – I talked to the young Bavarian brewer Albrecht von Wallmoden. He told me that in his country wheat-beer shandies are popular, such as a combination of fresh lemonade and wheat beer (slightly more beer than lemon), a Russian, which is wheat beer with Coke, and, unlikely though it sounds, a Goat – strong dark beer with a dash of whisky and cherry juice. Here is my favourite wheat-beer cocktail.

One of my favourite pre-dinner tipples is Kir Royale made, of course, with crème de cassis and champagne. Using beer is far cheaper, and with this pale, sparkling wheat beer, just as effervescent.

For 4 people chill 2 bottles of Hoegaarden wheat beer. Set out 4 large champagne flutes and put as large a measure as you like of crème de cassis in the bottom of each. Top up with chilled Hoegaarden, and hook a pair of linked cherries over the rim of each glass. A refreshing aperitif.

# Posset

| | |
|---|---|
| 3 medium eggs | 2 cardamom pods |
| 600 ml (1 pint) milk | powdered cinnamon |
| 300 ml (½ pint) strong brown ale | ground ginger |

Beat eggs into the milk, add cardamom pods, and heat gently, stirring, until the mixture thickens.

In a separate pan heat beer almost to boiling point and pour into a large warmed bowl. Quickly pour over the hot egg and milk mixture, cover, and leave in a warm place for 5 minutes to allow curds to set. Sprinkle the top with cinnamon and ginger.

# Beer Banquets

Putting beer on the menu is certainly food for thought – and requires a little more effort and judgment than designing other menus. It is a delicate balancing act. Beer can be a heavier drink than wine and some beer dishes are rather filling, perhaps lending themselves to a hearty one-course meal.

On the whole, you should start with a lighter course and a lighter beer, work up to the strong brews and either continue in that vein, until you reach the big cheeses and barley wine, or let diners down gently with a frothy fruit beer dessert and accompanying pale, effervescent beer.

Obviously, you would not serve an entire meal of dishes made with stout or porter, or with all fruit beers, or exclusively pale wheat beers and pilsners. Otherwise, the usual menu rules apply. Contrast filling, hot main courses with lighter, chilled starters and desserts. Some beer dishes are extremely rich, so partner them with plain vegetables and simple starters. Large beer casseroles can be satisfying meals on their own simply followed by beer cheese; big bowls of mussels cooked with beer and bacon, accompanied by beer bread, then fresh fruit, should suffice.

There are those who say that one or two beer dishes in a meal are quite enough, and that other courses should be ale-free. I concede that from a gastronomic point of view they are probably right, but, if I'm cooking with beer, frankly I like to go for the Full Monty. When I invite friends round for a beer banquet, they know that is precisely what they're going to get – besides, you should never mix the hop and the grape!

However, recipes in this book are also designed to stand alone, and can be enjoyed as the only beer course in a meal – and you can certainly serve beer-cooked vegetables alongside plain roasts. The following menus are unashamedly beer feasts, though obviously you can stick to only one or two beer dishes if you choose.

## Winter Dinner Party

Bortsch and beer (small wine glass of smoked beer or cherry beer)

Duet of smoked salmon and halibut with stout vinaigrette
(Ushers' White Beer or a lightly chilled dark mild)

Steak and oyster pudding or wild mushroom pudding with
Oyster Stout (Marston's bottle-conditioned Oyster Stout)

Porter jelly with figs (spicy Festive Ale)

## Vegetarian Summer Supper

Boozy fennel baskets (chilled wheat beer)

Penne with plum tomato and plum beer sauce
(strong Trappist beer or honey beer)

Cherry beer syllabub (Liefmans Kriek)

## Sunday Lunch

Chilled melon with cherry beer (Hoegaarden weissbier)

Albert Roux's boeuf aiguillette accompanied by braised
chicory, creamed potato and small beer-batter
Yorkshire puddings (India Pale Ale)

Vegetarian alternative: Winter warmer wellington (IPA)

Beer-baked Bramleys (Dark Mild)

## Informal Get-together

Toad-in-the-barrel with venison sausage accompanied by
beer and onion gravy (a full, hearty, cask bitter)

Rice pudding made with Traquair Ale

## Celebration Buffet
Centrepiece: Whole salmon glazed in Hoegaarden aspic
and a large joint of gammon in Mash Tun marmalade,
beer mustard and chutney to accompany

Bite-sized: ale choux buns filled with horseradish cream; little beer
pancakes with range of fillings; red onion and beer flan recipe
made as tartlets; bowls of non-beer green, potato and pasta salads

Raspberry beer and cream tartlets; Elderbeer trifle;
chocolate beer truffles; beer cheeses.

If this is a formal cake occasion, use the recipe for Owd Rodger's
Christmas Cake with traditional marzipan and white icing covering

To drink: chilled raspberry beer; magnum bottles of Chimay
Grande Réserve

## Festive Dinner
On arrival: small tumblers of spiced beer soup and hot beer-glazed
chestnuts, accompanied by chilled (effervescent) wheat beer

Chicken liver and porter pâté or mushrooms
marinated in spiced beer (Old Ale)

Hop and lemon sorbet

Delia's venison with port, Guinness and pickled walnuts
accompanied by roast parsnips and potatoes; tiny Brussels
sprouts and fine green beans (King and Barnes's Festive Ale,
Fuller's 1845 and Ushers' Ruby Ale)

Christmas pudding made with brandy and barley wine (barley wine)

Coffee and plain chocolate mints (Gordon's Scotch Ale)

When you don't want to have a whole banquet, have a tasting.
Choose six to eight different beers, mixing a range of styles as well
as bottled and draught, and choose cheeses and breads that go
with them, or different shellfish and smoked fish, or a delicious
platter of cold meats with the beer mustard and chutney, or all
sorts of salads and cold dips. Bon appetit!

# Classic Bottled Beers

These are my Desert Island Beers, only I'm going to choose two dozen. They have been used in recipes in this book but are really drinking beers and what I would call absolute classics of their style; the majority are bottled-conditioned so you can lay them down. Several really fall into the category of end-of-the-meal beers. Most are fairly easy to find – some you'll have to seek out.

**Aventinus (Schneider)**: extraordinary chewy, dark doppelbock at a serious 8 per cent, harmonizing a great mix of Bavarian wheat-beer flavours from banana to bubblegum into a complex whole.

**Ballard's Old Pecker**: an end-of-the-meal, strong, vintage ale changed every year and given the gravity of the year. So 1999 should be a skull-cracking 9.9, but what on earth will happen in the year 2000?

**Bateman's Salem Porter**: classic dark brew, building through fruit and malt layers to a dry finish.

**Black Sheep**: special bitter brewed by Paul Theakston, an offshoot of the famous Theakston brewers, at Masham in North Yorkshire. A superbly balanced beer, underlying roast flavours dominated by hops.

**Bodger's Barley Wine (Chiltern Brewery)**: small bottle, big taste – a classic thick, malty barley wine gorgeous with game.

**Budweiser Budvar:** the classic Czech long-conditioned lager, with a quenching, rounded flavour mixing malt and hops.

**Chimay Grande Réserve:** a towering Belgian Trappist beer which is the 'wine bottle' size of their 9 per cent Chimay Bleu in a wire corked bottle. Glorious with strong meats and cheese or where you would normally have a Burgundy.

**Double Chocolate Stout:** from London brewer Young's, it combines chocolate malts with genuine chocolate to put a whole box of chocs in a bottle.

**Duvel:** Flemish for Devil, appropriate because this pale golden ale looks positively angelic but has a devilishly seductive follow-through.

**Fraoch Heather Ale:** brewed to an old Gaelic recipe, mixing flowering heath with barley malt to give a lilting, floral aroma and taste with a spicy aftertaste. Unique. (I think their 7.5 per cent Alba, flavoured with Scots pine and spruce, dark, intense and just released as I write, could become a classic.)

**Fuller's 1845:** produced by the London brewer to commemorate their 150th anniversary in 1995. Like a barley wine and Christmas Ale in one.

**Gordon's Highland Scotch Ale:** strong, hugely malty and brewed in Scotland but perversely imported from Belgium – as good as a fine Highland malt at the end of a meal.

**Hoegaarden White:** classic Belgian wheat beer, pale, sparkling and imbued with luscious citrus and spice flavours; refreshing with fish.

**Jenlain Bière de Garde:** chestnut-hued, classic, strong example of the genre from northern France in a wire-corked bottle just begging to be on the table.

**King and Barnes's Festive:** makers of many fine bottle-conditioned ales, including a keepable annual Christmas beer, but the Festive is like a spiced fruit pudding any time.

**Liefmans Kriek:** my favourite Belgian cherry beer, macerating the fruit in this sour, brown Flemish style to achieve a tipple that is sweet edged without being syrupy.

**Old Growler:** smooth, bitter-sweet, powerful black porter with lots of roast malt and fruit from the Nethergate brewery in Suffolk.

**Orval:** not just a heavenly drink – I sip it and think of its Trappist brewers in Florenville at an abbey also producing Orval cheese, bread and honey.

**Owd Rodger:** port-hued strong barley wine brewed by Marston's, great in – and with – Christmas cake.

**Prize Old Ale:** an unusual deeply vinous dark old ale full of character and handsomely presented in a corked bottle sealed with red wax. Gale's gorgeous meal ender or haunch of venison accompaniment.

**Schneider Weisse:** the archetypal exuberant Bavarian wheat beer with its acid-drop sweetness, banana and pear. Dangerously quaffable on a hot day.

**Thomas Hardy's Ale** – formerly brewed by Eldridge Pope and my all-time favourite. A contender for the strongest beer in the world, and at 12 per cent it improves with ageing over many years. Named after the great Wessex novelist, who used the words 'the most beautiful colour that the eye of an artist in beer could desire'. My own description might be 'like angels walking over your tongue'.

# Other Beer Products

You can now enjoy beer in your food without having to take out the mixing bowl or chopping board. Small producers are catching on to the flavour beer can add to everything from marmalade to chocolate, cheese to chutney. Take ham, bacon and sausages. Several English charcuteries have successfully added beer to the brine to produce hams of superb colour and flavour. Foremost is Richard Woodall of Waberthwaite near the Cumbrian coast, his family business dating back to 1828. He produces a superb copper-hued Cumbria Mature Royal Ham by using a cure containing Newcastle Brown Ale and molasses, then hanging the ham for fifteen months. Served wafer thin it is as good as any Parma or Prosciutto, and is sold in Harrods and Fortnum & Mason (Woodall's mail order 01229 717237).

Merrivale Charcuterie at Gweek near Helston in Cornwall (01326 221506), which also has a restaurant, uses the local strong ale Spingo (brewed at the Blue Anchor in Helston) mixed with molasses and muscovado sugar in the cure to give a hop flavour to both ham and bacon.

And at Emmett's Stores in Peasenhall, Suffolk, they make a pickle with treacle and Guinness for their ham and bacon (mail order 01728 660250). Black pudding, my favourite delicacy, got the Vaux treatment when the Sunderland brewer held a competition for the best pudding made with its Double Maxim beer. Entries came from as far apart as Norfolk and Ballycastle in Northern Ireland, but the winner was the Little Bury from real black-pudding country, Accrington, where butcher's A.C. Wild still makes it to Arthur Wild's winning recipe.

Many enterprising sausage-makers now flavour their sausages

with beer, using different combinations of meat with different styles of beer, such as beef with Guinness, lamb with apricot and a dash of fruity bitter, pork with a strong hoppy bitter. Ushers Brewery supplies its pubs with a hop sausage made with organic pork and gently flavoured with hops.

Best all-rounder is Chiltern Brewery on a farm at Terrick near Aylesbury in Bucks. Where to start? Born-again Christians Richard and Lesley Jenkinson with 'Fear God and Give Him the Glory' on their labels, are brewers par excellence who use their beers to create many delicious treats. Chiltern Ale Mustard blends their bitter with mild, coarsely ground mustard seed; Beechwood Hop-Leaf Mustard is a strong wholegrain blended with their Beechwood Bitter and Fuggles hop leaves for extra bite. (Several small producers now make mustard flavoured with beer, such as Wiltshire Tracklements. I also adore Lakeshore Wholegrain Mustard with Guinness made in Tipperary, and Jesse Smith of Cirencester's hot beer mustard with black mustard seeds.)

Chiltern Brewery's rich, chestnut-hued Three Hundreds Old Ale is in a chutney, just made for a ploughman's. Mash Tun Marmalade combines bitter Seville oranges with dark, roasted malt from the brewery, while Maris Otter pale ale malt goes into their sweeter blend of lemons, grapefruit and oranges in Three Fruit Maris Marmalade. Spicy pickled onions in their brewery shop have hops in the vinegar; vanilla and chocolate fudge are sweetened with brewer's crystal malt; and their classic Bodger's Barley Wine (in a pie on page 87) enriches a fruit cake.

And they do two amazing cheeses – Chiltern Beer Cheese and Terrick Truckle (see p. 180). You can buy beer, too, and visit their pint-sized museum (01296 613647). Latest temptations are Chiltern chocolates – little dark chocolate barrels with a dark cream filling flavoured with their Old Ale. 'Seriously chocolatey,' says Lesley.

And talking of chocolates, the highlight of one of our Beer Banquets were Hopolates, a bitter dark after-dinner chocolate made from equatorial chocolate beans Trinitario and Forastero with hop oil. Still on sweets, as I write I have in my freezer some really grown-up ice cream made by Lovington's of Castle Cary in Somerset, a deep toffee shade flavoured with award-winning local ale Norman's Conquest from the Cottage Brewery in a former dairy, which seems to complete the circle.

# Specialist Beer Shops

Beer is now widely available, both bottled and draught. You will find good ranges in the main off-licence chains – Oddbins has a good selection including guest beers of the month – and supermarkets, including Tesco, which has actively been helping smaller UK brewers and overseas brewers to get their beers into the chain, as well as launching the Tesco Beer Challenge competition to create new beers, Safeway, which has been holding tastings to launch its beer lists, and Sainsbury and Waitrose.

In addition we now have beer superstores, brilliant emporiums gathering beers from breweries all over the world as well as collectors' ales, and small, independent, specialist beer shops, where you can spend many a happy hour seeking out the more unusual beers. It would be impossible to give an exhaustive list, but here are some of them.

**Belfast** The Vineyard, 375 Ormeau Road (01232 645774)

**Bexley:** Cork and Cask, 3 Bourne Parade, Bourne Road (01322 528884)

**Bromley:** Bitter End, 139 Masons Hill (0181 466 6083)

**Birmingham** Rackhams, 35 Temple Row (0121 236 3333)

**Cambridge:** Jug and Firkin, 90 Mill Road (01223 315034)

**Canterbury:** Canterbury Beer Shop, 83 Northgate (01227 472288)

**Cardiff:** Full Moon, 88 Ty'n y Pan Road, Rhiwbina (01222 623303). Range includes bottle-conditioned and seasonal cask beers.

**Corbridge:** Corbridge Larder, Hill Street (01434 632948)

**Darlington:** Binns off-licence in House of Fraser, 1–7 High Row (01325 462606)

**East Boldon (Tyne & Wear):** Beaumont Wines, Station Road (0191 536 7152)

**Edinburgh:** (Oats and Toasts, 107 Morrison Street, Edinburgh (0131 228 8088)

**Glasgow:** Peckham and Rye Ltd, 18 Bogmoor Place, Glasgow (0141 445 4339)

**Hexham:** Edible Options, 24 Market Street (01434 605090)

**High Wycombe:** Wycombe Wines, 20 Crendon Street (01494 437228)

**Kendal:** Beers in Particular, 151 Highgate (01539 735714)

**Knaresborough:** Beer Ritz, 17 Market Place (01423 862850)

**Leeds:** Beer Ritz, 14 Westwood Lane (0113 275 3464). Huge choice of bottled beers in a converted chapel, plus cask ales from small local breweries.

**Lincoln:** Small Beer, 91 Newland Street West (01522 540431)

**London:**
Grog Blossom, 253 West End Lane, West Hampstead (0171 794 7808).

Pitfield Beer Shop and Brewery, 14 Pitfield Street, Hoxton, London N1 6EY (0171 739 3701). Fantastic collection of some of the best beers in the world, including rare and collector beers –

plus an adjoining micro-brewery producing own-label beers.

Selfridges, 400 Oxford Street W1A 1AB (0171 629 1234). Adjoining the gourmet food hall, the extensive wine and spirit department also takes beer seriously. I was even able to buy the damson beer brewed at the Mason's Arms in Cartmel Fell, Cumbria, which donated a recipe to this book – and which has its own beer shop, Inter Ale.

**Luton:** Hart Lane off-licence, 12 Hart Lane (01582 726279)

**Lutterworth:** Off-Licence and Beer Room, 35 Station Road LE17 4AP (01455 554 943)

**Newton Abbot:** Tuckers Maltings, Teign Road (01626 334734)

**Preston:** Real Ale Shop, 47 Lovat Road (01772 201591)

**Peebles (Borders):** Villeneuve Wines, 37 Eastgate (01721 722500)

**Scarborough:** Wells Wine Cellar, 94 St Thomas Street (01723 362220)

**York:** York Beer Shop, Sandringham Street, off Fishergate (01904 647136). Draught cask beer plus UK – and foreign-bottled beers – nice cheese counter, too.

**Westcliff-on-Sea:** Beers Unlimited, 500 London Road (01702 345474)

# Index